George Sand
and
Idealism

GENDER AND CULTURE

Carolyn G. Heilbrun and Nancy K. Miller, editors

George Sand

and

Idealism

N A O M I S C H O R

Columbia University Press
New York

Columbia University Press
New York   Chichester, West Sussex

Copyright © 1993 Columbia University Press
All rights reserved

Library of Congress Cataloging-in-Publication Data
Schor, Naomi.
George Sand and idealism / Naomi Schor.
p.   cm. -- (Gender and culture.)
Includes bibliographical references and index.
ISBN 0-231-06522-1
1. Sand, George, 1804–1876--Criticism and
interpretation.   2. Feminism and literature--
France--History--19th century.   3. Women
and literature--France--History--19th century.
4. Idealism in literature.   I. Title   II. Series.
PQ2417.S36   1993
843'.7--dc20   92-34449
                                            CIP

Casebound editions of
Columbia University Press
books are printed on
permanent and durable
acid-free paper.

Printed in the United States of America
c   10   9   8   7   6   5   4   3   2   1

For my mother,
Resia Schor

CONTENTS

ILLUSTRATIONS

Cover photograph by Félix Nadar, Bibliothèque Nationale

ACKNOWLEDGMENTS

I take it as a sign of the fascination George Sand continues to exert on my colleagues and peers that this project has been so magnificently supported from its inception to its completion. I am almost embarrassed to thank the following institutions and foundations for their generous support over the years it took to write this book: Brown University's Pembroke Center for Teaching and Learning on Women (1983), the American Council of Learned Societies (1986), the National Endowment for the Humanities (1990), and the John Simon Guggenheim Memorial Foundation (1990).

I wish also to thank the students in my undergraduate Sand seminar at Brown (Spring 1982), as well as my graduate Sand seminar at Duke (Spring 1990) for allowing me to learn Sand along with them. At different stages various sections of the manuscript benefited from the encouragement, editing, questioning, invitations, and suggestions of these friends and colleagues, in near-chronological order: Charles Bernheimer, Joan DeJean, Leslie Rabine, Susan Suleiman, Martine Reid, Jane Gallop, Marianne Hirsch, Philippe Hamon, Joan Scott, Judith Butler, Isabelle Hoog Naginski.

Though they never got to see the manuscript as a whole, the members of my original Providence reading group—Karen Newman, Mary Ann Doane, Ellen Rooney, and Christina Crosby—provided insightful commentary on various chapters. Much of this book was written after I left Brown; nevertheless, it is indebted to that institution, its students, its faculty, and its administration (1978–89).

Abigail Solomon-Godeau and Vanessa Schwartz, my Gymnase Club partners in Paris, were the first real and tough readers of the completed draft, Toril Moi, the last and most constructive. Fredric Jameson volunteered to read the book and made sense of the project. Ross Chambers and Nicole Mozet produced the sorts of readers' reports that make one feel that one's best years have not been entirely wasted.

Elizabeth Weed, who was always too busy to read my manuscript but never too busy to lavish her friendship on me, helped me stay relatively sane throughout the eighties and into the nineties. By generously relieving me of the burden of the daily grind of producing *differences*, she made it possible for me to devote time to my own writing. I can never thank her enough for this gift.

My greatest debt, however, is to the three people who in the most literal sense helped me complete this book. Nancy K. Miller, *amie de toujours* and occasional Sandiste, signed on the project when it was just a glimmer in my eye (and she identified with Daniel Stern). An incisive and engaged editor when the manuscript was in its final stages, in the very end she went far beyond what one can expect of a friend or editor. My immense debt to Janell Watson, my research assistant, is offset only by the hope that she has at least learned from the experience of preparing this manuscript for publication an invaluable lesson they don't teach in graduate school: the virtues of getting one's bibliographical references right the first time. Third, I am grateful to Jennifer Crewe who was as warm, unflappable, and above all patient an editor as any author could wish for.

But no one was more patient than Paol Keineg, who could never understand why I wouldn't work on his favorite text by Sand (*Les Dames vertes*). Gizella and Guy Etienne, as well as the chief conservator of the Sand Museum at Nohant, Monsieur Franco, helped make my visit to Nohant and the Berry memorable. Finally, Sarah St. Onge, my copy editor, deserves thanks for her attentive reading and light-handed editing, as do Sharon Marcus and Elizabeth Houlding for their generous gift of youthful energy in helping me tie up loose ends.

Paris, June 1992

Credits

Several parts of the book have been previously published, and all of these have been substantially revised. Chapter 1 originally appeared under its current title in *Yale French Studies* (1988), 75: 56–73, and was subsequently reprinted in *Displacements: Women, Tradition, Literatures in French*, ed. Joan DeJean and Nancy K. Miller (Baltimore: Johns Hopkins University Press, 1991). Chapter 2 is made up of two articles, "*Lélia* and the Failures of Allegory," which was published in *L'Esprit Créateur* 29 (1989), and a piece that appears in French as "Le Féminisme et George Sand: *Lettres à Marcie*," in the *Revue des sciences humaines* 226 (1992) and in English in *Feminists Theorize the Political*, edited by Judith Butler and Joan W. Scott (New York: Routledge, 1992). Chapter 4 is a retitled and reframed version of "Reading Double: Sand's Difference," which appeared in *The Poetics of Gender*, edited by Nancy K. Miller (New York: Columbia University Press, 1986).

George Sand
and
Idealism

The

Importance

of

Being

George

Sometime in the mid-fifties I spent an evening baby-sitting for my younger sister reading (in French, of course, as I was a student at the Lycée Français de New York) *Lélia*, André Maurois's recently published biography of George Sand (1952). I have a very vivid vision of myself standing by the pink Formica table with wrought-iron legs in my parents' kitchen, one of those emblematic artifacts of the fifties now for sale in trendy SoHo boutiques, having a sort of epiphany about George Sand. An inveterate reader of biographies of famous women—I can trace my feminism at least as far back as my devouring the "famous women of America" series at the local St. Agnes's branch of the New York Public Library on Friday afternoons after school—I had never read a biography of a woman such as Sand. Not a nurse, not an aviator, not a scientist, not the first woman lawyer, not the consort to a king, but a French woman writer of international fame whose friends and lovers included some of the most celebrated artists, writers, and musicians of her time. Although it is hard at this distance to reconstruct exactly what it was that fascinated me most about George Sand, I know this much: the book inspired in me a desire to *be* George Sand. And being George Sand meant mainly, as I understood it then—I must have been around eleven or twelve at the time—having famous lovers. I know now that if my identification was misplaced, I had gotten the sense of the biography exactly right, since Maurois's misogynistic view of Sand involved stressing her scandalous love life and diminishing her accomplishments as a writer and thinker. By identifying with Sand the lover I had inadvertently (and perhaps inevitably) reproduced the first stage of Sand studies, the biographical.

It took me almost as long as Sand studies to mature and move on to the second stage. In graduate school, where it was possible in the sixties to do advanced work in nineteenth-century French literature in the most highly rated department in the United States (Yale University) and never encounter a single text by Sand (or by any other woman writer of the period, for that matter, with the possible exception of Staël's *De l'Allemagne*), I flirted briefly with the idea of writing my dissertation on Sand but never considered reading her. The only progress I made was to purchase the Garnier edition of *Lélia*, a wise move for it was soon to go out of print for some twenty years. But it remained unread on my shelves.

As a young assistant professor charged with teaching a graduate survey course on the nineteenth-century French novel and caught up in the excitement of the beginnings of feminist literary studies, I unthinkingly reproduced the canon as I had received it, though I did begin to question its representations of women. Meanwhile, I directed my energies toward turning my imaginary identification with the scandalous Sand into reality, by taking—*toutes proportions gardées*—a famous lover. We even joked about rewriting *Elle et Lui* (*She and He*).[1] As it turned out, he was not joking.

And so it went until on moving to Brown University in 1978, a bright senior named Robert Riger asked me if I would guide him in an independent study on George Sand. So in my mid-thirties, having renounced my adolescent fantasy of *being* Sand, I finally progressed to the second stage of Sand studies: *reading* her.

Paradigm Shifts

Originally conceived under the regime of Elaine Showalter's programmatic identification of feminist criticism with gynocriticism (which exiled the work I had been doing up to then on women and representation to the Siberia of feminist critique) significant portions of this book were written and the entire work revised in the era of the rise of cultural studies—which has made those earlier debates seem like quaint relics of a more innocent, neoformalist past. I had begun with the idea of trying to define the specificity of women's writing in the light of feminist theory (especially the French), but the last stages of the book were composed at a time when the very notion of studying literary texts exclusively has been displaced by the study of all manner of paraliterary materials. Situated then between the receding horizon of gynocriticism and the looming horizon of cultural studies, this book most accurately reflects the moment—around 1985[2]—at which most of it was in fact conceived, a moment when under multiple political pressures issues of canonicity came to the fore and when the pervasive critique of essentialism made it imprudent to assert anything at all about women's writing that was not rigorously contextualized and particularized. *George Sand and Idealism* is then about a woman writer but makes no claims about a specificity of women's writing; its concern is rather the gendering of aesthetic categories and the ways in which that gendering impinges on the reception and (de)valorization of female-authored texts.

From Detailism to Idealism

Many years ago, in *The Degree Zero of Writing*, Roland Barthes proposed a triadic genetic model of writing, ranging from the suprapersonal *langue* to the most intimately personal and corporeal *parole*. If I may appropriate this model I would add to the two levels I have just mapped out—my personal history (*parole*) and the critical context (*langue*)—a third, intermediary register equivalent to Barthes's *écriture*, that is, my own critical trajectory, which has moved from Zola's crowds to the detail and now to the ideal.

Throughout many of the years I was thinking and writing about the detail (*Reading in Detail*), I was also engaged as a professor of courses on women's writing in rethinking the French canon and its politics of inclusion and exclusion. For all the reasons mentioned above, my interests came to focus on the case of George Sand, the preeminent French woman writer of the nineteenth century. But it was only after I had completed my work on the detail that I began to see how the two projects were in fact connected, part of the same ongoing reflection on aesthetics and the feminine, on detailism and its polar opposite, idealism.

In the summer of 1985, while browsing through the French section of a bookstore in Hay-on-Wye, an extraordinary English village made up almost entirely of secondhand book shops, I came upon an old text-book entitled *La Littérature française par la dissertation*.[3] As I was already working on George Sand at the time, I flipped to the table of contents to see if she was included. It was then that I made an important, indeed a decisive discovery: she was included, but under what struck me as a strange and unfamiliar heading, *Le Roman idéaliste*. This was, as it were, my second Sandian epiphany. I knew, of course, in a general sort of way—as anyone working on Sand would—that an important idealistic strain existed in Sand's fiction, and I had even touched on it in some of the work I had already published on Sand. But this moldy and outdated study aid suddenly made palpable for me the force of that category and the extent of its disappearance. From that moment on I knew that my reading of Sand would be inseparable from my attempt to come to terms with the disappearance of the "idealist novel," to understand its relationship to its more, infinitely more familiar binary opposite, the "realist novel." To retrieve the idealist novel from the oblivion where it has languished at least since the 1920s, to try in the era of postmodernism to theorize idealism in the novel is not—let me state this categorically—to plead for its return. This book is not called: *for* an idealist novel. My concern (again) lies elsewhere: it is with un-derstanding how Sand came to be positioned in, or rather on, the margins of the canon, and that understanding is bound up with (re)thinking idealism in the novel.

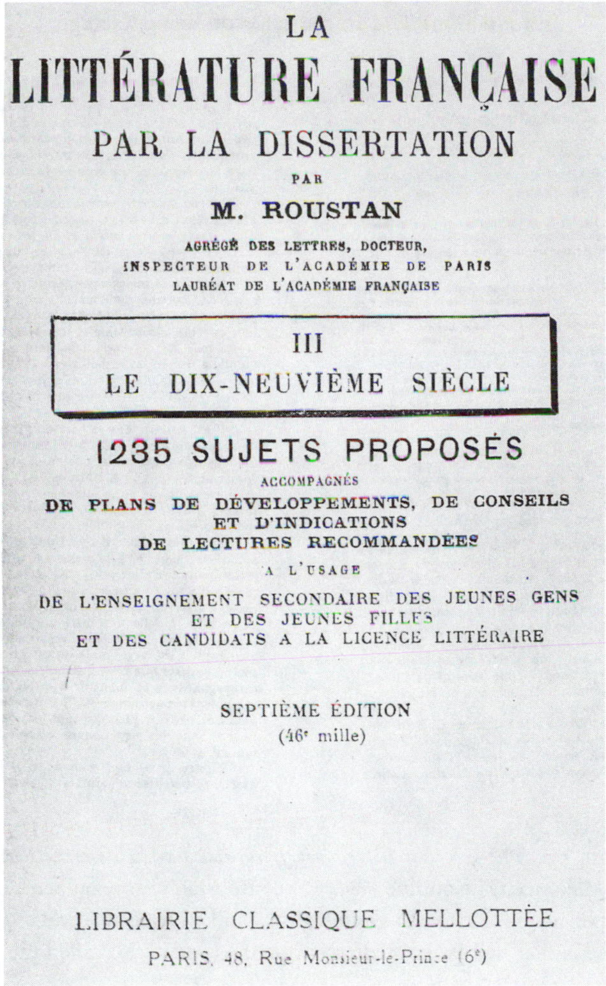
LA
LITTÉRATURE FRANÇAISE
PAR LA DISSERTATION
PAR
M. ROUSTAN
AGRÉGÉ DES LETTRES, DOCTEUR,
INSPECTEUR DE L'ACADÉMIE DE PARIS
LAURÉAT DE L'ACADÉMIE FRANÇAISE

III
LE DIX-NEUVIÈME SIÈCLE

1235 SUJETS PROPOSÉS
ACCOMPAGNÉS
DE PLANS DE DÉVELOPPEMENTS, DE CONSEILS
ET D'INDICATIONS
DE LECTURES RECOMMANDÉES
A L'USAGE
DE L'ENSEIGNEMENT SECONDAIRE DES JEUNES GENS
ET DES JEUNES FILLES
ET DES CANDIDATS A LA LICENCE LITTÉRAIRE

SEPTIÈME ÉDITION
(46e mille)

LIBRAIRIE CLASSIQUE MELLOTTÉE
PARIS, 48, Rue Monsieur-le-Prince (6e)

FIGURE 1.

M. Roustan, title page, *La littérature française par la dissertation.* Librairie Classique Mellottée. Geared to serve the needs of students participating in France's highly competitive and standardized national qualifying examinations (*baccalauréat, licence*), Roustan's study aid bears all the insignia of authority and coverage. Roustan was the author of many works on pedagogy (e.g., *La Scolarité jusqu'à* 14 *ans* and the intriguingly titled *Hitler éducateur. Racisme ou démocratie. Dressage ou liberté!*) and an editor of "morceaux choisis" of major French canonic authors (e.g., La Fontaine, La Rochefoucauld, Montesquieu), as well as of *"manuels."*

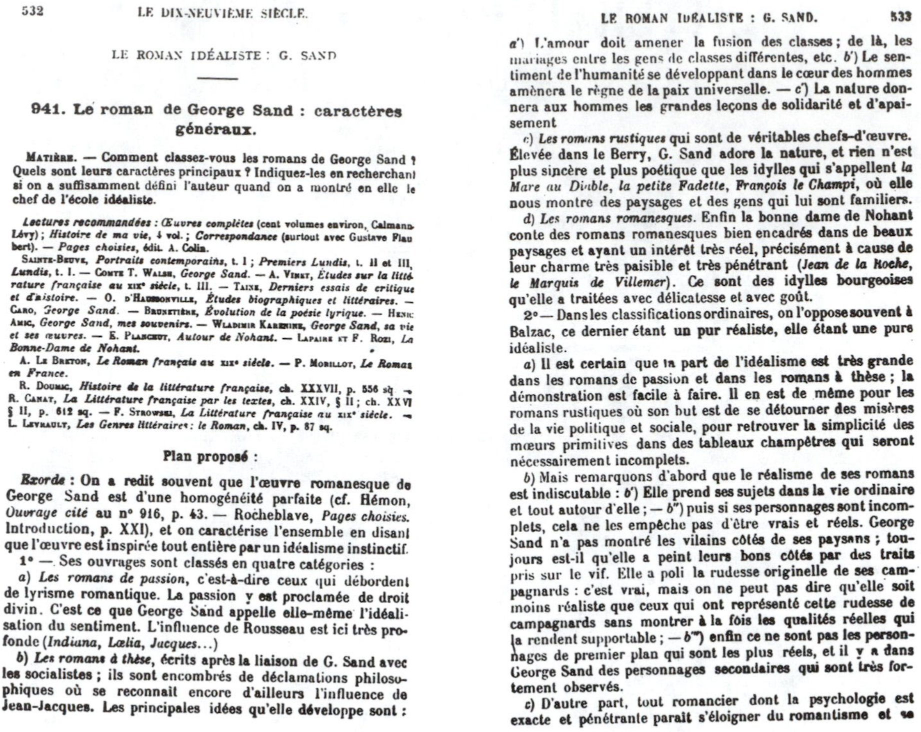

532   LE DIX-NEUVIÈME SIÈCLE.

LE ROMAN IDÉALISTE : G. SAND

941. Le roman de George Sand : caractères généraux.

Matière. — Comment classez-vous les romans de George Sand ? Quels sont leurs caractères principaux ? Indiquez-les en recherchant si on a suffisamment défini l'auteur quand on a montré en elle le chef de l'école idéaliste.

Lectures recommandées : Œuvres complètes (cent volumes environ, Calmann-Lévy) ; Histoire de ma vie, 4 vol. ; Correspondance (surtout avec Gustave Flaubert). — Pages choisies, édit. A. Colin.
Sainte-Beuve, Portraits contemporains, t. I ; Premiers Lundis, t. II et III, Lundis, t. I. — Comte T. Walsh, George Sand. — A. Vinet, Études sur la littérature française au xixe siècle, t. III. — Taine, Derniers essais de critique et d'histoire. — O. d'Haussonville, Études biographiques et littéraires. — Caro, George Sand. — Brunetière, Évolution de la poésie lyrique. — Henri Amic, George Sand, mes souvenirs. — Wladimir Karénine, George Sand, sa vie et ses œuvres. — E. Plauchut, Autour de Nohant. — Lapaire et F. Roz, La Bonne-Dame de Nohant.
A. Le Breton, Le Roman français au xixe siècle. — P. Morillot, Le Roman en France.
R. Doumic, Histoire de la littérature française, ch. XXXVII, p. 556 sq. — R. Canat, La Littérature française par les textes, ch. XXIV, § II ; ch. XXVI, § II, p. 612 sq. — F. Strowski, La Littérature française au xixe siècle. — L. Levrault, Les Genres littéraires : le Roman, ch. IV, p. 87 sq.

Plan proposé :

Exorde : On a redit souvent que l'œuvre romanesque de George Sand est d'une homogénéité parfaite (cf. Hémon, Ouvrage cité au n° 916, p. 43. — Rocheblave, Pages choisies. Introduction, p. XXI), et on caractérise l'ensemble en disant que l'œuvre est inspirée tout entière par un idéalisme instinctif.

1° — Ses ouvrages sont classés en quatre catégories :
a) Les romans de passion, c'est-à-dire ceux qui débordent de lyrisme romantique. La passion y est proclamée de droit divin. C'est ce que George Sand appelle elle-même l'idéalisation du sentiment. L'influence de Rousseau est ici très profonde (Indiana, Lélia, Jacques...)
b) Les romans à thèse, écrits après la liaison de G. Sand avec les socialistes ; ils sont encombrés de déclamations philosophiques où se reconnaît encore d'ailleurs l'influence de Jean-Jacques. Les principales idées qu'elle développe sont :

LE ROMAN IDÉALISTE : G. SAND.   533

a') L'amour doit amener la fusion des classes ; de là, les mariages entre les gens de classes différentes, etc. b') Le sentiment de l'humanité se développant dans le cœur des hommes amènera le règne de la paix universelle. — c') La nature donnera aux hommes les grandes leçons de solidarité et d'apaisement.
c) Les romans rustiques qui sont de véritables chefs-d'œuvre. Élevée dans le Berry, G. Sand adore la nature, et rien n'est plus sincère et plus poétique que les idylles qui s'appellent la Mare au Diable, la petite Fadette, François le Champi, où elle nous montre des paysages et des gens qui lui sont familiers.
d) Les romans romanesques. Enfin la bonne dame de Nohant conte des romans romanesques bien encadrés dans de beaux paysages et ayant un intérêt très paisible et très pénétrant (Jean de la Roche, le Marquis de Villemer). Ce sont des idylles bourgeoises qu'elle a traitées avec délicatesse et avec goût.
2° — Dans les classifications ordinaires, on l'oppose souvent à Balzac, ce dernier étant un pur réaliste, elle étant une pure idéaliste.
a) Il est certain que sa part de l'idéalisme est très grande dans les romans de passion et dans les romans à thèse ; la démonstration est facile à faire. Il en est de même pour les romans rustiques où son but est de se détourner des misères de la vie politique et sociale, pour retrouver la simplicité des mœurs primitives dans des tableaux champêtres qui seront nécessairement incomplets.
b) Mais remarquons d'abord que le réalisme de ses romans est indiscutable : b') Elle prend ses sujets dans la vie ordinaire et tout autour d'elle ; — b") puis si ses personnages sont incomplets, cela ne les empêche pas d'être vrais et réels. George Sand n'a pas montré les vilains côtés de ses paysans ; toujours est-il qu'elle a peint leurs bons côtés par des traits pris sur le vif. Elle a poli la rudesse originelle de ses campagnards : c'est vrai, mais on ne peut pas dire qu'elle soit moins réaliste que ceux qui ont représenté cette rudesse de campagnards sans montrer à la fois les qualités réelles qui la rendent supportable ; — b"') enfin ce ne sont pas les personnages de premier plan qui sont les plus réels, et il y a dans George Sand des personnages secondaires qui sont très fortement observés.
c) D'autre part, tout romancier dont la psychologie est exacte et pénétrante paraît s'éloigner du romantisme et se

FIGURE 2.

M. Roustan, pp. 532–33, *La littérature française par la dissertation.* Librairie Classique Mellottée. The outline (*"plan"*) of Roustan's essay on Sand is a model of French pedagogy. Classified as an idealist, Sand's idealism serves as the essay's thesis, a thesis that will be immediately qualified, nuanced, called into question (anti-thesis).

The Life, Death, and Resurrection of the Author

What is the status of the author today? Coming after Barthes, Foucault, and the feminist response to the "death of the author" first articulated by Nancy K. Miller,[4] undertaking to write a book on an individual author or what is known in publisher's parlance as a "single-author" book requires some explanation. The allusion to the classification of such books in the world of publishing raises an important point never mentioned in lofty theoretical discussions about the status of the author: one of the major arguments against writing single-author books today is not so much theoretical as it is commercial. It is not only because the author was severely discredited by (post)-structuralist male theoreticians of the late sixties that one is ill-advised (at least in the United States) to write on a single author; such books—there are always exceptions, of course—also have limited market appeal: single author books don't sell, are not candidates for course adoption, do not in the parlance borrowed from show biz have "legs." And when a single author is part of what is oddly referred to as a national literature the problems of marketing grow even more acute. We cannot claim to do materialist analyses of the production and circulation of books in print without reflecting a little on the laws of the marketplace within which we as writers of critical and theoretical prose function, without breaking the polite silence that surrounds our own efforts to capture for ourselves a share of the admittedly small audience for academic publications.[5] Though most academics do not depend on the sale of their books to support themselves and can at least in theory afford the luxury of disinterestedness—especially once they are tenured—like all producers of discourse they are nevertheless constrained by and subject to the laws of the marketplace (however restricted).

I am, of course, perfectly aware that Barthes's and Foucault's convergent (but in many respects antithetical) critiques of the author were not couched in economic terms. Indeed, as Molly Nesbit has remarked: "When Foucault described the circulation and operation of discourses, he neglected to explain that this takes place within a market economy even though this economic condition . . . defined the author in the first place. But the economy is Foucault's blind spot."[6] And yet despite Foucault's blindness to the economic, issues of value and hence marketability are very much at stake in his essay, for the legitimating "function" of the author exerts its influence in the arenas of both cultural prestige and commerce. Shakespeare sells; Racine doesn't. The relatively recent emergence of the author function in Western literature serves—and this is not the least of its effects—to keep the value of certain discourses artificially high, while depressing the value of others. And this brings us to another glaring blind spot of Foucault's, at least at that stage in his thinking: what is singularly lacking in his "What Is an Author?" essay is any analysis of the imbrication of what he was later to call the power-knowledge circuit with the circulation of discourses. For, as recent ideological criticism has demonstrated over and over again, under the "empire of the author" (Barthes) only discourses produced by a tiny minority of writers have in fact benefited from the author function. The "privileges of the subject" Foucault's discourse analysis was intended to "re-examine" did not accrue to those producers of discourse not generally credited with subjectivity. Contrary to the utopic longing Foucault expresses in his final sentence for a time when the matter of "who is speaking" will not make a difference, feminist and other critics have argued and continue to argue that, for the time being and for the foreseeable future, it does indeed make a difference who is speaking and to whom.

While in complete agreement with the feminist critics who argue that given the uneven developments of men and women, the death of the Author is not applicable to the newly born female writer and may indeed be viewed as a demise opportunely timed to deny the privileges of authorship to emergent subjectivities, I have no wish to claim for Sand the attributes of the departed Author, nor could I. To write on a woman author in a feminist perspective is by definition not to resurrect the so-called dead white male European Author. The very act of mapping the mechanisms of canonization implies a rupture with the glorified image of the humanist Author. Once the contingencies of literary value have been exposed, the mystified stature of the Author crumbles; once one lays bare the complex and often obscure means by which value is conferred on certain discourses and denied others—and in this field a case-study method is optimal—notions such as that of universal genius collapse of their own inanity. *This then is not in fact an "author book" though it does take the work of a single author as exemplifying a certain trend in fiction.*

But in that case why not simply write a book on idealism and use Sand's works as a privileged but by no means unique example of this trend? Other authors can be cited as idealists—Lamartine, Hugo, and

Dostoyevski, for example—indeed, if this were not the case, the very category would be disabled. The answer is that I am not willing to relinquish the author completely, however much reconfigured and shorn of her privileges, and not only because of her biological sex—Sand's signature is after all male. Unlike Nancy K. Miller, for whom, attending graduate school in the heyday of structuralism, "the notion of the author . . . had never been alive in the first place,"[7] for me, trained in the waning days of the Geneva school, it was, it is—not as a standard of value, not as a subject fully present to himself, not as a fount of intentionality and a guarantor of univocal meaning, but rather as a nebula of words, themes, desires, obsessions, recurrent scenarios, strategies somehow linked by a proper name, attached to a signature. What was attractive about the Geneva critics' author was the sense of the organic whole, the notion that shards of language culled from vastly different regions of the writer's production could be recombined to produce not the author, still less the man, but something like his simulacrum.[8]

Though unnamed, it is clear that the "modern literary criticism" Foucault targets at one point in his article is the then-dominant author-centered mode of continental criticism practiced by Georges Poulet, Jean Starobinski, and Jean-Pierre Richard among others, where the author "is a principle of a certain unity of writing."[9] I confess (I know the risks of this confession, but what is confession without risk?) that if my idealism resides anywhere—and it is surely at work here in other ways I have not fully mastered—it is in a certain nostalgia for the organic unity emblematized by the Geneva critics' authors. Though my Sand bears little relationship to Richard's Mallarmé, Starobinski's Rousseau, or Poulet's Pascal—she is notably lacking in the lush sensory apparatus of the author under phenomenology—my debt to these brilliant, now largely unread critics and to the professor (Victor Brombert) who taught me to read their works by his own example is real. Sand's idealism, her struggle with realism, might then be seen as constituting a sort of equivalent for what Foucault describes as the nodal point in phenomenological criticism, "where contradictions are resolved, where the incompatible elements are at last tied together or organized around a fundamental or originating contradiction" (p. 151). And yet, marked by gender, historically situated, inscribed in intertextuality, and theorized, Sand's idealism is disoriginated, detotalized; like all ideals, the organic unity that forms the utopian horizon of this undertaking is unattainable but enabling.

Definitions

At this point the reader is probably wondering when I am going to get around to defining my key term. I want to resist this imperative, at least for the moment, except to say that when I speak of Sandian idealism, I will not be referring to some sort of debased Gallic version of German idealism, yet another French (mis)prision of high German philosophy. It is a striking fact that when one pronounces the word *idealism*, one immediately provokes among one's listeners the unease but also the interest associated with that brand of idealism, for, however discredited by an overwhelming line of thinkers from Marx to Derrida, German idealism continues to represent in our postmodern Western culture the essence of philosophy and the dominant model of idealism. Given the fact that Sandian idealism as I understand it bears no significant relationship to the tradition of speculative idealism[10]—though it does bear a very explicit one to another strain of German idealism, that of Schiller, whom Sand much admired[11]—and that therefore my expectant readers can only be disappointed, one might well wonder why I did not choose a less troublesome title for my book. My response is that to do so would have been tacitly to reinscribe the banishment of women from what are widely held to be the most prestigious precincts of human thought. I mean first of all to do precisely the opposite by emphasizing the link between Sand and idealism; that is, my purpose is to call into question the reduction of idealism to the version that depends precisely on its exclusion of women from its purview, on its association of women with lesser forms of ideality (the pretty, the agreeable, the useful) to deploy its modes of thinking.[12]

What those who insistently equate idealism with a single moment in its long history often lose sight of is that even if one remains within the domain of philosophy, the boundaries of idealism are impossible to trace, for its purview is coextensive with philosophy itself. *Idealism is not one*: the idealism of Berkeley is not that of Kant, nor is that of Kant that of Hegel, nor that of Hegel that of Derrida, for that matter.[13] And if one expands the domain of philosophy to include aesthetics, the reductive equation of idealism with its high German instantiation becomes even less tenable. My claim throughout will be that idealism comes to function within the history of aesthetics as the opposite of realism and as such cannot be replaced by any other term if one is to make sense of that opposition. Thus, if my first reason for retaining this contested term is strategic, the second is archeological.

In an intellectual framework irrevocably marked both by deconstruction and by feminism, any attempt, however well founded, to revive a binary opposition such as (or perhaps especially!) idealism/realism, with its resonances of conservative Sorbonnard literary historicizing, cannot but evoke suspicion. To this suspicion, which I take very seriously—in fact share—I would offer two responses, one addressed to my largely imaginary (but occasionally embodied) deconstructionist interlocutor, the other, to the feminist.

First, no deconstruction can take place without a revalorization, in this case a veritable exhumation, of the previously devalorized term in the paradigm, and idealism has been repeatedly demonized, most recently by deconstruction itself (or at least by some of its epigones). Second, the deconstructive reversal of the opposition inheres, as we shall see, in its very revival, for *it is only in the process of reconsidering idealism as it functioned in nineteenth-century aesthetic debates that one becomes aware that in what we might call the paradigm of representation the term that now appears dominant* (realism) *was in fact subordinate*. Whereas in twentieth-century critical theory idealism appears, if it appears at all, as a reaction to realism, in the nineteenth century the opposite was true. What secures the superiority of realism within the paradigm of representation is the alignment of its terms with the paradigm of gender. To expose the ways in which aesthetics is articulated in gendered terms and thus to go beyond representation as we know it, one must be willing at the outset to revive old academic categories, however tired, however metaphysical. Third, as deconstruction has shown, perhaps the most effective mechanism for undoing binary oppositions is giving polysemy free reign, allowing the multiple meanings of words to break through the dam of univocal definitions. As Derrida has remarked to great effect, there is no *one* deconstruction.[14] And this in a sense brings me full circle:

the exclusive understanding of idealism as referring to the high German tradition of speculative philosophy obscures the multiple understandings of the term first in philosophy itself, second as it is used in everyday language, and third as it shifts across the boundaries of such discourses as aesthetics, Marxism, and psychoanalysis. Tracking the changing meanings of idealism in the three major discursive modes I have just identified is an organizing principle of this book: chapter 1 considers idealism as it signifies chiefly in nineteenth-century French aesthetic discourse, chapter 3 takes up the Marxist critique of idealism, and chapter 5 examines closely Freudian theories of the ideal and idealization. Of course, this inquiry does not pretend to exhaust the semantic field of the term— *idealization* (and *idealism* throughout will be inseparable from the term of its actual enactment) is, for example, a crucial term in epistemology— but it does extend it beyond its usual narrow acceptance.

If deconstructionists are suspicious of binary oppositions because of the metaphysical residues that may lurk there, certain feminists view binaries as irremediably tainted with the phallocentrism that is the very ground of metaphysical thinking. According to this view, the "bleak binaries"[15] inherited from structuralism collude with the mind/body split that inevitably results in the oppression of woman, who is always inscribed on the despised corporeal side of the slash. Though one must be exceedingly careful not to reinscribe unwittingly the oppressive hierarchies of patriarchal metaphysical thinking, one must equally beware of confusing a wished-for dismantling of this thinking in the present and future with scrupulous analyses of its operations in the past. It is not because late-twentieth-century feminism rejects Cartesian dichotomies that we must not take account of earlier feminist accommodations with binary logic.

It would be absurd to deny that in her aesthetic writings Sand (like other nineteenth-century women writers and aestheticians; see chapter 1) enthusiastically and unquestioningly subscribed to such metaphysical oppositions as that between the detail and the whole, and especially between idealism and materialism. This is not to say that these oppositions did not entrap her, for clearly they did. They constituted the epistemological horizon within which she and her contemporaries—male and female—necessarily and inescapably conceived the world and their missions as artists. In her remarkable long critical *Essai sur le drame fantastique* (Essay on fantastic drama) (1839), comparing Goethe's *Faust*, Byron's *Manfred*, and Mickiewicz's *Konrad*, Sand enlists a series of endlessly exfoliating oppositions to justify her evaluations, her critical choices, and her preferences.[16] These serial oppositions include but are not limited to the following: "metaphysical world" versus "real world" (p. 8), "the *naive* fantastic" versus "the deep fantastic" (pp. 11–12), artist versus philosopher (p. 16), "material beauty" versus "intellectual beauty" (p. 16), and "the unintelligent beauty of matter" versus "the loving wisdom of God" (p. 18). The rift between the spiritual and the material, passion and asceticism, poetic reverie and humanitarian action constitutes precisely the central existential and artistic dilemma facing Sand's metaphysical poets; riven by the seemingly irreconcilable forces and poles of attractions of the material and the spiritual, atheism and faith, the heroes of Goethe, Byron, and Mickiewicz are virtually doomed to failure. Far from undoing these oppositions, Sand sets up a clear hierarchy between them, consistently and eloquently privileging those she calls the "disciples of the ideal" (p. 27). She reserves her harshest critical judgment for Goethe, who is made to stand for an enlightenment naturalism that draws on the materialist philosophies of Descartes, Spinoza, and Leibniz: "Goethe does not seem to me to be the ideal of a poet, because he is a poet without an ideal" (p. 21). Not only is Goethe the materialist not a poet, he is not a philosopher either, because for Sand philosophy is "a philosophy of the future" and "chained to the present, he [Goethe] painted things as they are and not as they should be" (p. 31). Goethe, in other words, is the anti-Sand.

For feminist theorists suspicious about retrieving the paradigms of metaphysics, the idealism/realism opposition, when it is modulated as idealism/materialism, is particularly sensitive, since in the Western philosophical tradition idealism has always been opposed to the degraded materialism associated with femininity—or is it that materialism is degraded by its association with femininity? Much of feminist theory, at least after and in response to Beauvoir, has been engaged in reclaiming and revalorizing the allegedly feminine material, whether in the form of the body, especially the maternal body, the contingent culture of domesticity, or nature. Feminism, even in its non-Marxist occurrences, has almost always made common cause with materialism.[17] Hence any attempt, however cautious, however timely, to rethink idealism from a feminist perspective, is bound to be looked upon with extreme mistrust by the eyes of feminism.

For me, rethinking idealism is a way of reclaiming its utopian dimension, the ability of an ideal to empower and to mobilize the disenfranchised. The longest chapter in this book, the central chapter (chapter 3), concerns Sand's political fiction written during the decade leading up to the revolution of 1848, a time when atrocious social inequities (between rich and poor, as well as between men and women) produced a heightened utopian longing in Sand and so many of her contemporaries. As Paul Bénichou writes in conclusion to his magisterial study of romantic ideologies, *Le Temps des prophètes* (The time of the prophets): "Future *mal* was the real *mal de siècle*"(p. 566). Whatever the differences among the various doctrines Bénichou studies, ranging from liberalism to humanitarianism, they all share a common fund of ideas and values, among which features prominently what Bénichou calls "the sanctity of the ideal" (p. 11). What the crippling equation of idealism with Hegelianism, reinforced by the scientific Marxist critique of utopian socialism, has most effectively and disastrously succeeded in repressing is idealism's transformative, revolutionary potential. *Sandian idealism is a politics at least as much as an aesthetics.* The quest for the ideal, animated by an unshakable faith in the perfectibility of humankind and the social was throughout the nineteenth century a powerfully mobilizing force for change; intellectuals and workers, poet-magi and worker-poets all worshiped in what Bénichou calls "the great Church of the modern ideal" (p. 12).

Ideal, Idealization, Idealism

Idealism as an aesthetics is opposed to realism; as a politics, to materialism;[18] however, in psychoanalysis, the ideal is not opposed to the real but rather represents a compromise between desire and the reality principle. Put another way, in the realm of the psyche idealization is synonymous with an overestimation, an elevation of the loved object, while in the realm of art it signifies, according to the tenets of classical and neoclassical aesthetics, an amelioration, a heightening of the real through sacrifice, selection, and recombination. The idealized beloved, though embellished by fantasy, is modeled on a real person, and the goal of the psychoanalytic cure is to strip away or chip away at that fantasy to reveal the gap between the paragon and reality. By contrast, the artificial integrity of the idealized work of art, whose model in the real is nowhere to be found, is the very end point of classical and neoclassical aesthetics. Put still another way, both the revolutionary and the lover seek to recapture an earlier state of being fantasized as ideal, to suture an originary split between the real and the ideal, but while the utopian idealist wants to restore a state of collective perfection, an organic whole, the narcissistic idealist pursues an individual Eden, a blissfully unified and omnipotent Ego. A whole series of questions then arises: What are the paths that lead from a refusal of realism as a signifying practice to the embrace of utopianism as a political praxis? What are the connections between idealism as an aesthetic category and idealization as a mode of intersubjectivity? How can an aesthetic mode that draws its impetus from Plato be articulated onto a political philosophy that owes as much to the Gospel as to the Enlightenment? Is utopianism the (regressive) social thought of the narcissist?

The crossovers are dizzying and must be negotiated with extreme caution, but it is my conviction that, at least in the age of romanticism, the ideal, idealism, and idealization traverse aesthetics, politics, and Eros and provide important links among them. Nor are some of these links confined to the age of romanticism; they are at work as well, for example, at the dawn of the age of fascism and totalitarianism. Thus, for example, in *Group Psychology and the Analysis of the Ego*, Freud makes the connection between individual and collective forms of idealization a centerpiece of his theory of mass psychology.

If tracking the subtle and not so subtle differences in meaning the term *idealism* acquires as it shifts across disciplines and discourses is a daunting task, that difficulty is compounded by the obvious distinctions to be made among the three terms I have just aligned—the ideal, idealism, and idealization—and the fourth that I add now, the Idea. Each of these terms has its own semantic field and commands its own set of connotations, yet all four are inextricably linked. Idealization, for example, is the process whereby the ideal is enacted, yet it can also signify the idealized object, the end product of the process itself.

The ways in which these terms operate on a continuum in nineteenth-century thought are illustrated in the work of the utopian socialist Pierre

Leroux, whose influence on Sand has been amply asserted if inadequately studied. In his *Troisième Mémoire: Des rapports du christianisme avec la doctrine philosophique du progrès* (Third memoir: The relationship between Christianity and the philosophical doctrine of progress), Leroux seeks to establish the role of ideas in bringing about progress. This is how he defines idealism:

> Let us call *idealism* the belief in the power and the benevolence of *ideas*. An *idealist* will be he who *believes in tomorrow*, that is, who believes *that today's reality is the result of yesterday's thought* and that *tomorrow's reality will be the result of today's thought*.[19]

Idealism according to Leroux implies a belief in the inscription of ideas in a progressive temporality, and that belief entails in turn a belief in the embodiment of ideas in individual human beings. Leroux situates himself between two rival philosophies, the "double rut of Descartes and Locke" (p. 165), materialism and spiritualism. Materialism denies the existence of ideas and subsumes them in sensationalism, whereas spiritualism is an extreme form of idealism that asserts the absolute autonomy of ideas. Thus to the question: *"How is progress achieved in Mankind? How is perfectibility brought about?"* Leroux answers, *"By the birth in the bosom of Humanity of ideas that are realized and incarnated"* (p. 169). This produces the "formula of perfectibility": "REALITY—IDEAL—PROGRESS" (p. 169), where what Leroux calls the ideal is the "Idea which [reality] engenders" (p. 149). What interests me here—and we shall return to Leroux's social thought later—is the smooth, entirely unselfconscious way Leroux shifts from ideas to the Idea, from the idea to the Idea, from ideas to idealism, from idealism to the ideal, from the Idea to the Ideal.

It would be disingenuous to claim that *the ideal, idealism,* and *idealization* are not related terms that all refer back to *the Idea;* using these terms if not interchangeably, at least as part of a semantic continuum, seems to me entirely justified by current as well as nineteenth-century usage, with one caveat: whereas the words *idea, ideal,* and *idealization* occur in Sand, the word *idealism,* to my knowledge, does not or, if it does, so infrequently as to escape all but the lexicologist's all-seeing eye. It is useless to speculate on the reasons for its absence, especially surprising in the writings of so astute a critic of realism as Sand, but I would suppose it is part of a general refusal by the poets and novelists of the period to endorse the metacritical categories affixed to their writings by critics. I am thinking, of course, of Flaubert and his vehement rejection of the descriptive epithet *realist* that critics insisted on applying to him. In a similar vein, speaking of Balzac and his refusal to adhere to "an absolute system," Sand notes approvingly:

> He tried everything. . . . He further developed what he felt were his strongest assets, and made fun of wrong-headed criticism that seeks to impose on artists a framework, a subject, and methods. This is an error to which the public still subscribes, not realizing that this or that arbitrary theory is always the expression of a single individual, hence would be the first to declare its independence by contradicting the point of view of an adjacent or opposing theory. We are struck by these contradictions when we read half-a-dozen critical articles on the same work of art; we then see that each critic has his own criteria, his own passion, his own particular taste.[20]

The critics Sand is referring to here are the journalists writing in the contemporary press, those who evaluate works of art in the name of some aesthetic dogma: academic idealism for the enemies of realism, strict mimetic realism for its promoters (among them, Sainte-Beuve).

Idealism in the Canon

By pinning the term *idealist* to Sand I do not wish to channel the diverse and contradictory trends in her multifaceted oeuvre, still less to project or impose my own passions and tastes onto her, for if anything they run in the opposite direction. By investigating idealism in the novel (but not only the novel) as it is exemplified by Sand, I want instead to contribute to her recanonization by taking at face value the very categorization that has enabled her decanonization. The critical cliché has a conservative function; at any given moment, it helps maintain extant hierarchies. At the same time, these clichés offer perfect starting points for projects of transvaluation.

Not all critics of Sand, indeed not all critics engaged in the positive reevaluation of her work, would agree, however, that idealism is the category most responsible for Sand's loss of canonic status. Though one would be hard-pressed to find a book on Sand that does not mention her idealism, one would be equally hard-pressed to find one that in any way problematizes this category, because like so many critical stereotypes, Sand's vaunted idealism is often invoked to obscure rather than illuminate what is most worthy of investigation, to close off rather than open up the discussion. Instead, romanticism, and the degree of Sand's participation in it, has been to date the major category informing efforts to reevaluate Sand's writings. Thus in her feisty book, *George Sand: A Brave Man, the Most Womanly Woman* (1988), Donna Dickenson sets out to prove that George Sand has been mislabeled a romantic, while in her pioneering study, *George Sand: Writing for Her Life* (1991), all the while recognizing the centrality of idealism in Sand, Isabelle Hoog Naginski purposely gives short shrift to the overstudied pastoral, idyllic novels to give the more romantic (Gothic, metaphysical, mythological) aspects of Sand's fiction full play.

Just as *"idealist" is not the only label affixed to Sand, Sand is not the only author in the French canon to be labeled "idealist"* and by the same gesture exiled to the margins of canonicity. Indeed, as realism has become hegemonic and idealism, as its countervailing representational mode, forgotten, the epithet has reverted to its more strictly philosophical meaning and is perhaps most often used today to characterize fin-de-siècle French writers closely identified with the importation of high German speculative philosophy, particularly symbolists promoting an aesthetic idealism in reaction to the triumph of naturalism. The term has, for example, been applied with equally devastating results to *L'Eve future*.[21] Villiers is, I hasten to add, hardly comparable to Sand either in terms of his productivity or national and international stature during his lifetime. However, this comparison emphasizes *the instability of this categorization even within the parameters of the literary institution*, indeed the French literary institution, for Villiers's idealism is not Sand's—in many ways it offers a striking counterexample that brings to the fore the *play of gender in the realm of the ideal*. Villiers's future Eve is an ideal woman called Hadaly, a sort of anagram of *idéal*. And Hadaly is an automaton built according to the tenets of classical idealism: that is, she is an artificial composite of the best features of a number of natural women. Now it may well be that *the logic of idealization always entails disembodiment*, so the difference between Sand's idealism and Villiers's appears on close inspection not to be as great as one might imagine or wish—and yet there is a world of difference between Sand's desexualized ideal women and Villiers's decorporealized replicant. The former, as we shall see, participate in a feminist postrevolutionary strategy of dualistic representations of women as either sensuous or rational, the latter, in rising capitalism's inflation of misogynistic representations of women as made up of fetishized spare parts. It will be important in what follows to distinguish carefully what I will call *feminist idealism* from its masculinist homonym—for if, like all perversions, fetishism always comports a degree of idealization, Sand's idealism is bound up with a radical subversion and rejection of male fetishism and the misogynistic idealism that it underwrites.

From Female Fetishism to Feminist Idealism

According to Freud, fetishism is a uniquely male perversion, and even though feminists have over the last decade mounted increasingly sophisticated and effective appropriative raids on this notion, the association between what we might call "classical fetishism"—the eroticization by certain men of a part object meant to compensate for but also certify woman's alleged castration—the birth of equally classical realism, and a certain stage of capitalism, is by now an established historical fact. Beginning to write in the 1830s, Sand bears witness to the affinity of emerging realism in Louis-Philippe's France for details of female mutilation. It is precisely in her most overtly feminist early fictions—*Indiana* (1832), *Valentine* (1832), and *Mauprat* (1836)—which are not yet fully disengaged from realistic representational codes, that we find recurrent scenes of fetishistic eroticism, for in these highlighted details of female anatomy—eroticized plaits of hair, burned and scratched parts of the body—are lodged the entire gender power system Sand struggles to dismantle.[22] And it is no accident that among the details Sand eventually places "under erasure" in her mature idealistic fiction are precisely these details referring to violence done to female bodies. It is by electing to turn away from this category of fetishistic details embraced by detailists from Balzac to Barthes, from Flaubert to Robbe-Grillet, that Sand most clearly distinguishes herself from her (realist) male counterparts. *Feminist idealism is an antidetailism, an antifetishism*, to the extent that the realist detail is bound up with a fetishistic economy that values only women who are wounded, in pieces, and/or phallic.

If, as I argued in *Breaking the Chain*, a century of fetishization of the female body by male writers culminates in the creation of Villiers's female android, then we might say that decades of female idealism culminate in a text by a fin-de-siècle woman writer who proposes a telling countermodel to *L'Eve future*, Rachilde's *Monsieur Vénus*. At the end of this famously scandalous novel, which presents itself from its first chapter as a deliberate rewriting of the story of Adam and Eve and throughout as a radical experiment in idealizing Eros, the dead new Adam is preserved by his wife Raoule as a sort of cyborg, part embalmed body, part machine.

Rachilde, the author of an astonishing pamphlet entitled, *Pourquoi je ne suis pas féministe* (Why I am not a feminist), is hardly a spiritual daughter of George Sand's; it would therefore be difficult to call her idealism feminist or to do so without revising our understanding of feminism. And yet a male cyborg is not a female replicant: beyond the obvious element of role reversal, there is a significant difference in the process of production. Raoule is a necrophiliac, not a fetishist; by first feminizing her proletarian lover and ultimately husband, Jacques, and then having his dead body—she has more or less arranged to have him killed off in a duel—kept on in a reconstructed form, she wishes less to deny castration than to go beyond it altogether. Undecidability is present in this novel, but it does not center on whether woman is castrated (which is to say whether man is phallic), but rather on whether any meaningful difference (not to say relation) at all exists between men and women. When Raoule visits the shrinelike chamber where Jacques's body is preserved, she dresses alternately as a woman or in drag. Not only is the object's ontological status undecidable, so, too, is the subject's gender. In this extreme troubling of gender that is also a sort of cyborg manifesto, Rachilde plays out the most radical consequences of Sand's female fetishism, which always involve a destabilization of sexual roles, as well as the undermining of individuality itself through the use of travesty.

What Follows

Whatever other conclusions we can draw from what precedes, this much is clear: we cannot easily resolve the question of the relationship between feminism and idealism. That question is incredibly complex, and sorting it out can be said to have been, or, more accurately, to have become in the process of writing, the aim of this book. Pursuing my feminist inquiry into and critique of the gendering of aesthetic categories, I take it as axiomatic that neither realism nor idealism is intrinsically gendered; nevertheless, at various moments in their histories, I argue, they have come to be associated with or claimed by one sex or the other. Sand names such a moment of linkage between the feminine and the ideal. But if bringing to light and reexamining the way this concatenation functions also contributes to solving the riddle of Sand's posthumous loss of canonic status and thus to recanonizing her (chapter 1), it also exposes the multiple tensions between Sand's feminism and her idealism (chapter 2). For if idealism as an aesthetic mode tends toward the abstract and the metaphysical (e.g., allegory), a certain feminist protest necessarily entails an immersion in the concrete and the corporeal. Similarly, if idealism as a politics tends toward a utopian fraternal community, feminism, especially in France with its revolutionary heritage, is at odds with the republican ideal of a society of brothers (chapters 2, 3, 4). Finally, if idealization as a psychic process involves the disqualification of the mother and more generally women as agents of morality and citizens of the polis, feminism asserts women's equality with men as members of civil society and upholders of civilization (chapter 5).

Even by nineteenth-century standards, Sand's oeuvre is immense, and its very size and scope are an intrinsic aspect of her reputation, for better and for worse. So unwieldy is the Sand corpus that even the most serious Sand scholars resort to approximation when attempting to give a sense of her production, speaking of "some" eighty novels, as though it were literally impossible to count them or to count them with any precision. This imprecision may be traced back to the fact that the only nineteenth-century edition of Sand's works that purports to be complete (112 volumes published by Michel Lévy, later Calmann-Lévy) is neither complete nor numbered. Despite remarkable strides made in recent years to remedy this situation—notably the exemplary 25-volume *Correspondance* edited by Georges Lubin—large sections of the Sand oeuvre remain uncharted, unmapped territory.

Arising at this juncture is the classic academic question of the constitution of one's corpus. Not the least of my differences from my predecessors in the Geneva school—and here I am perhaps more structuralist than thematic in my founding postulates and methodology—is that I do not take the entirety of Sand's oeuvre for my corpus. Though I have read a great many more works by Sand than those I actually discuss, my approach is purposely selective. The works I read closely span Sand's career as a writer from her early novellas through her late correspondence with Flaubert. And though I have tried to avoid the well-known pitfalls of the chronological approach—notably the developmental fallacy that posits a progression from the juvenilia to the works of maturity—I have not altogether refrained from involving myself in certain by now well-rehearsed debates within Sand criticism, notably those regarding the role played by 1848. It would be difficult to do otherwise, given the shape of Sand's career and the historical context within which she wrote. But my concern has not been with Sand's career and its vaunted stages or periods. Hence in my final chapter I am concerned with Sand's posterity: her posthumous encryptment and vicarious canonization in Flaubert's most celebrated and idealizing novella, *Un Coeur simple* (*A Simple Heart*), which he claimed to have written expressly for Sand.

Some of the questions that animate this project throughout but are not all answered in the end are: Is there a place within the canon of nineteenth-century literature for a woman author who combines, however uneasily, feminism and idealism? Can a better understanding of the circumstances of Sand's loss of canonic favor help both to reclaim her writings and to recast our conventional histories of nineteenth-century (French) literature and the hegemonic place therein of realism and its male practitioners? Can a better understanding of the difficulties of reconciling idealism and feminism enrich our understanding of both terms? Is a feminist idealism *possible*? Further, is a feminist idealism any more or any less *desirable* than a feminist realism or materialism? What can theorizing feminist idealism on the basis on a single example *do* for feminism, especially in the age of postmodernism?

Idealism

in the Novel:

Recanonizing Sand

L'amour où le prendrons-nous? Telle femme l'irait chercher dans
Balzac. Mieux vaudrait madame Sand. Il y a là du moins toujours
un élan vers l'idéal.   Michelet, *La Femme*

Cette querelle des réalistes et des idéalistes est fatigante et sans
fin. Il y a de grands esprits et de petits esprits, il y a des esprits
masculins et des esprits féminins.   Champfleury,
Souvenirs et portraits de jeunesse

Je crois que dans cinquante ans je serai parfaitement oubliée et
peut-être dûrement méconnue. C'est la loi des choses qui ne
sont pas de premier ordre et je ne me suis jamais crue de premier
ordre. Mon idée a été plutôt d'agir sur mes contemporains, ne
fût-ce que quelques-uns, et de leur faire partager mon idéal de
douceur et de poésie.   George Sand,
Correspondance Flaubert-Sand

Let me begin with an anecdote: in June 1986, I participated
in a conference at Georgetown University on "The Representation of the Other." My paper dealt with the representation of men in women's writing, and I drew my examples

from the fictions of several major French women writers, among them George Sand, whose novel *Indiana* I discussed in some detail. When I sat down after having delivered my talk, a fellow panelist, a respected male professor at a major Ivy League institution, leaned over and whispered confidentially in my ear, "That was very nice, Naomi, but you still haven't convinced me to read *Indiana*." I begin with this comical but unfunny episode because it has everything to do with the reasons why I have undertaken to write a critical study of George Sand. Baldly stated: in 1986, sixteen years after Kate Millett's *Sexual Politics*, thirty-seven years after Simone de Beauvoir's *The Second Sex*, fifty-seven years after Virginia Woolf's *A Room of One's Own*, to cite some of the landmarks of feminist criticism and theory, many if not most of my colleagues still believed that it was incumbent upon us—and when I say "us," I refer in general to us feminist critics, in particular to us Sand scholars—to convince them that Sand (but also many other major women writers) are worth reading. Ours is of necessity a rhetoric of persuasion.

We may meet this challenge with a number of responses: disbelief, derision, dismissal, deconstruction, but the question of the canon remains, and it will not go away, for as Leslie Fiedler has observed: "We all know in our hearts that literature is effectively what we teach in departments of English; or conversely, what we teach in departments of English is literature."[1] If we assume for the moment that we can simply substitute French for English—no small assumption—then the situation becomes quite clear: as long as works by Sand are not included routinely in surveys of nineteenth-century French literature, on reading lists for prelims and orals, on the program for the Agrégation, and so on, however many colloquia we may hold on Sand, however many studies we may devote to her oeuvre, however many texts of hers we may reedit, she will remain beyond the pale of literature, in its strong institutional sense. Two possibly controversial assumptions ground that statement. First, that the task, rather one of the tasks, of feminist criticism is to infiltrate and remodel the existing canon. My quarrel here is with the position provocatively argued by Lillian S. Robinson in her much-anthologized article "Treason Our Text: Feminist Challenges to the Literary Canon." Robinson claims that upgrading women writers already marginally in the canon from second to first rank is a misguided feminist enterprise, as it leaves the criteria for canonization in place:

> The case here consists in showing that an already recognized woman has been denied her rightful place, presumably because of the general de-valuation of female efforts and subjects. . . . Obviously, no challenge is presented to the particular notions of literary quality, timelessness, uni-versality, and other qualities that constitute the rationale for canonicity. (104)[2]

My effort here is to show that on the contrary a reflection on the particular circumstances of a *de*canonization can produce results that exceed the case of an "already recognized woman" and call into question the value system grounding the canon.

The second assumption is that Sand deserves a place in the new, revised French canon of nineteenth-century literature. More precisely, Sand deserves to recover the eminent place she occupied in the old, unrevised French canon established by the Sorbonne between 1871 and 1914 during a period of intense national reaffirmation following the humiliating defeat of 1871. As Elaine Showalter has remarked: "It is a curious fact of literary history that canon formation has been particularly aggressive following wars, when nationalist feeling runs high and there is a strong wish to define a tradition."[3] The ideological constraints that presided over the formation of the French canon at the turn of the century are clearly at work in the promotion of Sand's so-called rustic fiction that went hand in hand with her canonization. It is after all as a novelist of the *terroir*, or country, the author of such classics of French children's literature as *La Petite Fadette* (*Fanchon the Cricket*), *François le champi* (*The Country Waif*), and the adult's favorite, *Les Maîtres sonneurs* (*The Bagpipers*), that Sand was initially inscribed into the canon.[4] Somewhere around 1890 a consensus was reached regarding the canonicity of Sand's pastoral mode. Already in 1887, Emile Faguet had written: "Hers was the genius of the idyll." According to him it is the works written in what he terms Sand's "third manner," the peasant idylls sited in her home region, the Berry, that are destined for immortality: "She found there her superior works, the ones that will endure, *Fadette*, *Le Champi*, *Jeanne*, and above all, *la Mare au Diable* [*The Devil's Pool*] and *les*

Maîtres Sonneurs."[5] And, in an important and thoughtful assessment of Sand's literary achievement, Georges Pellissier asserted in 1889: "What will remain of George Sand are her pastorals, a few simple and touching love stories set in a natural framework. . . . She is par excellence a painter of the fields."[6]

Clearly, to recanonize Sand at the end of the twentieth century cannot merely be to reinstate her earlier position and positioning; it must entail a reexamination of the premises of her earlier canonization, as well as a recognition of new ideological pressures. Although discontinuous, the history of Sand's critical reception shows that each successive generation of Sand scholars has contested not only or so much her global exclusion from the canon as the selective terms of her inclusion. Or to put the matter another way, no argument for inclusion has been without its own exclusionary gesture, as though only one Sand could claim our attention at any time. Thus the ground for Pellissier's promotion of the rustic tales is prepared by his clearing away of the debris of Sand's romanticism: "Mid-century marks the irremediable decadence in all genres of the exalted romanticism from which her passion-filled novels proceed. For some time now her socialist novels make us smile with their humanitarian tirades and their chimerical optimism" (p. 243). Thus, in 1974, Léon Cellier wondered whether it is a good thing that only the rustic novels have been saved from oblivion: "Did this choice represent a qualitative selection? Or was it rather a partisan selection, an underhanded maneuver designed to eliminate a certain image of George Sand, the rebellious, the socialist George Sand?"[7] Signaling a new era in Sand studies, Cellier proposed to retrieve another, the other Sand, by reediting *Consuelo*. In recent years Sand has begun to be reinscribed into the canon largely as the exemplary feminist author of such novels as *Indiana*, *Valentine*, and *Lélia*. *George Sand and Idealism* may well be seen with the wisdom of hindsight as participating in the cyclical return of the utopian Sand, and yet these few remarks on the history of Sand criticism suggest that a more satisfying (more utopian) outcome would involve inclusion that is not accompanied by exclusion, reduction, and selection.

To create the conditions favorable for such a comprehensive recanonization of Sand, we need a better understanding than we now have of the conditions of her decanonization. For Sand's fall from aesthetic grace has been spectacular. Writing in 1949, Van Tieghem declared: "Sand's fictional oeuvre has singularly declined. It is difficult to imagine the glory and the esteem that surrounded her."[8] Indeed, a writer of international stature in her lifetime, Sand was widely read, admired, and imitated by such far-flung readers as Margaret Fuller, the Brontë sisters, and Fyodor Dostoyevski, as well as by the greatest of her French contemporaries.[9] Allowing for the season in purgatory all French writers are said to endure in the immediate aftermath of their deaths—Sand's occurred in 1876— Sand's place in the pantheon of great nineteenth-century French authors appeared secure. In the introduction to selected passages from her writings published in 1924 in a series called *Pages choisies des grands écrivains*, the editor wrote: "The century that witnessed the birth and death of George Sand is scarcely over, and already she takes her place among our classics."[10] And yet, already in 1889, Pellissier concluded his exceptionally intelligent and sympathetic assessment of her achievement, by saying: "George Sand is hardly read any longer."[11] And, by 1938, Virginia Woolf spoke of Sand as a "half-forgotten novelist."[12] Unread in 1889, half-forgotten in 1938, what happened to George Sand?

I

The steady decline of Sand's artistic stock during the twentieth century is inextricably bound up with a major remapping of the topography of the nineteenth-century French novel. For, in the critical tradition instituted and widely disseminated by the Sorbonne, Sand's works are classified under a rubric that has since disappeared, seemingly without leaving a trace: the idealist novel.

It is difficult to date with any precision the establishment of the realism/idealism opposition first in the theory of art, then in aesthetics in general. But according to Erwin Panofsky's history of the idea from Plato to Michelangelo and Dürer, the founding opposition between idealism and naturalism was a relatively late occurrence (1664), an innovation of the neoclassical theoretician Bellori, which was bound up with the metamorphosis of the idea into the Ideal.[13] It is this neoclassical antinomy that persists to this day: "Thus the opposition between 'idealism' and 'naturalism' that ruled the philosophy of art until the end of the nineteenth century and under multifarious disguises—Expressionism and Impressionism, Abstraction and Empathy—retained its

Combat des écoles. — L'Idéalisme et le Réalisme.

FIGURE 3.

Honoré Daumier, *Fantaisies. — L'Idéalisme et le Réalisme*. Bibliothèque Nationale. Published in the *Charivari* in 1855, this caricature represents the ongoing battle between the rival aesthetics of idealism and realism as a parodistic duel between two mismatched male figures. Realism is portrayed as belonging to the lower orders; he wears rustic wooden clogs and an ill-fitting clownlike checked suit. In his left hand he holds a small square palette and in the right his weapon: an ineffectual paint brush, pointed downward. Boldly poised in the foreground is the embodiment of the idealist school. Naked and well-proportioned like an ancient Greek athlete-warrior, he holds his great oval palette before him like a shield. His head capped by a martial helmet, the representative of classical values stands ready to attack Realism with a maulstick, the long thin wooden stick used to rest the paintbrush on in Academic painting. The contrast between the figures of contemporary realism and neoclasssical idealism is somewhat undercut, however, by the very modern eyeglasses that sit squarely on Idealism's nose.

place in the twentieth, must in the final analysis appear as a 'dialectical antinomy.' "[14] In the nineteenth century, following the invention of aesthetics in Germany, the writings of Schiller, and especially Kant's formulations in *The Critique of Judgement* (and *The Critique of Pure Reason*), realism was yoked to idealism. Indeed initially realism appeared as idealism's binary opposite, as in G. H. Lewes characteristic formulation: "Of late years there has been a reaction against conventionalism which called itself Idealism, in favor of *detailism* which calls itself Realism."[15]

Realism in the nineteenth century signified overwhelmingly in relation to idealism, so much so that to consider one term in isolation from the other is to deplete, even distort its significance. Realism, cut off from idealism, is a radically decontextualized representational mode, a perennial trend rather than a historically specific literary, aesthetic, and political movement. Uncoupled from its binary other, realism is caught up in an endless semantic drift.[16]

Because the opposition between idealism and realism was viewed as an immanent mental structure, it is a commonplace of nineteenth-century literary criticism.[17] Pellissier's account of the evolution of the novel is in this respect typical: After passing through a lyrical, then a historicist stage, the novel

> in the end divided itself, without exceeding this very framework, into two very distinct genres corresponding to two irreducible tendencies of the human spirit: some, viewing real life through their imaginations enamored of beauty, virtue, happiness, produced a portrait always idealized in its very truth; the others, fortified with a wise and penetrating analysis, directed their energies at seeing reality as it is and at representing it as they had seen it.[18]

And yet so massive, so crushing has been the triumph of realism that at least in the field of literature—in painting and the theory of art where the opposition first arose, the story is quite different—idealism has all but vanished from our critical consciousness, taking with it the literary reputation of its most eminent French representative, George Sand.[19]

Sand's posthumous promoters generally recognized that her declining literary fortunes were linked to the triumph of Balzacian realism over the idealism associated with her name:

> For the last twelve or fifteen years her success diminished, though her talent had not flagged; it is just that fashion had shifted elsewhere. The positivist and scientific spirit has taken over literature; today a more exact imitation of things, characters more like those one encounters daily, absolutely precise descriptions recorded on the spot, in short a detailed, literal and micrographic copy of reality are what is wanted. The novel is in the hands of Balzac's successors.[20]

Consequently, around the turn of the century, all hopes for and predictions of Sand's return to favor are tied to a return to or of idealism, a turning away from a spent realism. In his *Cours de littérature*, Félix Hémon announces that that double return is imminent:

> Since Balzac, we have for so long savoured the humiliating pleasure of contemplating our portraits as we are, that we are seized by a violent desire to be flattered, idealized, fooled if need be about our poor human nature. And that is why favor is returning to this mixed oeuvre [Sand's], within which one nevertheless asks to pick and choose.[21]

And idealism did return. In an important (and, in the confused political context of the time, controversial) talk he gave in Besançon in 1896, entitled *La Renaissance de l'idéalisme*, Ferdinand Brunetière reported detecting symptoms of idealism's renewal not just in the arts (painting, literature, music) but in the sciences and politics as well.[22] Sometime around 1886, according to Brunetière, the exhaustion of the positivist paradigm, the reaction against naturalism, and the dissatisfaction with individualism combined to provoke a turn toward idealism in its manifold fin-de-siècle manifestations: a science of ideas and not facts, Wagnerianism, symbolism, socialism, and, pushed to an extreme, mysticism. But beyond the reactive character of this neoidealism, for Brunetière the move away from naturalism and the revival of idealism participated in a larger transhistorical cycle, the perpetual (and predictable) swing between the two extremes of this eternal polarity. *"Corsi e ricorsi*. Turn and return, action and reaction" (p. 56) writes Brunetière, citing Vico. The eminent French Academician therefore concludes: "Naturalism has its dangers, but so too does idealism. . . . Which is to say, gentlemen, that there is a time to be an idealist, and there is a time to be a naturalist (p. 85)." "Now is the time to be an idealist, and to react in all ways

Ferdinand BRUNETIÈRE

DE L'ACADÉMIE FRANÇAISE

La Renaissance
de l'Idéalisme

PARIS

LIBRAIRIE DE FIRMIN-DIDOT ET CIE

IMPRIMEURS DE L'INSTITUT, RUE JACOB, 56

1896

FIGURE 4.

Ferdinand Brunetière, cover, *La Renaissance de l'Idéalisme.* Firmin-Didot. On a cold wintry Saturday in Paris, just as I was preparing to send off the completed manuscript of this book, I took a late afternoon stroll to the Latin Quarter with my husband. While he eagerly examined the used books in the vast bins arrayed on the sidewalk in front of the great bookstore, Joseph Gibert, I whiled away the time sifting through the smaller bins in the first floor literary section. There, like a siren that had been obscurely calling me all afternoon, was Brunetière's little yellow pamphlet, the last piece in the puzzle I had been assembling since my first "find" in Hay-on-Wye.

and in all directions against that strain of naturalism we all have in our blood" (p. 86). "Let us then be idealists!" (p. 87).

Now, Sand is not absent from this pamphlet, where few artists are cited by name. But her work is not evoked as an instance of the new idealism, or even of the old; instead, it is linked to idealism's earlier incarnation, romanticism. Sand's very success in the late 1860s—the *Marquis de Villemer* is singled out as the "masterpiece" of her late manner (p. 55)—along with that of *Les Misérables* and of Musset's *Comédies*, is viewed by Brunetière as a sign of the incipient reaction against realism. The coming of the new idealism is heralded by the success of Sand's work, but that work is seen as part of the dying fall of romanticism, of a decadence not a renaissance.

My thesis then is this: Sand's spectacular aesthetic devaluation cannot be ascribed in any simple terms to her gender; it is not because Sand was a woman but rather because (like so many other woman authors) she is associated with a discredited and discarded representational mode that she is no longer ranked among the canonical authors.

The question then becomes: what is the relationship if any between femininity and idealism as a representational mode? This is by no means an easy question to decide, but we might begin by observing that the very notion of femininity already contains within it part of the answer. Femininity is a cultural construction, and as Simone de Beauvoir points out, one of the consequences of women's acculturation in patriarchy is their compensatory tendency to situate themselves on the side of the Ideal: "Because she is condemned to know only the factual contingencies of life, she makes herself the priestess of the Ideal."[23] It is this culturally induced idealism that, according to Beauvoir, accounts for women's romanticism as well as their hysteria, their "naturalism" as well as their narcissism, their optimism: "woman has a profound need to be ontologically optimistic" (p. 690).

Reading the romance is perhaps the most prevalent expression of feminine idealism in contemporary mass culture. Thus, one of the readers of romance Janice Radway interviewed confirms Beauvoir's analysis when she exclaims: "Optimistic! That's what I like in a book. An optimistic plot. I get sick of pessimism all the time."[24] Romance novels cater to their many female readers' powerful, culturally determined need to escape "ugliness, despair or serious human problems"[25] by fantasizing about a more perfect world inhabited by idealized characters and ordained by a logic of wish fulfillment.

The idealism at work in popular romance literature—a genre overwhelmingly produced and consumed by women—as well as in its more "elevated" high-culture avatars, is bound up with contingent circumstances, a specific historical situation and form of socialization. Consequently, its popular expression does not prove that idealism in general is essentially feminine. Further, if idealism is an aspect, a corollary, of the romance and romance a frequent by-product of idealism, the two cannot be collapsed into each other. There is overlap here, but not perfect congruency. Romance, like realism (and unlike idealism), is traditionally held to be a major literary mode, albeit one discredited by its coupling with the feminine and/or the popular. And, as Laurie Langbauer has persuasively argued, even women novelists felt the need to disassociate themselves from this devalorized, feminized form of writing—none more so than George Eliot. Indeed, a brief comparison of the literary fates of "the two Georges" should serve to dispel at the outset any notion of the essential femininity of idealism or romance as a literary practice. Or rather, to anticipate somewhat and to reassert the difference between the two terms, whereas Eliot repudiates (more or less successfully) *both* idealism and romance—often conflating them—Sand repudiates romance (Eliot's "silly women's novels"), while (re)inventing idealism.[26] Speculating on the reasons for George Eliot's easy superiority over the other George, whom she read so admiringly and to whom she owed so much, Patricia Thomson writes:

> In the long run, George Eliot has easily outdistanced the other George to whom she was indebted for so many insights and such a great enlargement of her horizons. It is not simply that *the idealist, optimist and romantic* has less of value to communicate than *the writer with a deep and realistic sense of the irony and tragedy of life*—although for modern readers this is surely a vital distinction.[27]

The difference in the literary fates of "the two Georges," while not reducible to the opposition idealism/realism, does overlap with it in interesting ways. For Eliot's poetics was, it will be recalled, explicitly anti-idealist, classically realist, bearing out Harry Levin's apt observation that, to a large degree, "realism presupposes an idealism to be corrected."[28] In chapter 17 of *Adam Bede*, entitled "In which the story pauses a little," Eliot stops to explain why, deliberately frustrating her implied readers' desire, she chooses not "to represent things as they never have been and never will be," not to "touch" up the world with a "tasteful pencil," not to "make things better than they were."[29] She prefers instead to offend her "idealistic friend" (p. 223) with the vulgar details that inhere in the representation of the commonplace and the homely. As Eliot writes in "The Natural History of German Life," "the unreality" of the representation of the common people is a "grave evil," for it directly prevents "the extension of our sympathies" that is art's "greatest benefit":

> Appeals founded on generalizations and statistics require a sympathy ready-made, a moral sentiment already in activity; but a piece of human life such as a great artist can give, surprises even the trivial and the selfish into that attention to what is apart from themselves, which may be called the raw material of moral sentiment.[30]

For Eliot the superiority of realism over idealism is moral; only a dei-dealized portrayal of the people can enable the sympathy for the Other that great art can uniquely inspire.

> There are few prophets in the world; few sublimely beautiful women; few heroes. I can't afford to give all my love and reverence to such rarities: I want a great deal of those feelings for my everyday fellow-men, especially for the few in the foreground of the great multitude, whose faces I know, whose hands I touch, for whom I have to make way with kindly courtesy. . . . It is more needful that I should have a fibre of sympathy with that vulgar citizen who weighs out my sugar in a vilely assorted cravat and waistcoat, than with the handsome rascal in red scarf and green feathers.[31]

The opposition between Eliot's realism and Sand's idealism is, however, neither simple nor neat. As many commentators have noted, Eliot is in her own way an idealist—the very figure of the common workingman, Adam Bede, who has been compared to Sand's meunier d'Angibault, is heavily idealized—and Sand's idealism is in turn informed by some of the same moral and social imperatives that animate Eliot's realism.[32]

But, finally, the question of the differences between Eliot and Sand is mooted by the recognition that the triumph of realism over idealism owes less to moral than to aesthetic considerations. Or, rather, the triumph of realism over idealism makes visible the interpenetration of the ethical and the aesthetic. If realism has triumphed over idealism, and Eliot and Balzac over Sand, this victory is in large measure because the aesthetic legacy linking referential illusion and political efficacy with the detailed representation of a blemished reality has remained with us in the age of the simulacrum. Even in those works, structuralist and poststructuralist, that have in recent years subjected the "order of mimesis" (Prendergast) to a radical critique, some of the underlying assumptions of classical realist aesthetics remain undisturbed. As Barthes observes in *S/Z*:

> Beauty . . . cannot be induced through catachresis other than from some great cultural model (written or pictorial): it is stated, not described. Contrariwise, ugliness can be abundantly described: it alone is "realistic," confronting the referent without an immediate code (whence the notion that realism, in art, is concerned solely with ugliness).[33]

Recanonizing Sand must of necessity entail a critical rethinking of both the aesthetic and ethical valorization of the ugly and the consensual equation of the real with the unsightly, for as we shall see it is on these linked assumptions that her decanonization rests.

II

So far, we have relied on a vague and commonsense understanding of idealism to ground our discussion. At this point, if we are to advance and to avoid the pitfalls that result from an indiscriminate use of the term *idealism*, we need to understand better how it was used in nineteenth-century aesthetic discourse. I will focus on two powerful French examples of that discourse, those of the philosophers P. J. Proudhon and Hippolyte Taine who, though writing from opposite ends of the aesthetic and ideological spectrum, both promoted idealism.[34]

An apologist of Courbet—whose portrait of Proudhon serves as an icon of nineteenth-century pictorial realism[35]—Proudhon devotes the third chapter of his *Du principe de l'art et de sa destination sociale*, "De l'idéal—But et définition de l'art," to undoing what he takes to be the false realism/idealism opposition, arguing that the two terms are inseparable:

> Realism, idealism, poorly explained terms that have become almost unintelligible, even for artists. I shall surprise more than one by asserting that art is, like nature itself, both realist and idealist; that Courbet and his followers are no exceptions to this rule; that it is equally impossible for a painter, a sculptor, a poet, to eliminate from his work either the real or the ideal, and that if he tried, by that very gesture he would cease to be an artist.[36]

Proudhon's demonstration of this natural interpenetration of the real and the ideal is even more surprising than his initial assertion, because it immediately displaces the ground of the discussion to the realm of representation, away from nature, as though nature were always already in representation. Proudhon's example is proffered as the paradigm of the realist image: a side of meat placed before a camera obscura:

> You may say, if you will, that the aesthetic feeling awakened by this representation of a side of beef is the lowest degree we can observe of the ideal, the one which is directly above zero; but don't say that the ideal is absolutely lacking here: you would be contradicted by the universal feeling. (p. 30)

The thrust of Proudhon's text is to disarm the idealist critic of realism à la Courbet by showing that the ideal is latent in nature, inherent in representation; there is no realism that is not also an idealism. In making his case for the primacy and prevalence of the ideal in art, Proudhon does not escape a dilemma he inherits from Plato and the Platonic tradition of aesthetics: the undecidability of the ideal, more precisely of the location of the idea. Either the idea is in the object—in which case mimesis is inescapably idealistic and the opposition between realism and idealism collapses—or it is located in the perceiving subject (the artist but also the spectator), in which case mimesis is incompatible with idealism, hence without redeeming value, abject—the photographed side of beef is just a side of beef.[37] Because Proudhon's goal is to redeem mimesis by demonstrating that it is shot through and through with idealism, he hedges his bets by having it both ways: the ideal is both in nature and in the artist. And yet, despite Proudhon's polemical assertion of inseparability, the opposition between the real and the ideal persists, the Platonic split between the idea of the ideal and its manifestations, nature and the spirit, immediately reasserts itself. Because the ideal is by definition an essence, a type, a perfection that cannot be realized, idealist art arises from the disjunction between the purely intellectual ideal and its sensory manifestations. The mechanisms for making the ideal perceptible are tropes, which Proudhon calls *idealisms*.

Proudhon's theorization of the ideal testifies to the centrality of the idealism/realism opposition in mid-nineteenth-century French aesthetic discourse, but because it is written from the perspective of the visual arts and in defense of Courbet and his followers, it is not all that helpful in understanding Sandian idealism. However, Proudhon's discourse cannot be enlisted here for another, not insignificant reason: Proudhon reviled Sand and the entire romantic (i.e., effeminate, Rousseauist) tradition that, according to him, she represented and in some sense capped. In his scurrilous series of essays published in pamphlet form, *Les Femmelins* (1858), Proudhon denounced romanticism as a perversion of idealist aesthetics. In the introduction, ominously entitled "Influence de l'élément féminin sur les moeurs et la littérature française" (Influence of the feminine element on the mores and on French literature), Proudhon rings the changes on the traditional association of femininity and decadence, writing: "If in either a society or a literature the feminine element comes to dominate or only to balance the masculine element, the society and the literature will come to a halt and decadence will soon set in."[38] This decadence takes the form of a clouding of the seminal, virile idea by an unseemly linguistic excess, because the association of effeminacy and decadence always implies a linguistic, indeed a rhetorical inflation:

> Any progressive or if one prefers developing literature is characterized by the movement of the *idea*, the masculine element; any decadent literature can be readily identified by the clouding of the idea, which is replaced by an excessive loquacity, which emphasizes falsity in thought, the poverty of the moral sense, and despite the artifice of the diction, the hollowness of the style. (pp. 27–28)

Proudhon, then, perceives two idealisms: the positive masculine form, which is faithful to the idea and which women can at best incarnate and promote, and the negative feminine form, a perversion of the masculine model that effeminate men as well as viriloid women—those belonging to that indeterminate intersexual category, the *femmelins*—propagate. Feminine idealism is not merely a literary pathology, it also affects or infects politics, as is demonstrated by Lamartine, upholder of the "Idealist Republic" (p. 42), but especially Madame Roland: "The Gironde, a bourgeois élite, made up of elegant and artistic subjects, inclining toward utopia by its admiration for antiquity, its literature and eloquence, was the idealist party of the Revolution and thus its feminine element" (p. 62). Paradoxically, the liberated woman that is Sand represents the ultimate perversion of the ideal by her idealization of love, that is, an Eros unsanctified by marriage, unbound by patriarchy:

> We have observed ourselves that the ideal had been given to man to invite him to love, and that love and the ideal are two elements by means of which woman exercises her share of influence in the education of humanity and the progress of Justice. But Mme Sand does not see things this way: for her there is no justice, no society so long as woman is not free, free in her love, free in everything. Indeed being sovereign, absolute, god, love is lawless; the consequence is then initially the condemnation of marriage. (p. 91)

What Proudhon's diatribe against Sand, whose obscene portrayals of Eros he ranks alongside those of Sade (!), points up is an important feature of misogynist theories of the ideal: it is precisely because in this system woman is made or makes herself into—of course, the distinction is not a minor one—a "priestess of the Ideal" (Beauvoir), that she is, that she must be, reviled for her naturalness. Thus all those misogynist idealists—Baudelaire, Proudhon, Nietzsche—who have attacked Sand have always done so by deidealizing her, by insistently emphasizing her bodily, animal functions: latrine, milk cow.[39] To steal a verse from Swift, Sand's misogynist critics might say: George, George, George shits.[40] Speaking of Sand's style, Proudhon makes a telling comparison:

> Her descriptions also have something lyrical about them that contrasts with Balzac's dissections. But, as all those who have studied the art of writing know, this blown-up style that our women of letters are vying to imitate, this bursting volubility that calls to mind the roundness of the Hottentot Venus, is not style: it's a fashion accessory. (pp. 103–4)

When one knows that the so-called Hottentot Venus functioned in the (racist, misogynist) nineteenth-century imagination as a symbol of hyperphysis/femaleness,[41], then one grasps exactly how irresistible is the impulse to degrade the woman writer who would rise above woman's assigned role in society, who would replace one form of idealism by another, by insisting on that writer's abject embodiment.[42]

In order to find a theorization of the ideal adequate to Sand, we must turn to a section of the French philosopher Hippolyte Taine's immensely popular and influential lectures on aesthetics, *Philosophie de l'art* (The philosophy of art), entitled *De l'idéal dans l'art* (Of the ideal in art). Now admittedly there is something circular about bringing to bear on Sand's literary practice the aesthetics of one of her most ardent admirers. Indeed, whereas Proudhon abominated Sand, Taine thought so highly of her that it is difficult to separate his theory from Sand's practice. No one was more keenly aware of the necessity to devise a poetics of idealism specially adapted to the idealist text that would allow readers with a realist horizon of expectations to read Sand with pleasure. "To take pleasure in them [Sand's fictions]," writes Taine, "we have to adopt their point of view, take an interest in the depiction of a more beautiful and better humanity."[43] Taine develops his notion of the ideal in two key chapters of *De l'idéal dans l'art*: "Le Degré d'importance du caractère" ("The degree of importance of the character") and "Le Degré de bienfaisance du caractère" ("The degree of goodness of the character"). What does Taine mean by "character"? Character, as he explains in the inaugural section of *Philosophie de l'art*, is an essential, salient feature of any object:

> This character is what the philosophers call *the essence* of things, and, because of that, they say that the purpose of art is to make manifest the essence of things. We will leave aside this word *essence*, which is technical, and we shall simply say that the purpose of art is to make manifest the central character, some salient and notable quality, an important point of view, a principal manner of being of the object.[44]

Despite his positivist trappings—Taine grounds his hierarchy of distinctive features in the realm of art on the notion of variability in the life sciences—in "Le Degré d'importance du caractère," Taine does little but reinscribe the main tenets of neoclassical aesthetics. The notable character that is the marker of the ideal is essential, unchanging, universal. The supreme work of art is installed in what modern historians call *la longue durée*; it arises from the bedrock over which the superficial and transitory products of the moment merely glide. As an example of such a perennial masterpiece Taine cites l'abbé Prévost's *Manon Lescaut*—so "durable" is the "type" created by Prévost that *Manon* has been repeatedly rewritten and adapted in response to the changing times. (It is here that Sand makes her first appearance in *De l'idéal dans l'art*, for in her novel *Leone Leoni* she rewrites *Manon* reversing the roles.)

Based on this section of Taine's work, the case for Sand as an idealist author seems weak, for it cannot be claimed that Sand ever created the sort of universal type Taine had in mind. Only when we turn to the second major section in Taine's text, "Le Degré de bienfaisance du caractère," can we begin to grasp the sense in which Sand could be described as an idealist novelist. In those pages Taine establishes a new hierarchy, one ordained by moral principles of goodness, rather than scientific principles of durability. Following this second classificatory system, the highest-ranked works of art are not those featuring universal types but rather those representing heroes and heroines: "All things being equal, the work that expresses a benevolent character is superior to the work that expresses a malevolent character" (2:289). It is according to this ethical scale of values that Sand is promoted as an artist of the ideal for, writes Taine, along with Corneille and Richardson, she undertakes deliberately ("de parti pris") to represent "noble feelings and superior souls."[45] Taine singles out for particular praise several of Sand's fictions, including *Mauprat* and *François le champi*, for their depictions of "native generosity" (2:295).

What Taine's lectures make apparent in a way distinct from that of a long line of theoreticians of the ideal in art stretching all the way back to Plato and up to Proudhon[46] is the necessary slippage between *the heightening of the essential* and *the promotion of the higher good* that constitutes idealism in the realm of aesthetics. Only in the light of Taine's double definition of aesthetic idealism does Balzac's celebrated statement to Sand regarding their differences become fully intelligible. Writing of her poetics of idealization in her autobiography, *Histoire de ma vie* (*Story of My Life*), Sand attributes the following remarks to Balzac:

> "You are looking for man as he should be; I take him as he is. Believe me, we are both right. Both paths lead to the same end. I also like

exceptional human beings; I am one myself. I need them to make my ordinary characters stand out, and I never sacrifice them unnecessarily. But the ordinary human beings interest me more than they do you. I make them larger than life; I idealize them in the opposite sense, in their ugliness or in their stupidity. I give their deformities frightful or grotesque proportions. You could not do that; you are smart not to want to look at people and things that would give you nightmares. Idealize what is pretty and what is beautiful; that is a woman's job."[47]

Initially Balzac casts his formulation of the difference between himself and Sand in terms all too familiar to generations of French *lycéens*: Balzac is to Sand as Racine is to Corneille. Theirs is but a replay of the paradigmatic French confrontation between realist and idealist writer. Almost immediately, however, Balzac undercuts this neat antithesis, arguing instead for an underlying commonality of purpose and method.

In keeping with Taine's first definition of the term, both Sand and Balzac are idealist novelists; *idealization* is here taken to be synonymous with *hyperbolization*, a form of excess in writing that strains the limits of verisimilitude. Enunciating her theory of writing earlier in the same section of her autobiography, Sand explicitly links idealization and implausibility:

> According to this theory, the novel should be a poetic, as well as an analytical work. It must have characters and situations that are true to life—even based on real life—that form a grouping around a type whose function is to embody the sentiment or main idea of the book. This character-type generally embodies in some way the passion of love . . . that passion, consequently that character-type, must be idealized . . . one must not be afraid to endow it with exceptional importance, powers beyond the ordinary, or subject it to delight or suffering that completely surpass the habitual, human ones, and that even surpass what most intelligent people think is believable. (p. 922/2:161)

The difference between Sand and Balzac's idealizations is in the end one of quality not quantity; it is of a thematic rather than a rhetorical order. The conflation in Sand's writing practice of hyperbolizing and meliorative idealization are what make of her in the eyes of Taine the paradigmatic idealist novelist, whereas Balzac, for all his larger-than-life character types, remains mired in the lower ethical spheres of realism.

Seen in this unfamiliar perspective, realism appears as a lesser, even a failed idealism. *In nineteenth-century French aesthetics* (whether it be that of Proudhon or Taine, Balzac or Sand), *it is idealism, not realism, that is the more inclusive term*. In Balzac's supposed remarks, however, the perceptible drift toward a stunning hierarchical reversal is checked when in the last sentence Balzac suddenly aligns idealization with gender. Earlier we asked what was the relationship, if any, between idealism and femininity. Balzac's statement offers the elements of an answer. Idealism in the novel is a priori sex-blind; the feminization of the idealist mode of representation is brought about by aligning sexual difference with a difference within idealism. This alignment produces a split: associated with masculinity, negative idealization becomes the positively valorized term, henceforth known as *realism*, while positive idealization, linked with femininity, becomes the negatively valorized term, a diminished and trivialized idealism.

This is perhaps the moment to stop and raise a cluster of troublesome questions, not to say objections: one, that by focusing on the realism/idealism opposition *I risk reifying realism*, reducing its complex meanings or, worse, endorsing one of many such meanings; two, that by insisting on the mutual exclusivity of the two terms, *I risk exaggerating the triumph of realism*; three, that by polarizing the binaries, *I risk overstating the differences between idealism and realism*. Let me take up each of these objections in turn.

Realism as such is not my concern here, except to the extent that realism and idealism are yoked together, that any attempt to (re)theorize idealism necessarily implies an understanding of the theory or theories of realism—indeed assumptions about what realism is as a representational mode. Since my concern is largely archaeological, that is, to reconstruct the workings of the idealism/realism paradigm in nineteenth-century aesthetics, I take as one of my assumptions that idealism, like realism, constitutes at some level a mode of apprehension and imitation of a referent posited as external and stable. In other words, the aesthetic discussions concerning both realism and idealism in the nineteenth century take for granted a conventional mimetic relationship between the word and the world—one that has, of course, been severely contested in recent years. Like the realist novelist, Sand drags a mirror behind her in which the world and the men and women that inhabit it are reflected, only her mirror is one that has, to paraphrase Woolf, the magical properties of blocking out the ugly and the mean and magnifying the beautiful and the good.

The mimetic theory of realism, especially in its Lukácsian modality, "reflection theory," has in recent years been subjected to sustained criticism by Althusserian-inspired Marxist critics, with the result that realism—and especially nineteenth-century realism—has come to be viewed in the late twentieth century not as the triumphant mode that it was in the late nineteenth century but rather as an embattled mode in need of "defense."[48] Without wanting here to become embroiled in these debates, I would like to observe that one striking aspect of the discrediting of traditional mimetic realism is the nearly complete lack of interest displayed by its most doctrinaire critics in the various representational modes that while contemporary with high realism insistently declared their own artifactuality, contesting from within, as it were, realism's claims to objectivity and universality, all of which share a common trait: a demeaning association with the feminine, i.e., sentimentalism, sensationalism, and idealism.[49] (The feminization of these modes, especially sentimentalism and idealism, should not blind one to their very real differences, not the least of which is hierarchical: that is, sentimentalism is subordinated to idealism and not the other way around. Sentimental fiction, to the extent that one can generalize about so shifting a category, deploys its cathartic strategies in the service of idealism, romantic or political.)[50]

This brings me to my third and final point: idealism and realism, while posited as binary opposites, in fact shared foundational assumptions as to plot, character, and verisimilitude. When viewed from the vantage point of postmodernism with its promotion of truly antirealist literary modes, idealism appears as more different in degree than in kind from realism. Sandian idealism may in certain instances blur the boundaries between characters, downplay "reading for the plot,"[51] challenge psychological verisimilitude, but there are no talking animals, no wild causalities, no incoherent wordplays, and other markers of the antirealistic in Sand's idealizing fictions.[52]

One thing is certain: the gendering of poetics inevitably results in their degeneration into stereotype. Thus, responding to a letter from the eighteenth-century woman novelist Riccoboni criticizing his alluring portrayal of the evil Mme de Merteuil in *Les Liaisons dangereuses* (*Dangerous Liaisons*), Laclos writes:

> To women alone belongs this precious sensitivity, this easy and cheerful imagination that embellishes everything it touches and creates objects as they should be, but . . . men, who are condemned to a harsher labor, have always acquitted themselves well when they have rendered nature exactly and faithfully.[53]

The division of literary labor along gender lines rests on two highly questionable assumptions: (1) Mimesis is man's work; the faithful representation of "nature," a sort of Adamic curse visited on male writers, condemns them to a literary life of referential servitude. (2) Women writers, congenitally unable to view the world without rose-colored glasses, are essentially idealists. Hierarchy insinuates itself into this paradigm less through its blatant naturalization of women's weakness than through its more insidious and far-reaching assumption that aesthetic value resides in the (virile) depiction of the horrors of unembellished nature. What is at stake here is, finally, woman's relationship to truth, which is always also a relationship to vision, observation, seeing. Thus Zola, a preeminent representative of the school of Balzac and critic of the "idealist school,"[54] attributes Sand's failure in her peasant novels to, "her idealist temperament that prevented her from *seeing true truth* and above all from reproducing it" (p. 772). The woman writer in rose-colored glasses stands as the necessary antithesis to that figure of the philosopher's imagining, woman-as-truth. For the logic of misogyny is a no-win logic where whatever is connoted as feminine—e.g., an excessive proximity to or distance from truth—is devalorized. Thus, the stereotypical association of women artists and the *ideal* is the obverse of an equally long and powerful tradition that condemns women to the servile *imitation of the nature* with which they are so closely identified, that views them as *congenitally incapable* of transcending immanence to attain the ideal.[55] For James, whose generally sympathetic account of Sand in *French Poets and Novelists* is a tissue of sexual stereotypes, Sand's disregard for truth is doubly determined by her sex and her nationality; like the heroine in the song, the French woman writer sees "la vie en rose":

> Women, we are told, do not value truth for its own sake, but only for some personal use they make of it. My present criticism involves an assent to this somewhat cynical dogma. Add to this that woman, if she happens to be French, has an extraordinary taste for investing objects with a graceful drapery of her own contrivance, and it will be found that George Sand's cast of mind includes both the generic and the specific idiosyncrasy.[56]

The essay concludes by enlisting a by-now-familiar color code, although in this instance the rosiness has been transferred from the lens of vision to reality itself:

> George Sand's optimism, her idealism, are very beautiful, and the source of that impression of largeness, luminosity and liberality which she makes upon us. But we suspect that something even better in a novelist is the tender appreciation of actuality which makes even the application of a single coat of rose-color seem an act of violence.[57]

Though we may today smugly mock the innocent sexism of a Laclos, a Balzac, a James, and though we may extend this list to include many other like-minded male authors,[58] the valorization of realism—the masculine mode—remains largely unexamined in contemporary theories of representation and the canonic hierarchies they serve to secure, for the theory of realism from Lukács to Barthes is essentially a theory of a single fictional practice, Balzac's. Despite repeated attacks on realism by some of the major avant-garde movements and figures of the twentieth century (surrealism, Brecht, the nouveau roman), critiques of mimetic representation stop well short of questioning the realist paradigm (and Balzac's status as the paradigmatic realist) and its underlying sexism.[59] Even those critics who have most acutely exposed the complicity of realism with bourgeois ideology, countering realism's claims to a specular objectivity by demonstrating the active part mimesis plays in legitimizing the apparatus of the Law, the network of disciplinary mechanisms that repress all exceptions to the norm, the sexual fix, even these critics have continued to be fascinated by the canonic figures, especially Balzac.[60]

To begin to grasp the not-so-subtle ways in which idealism has been feminized and hence devalorized is to begin to ask what it might mean to read otherwise, specifically, what poetics would have to be elaborated to take into account the Sandian text, to bring it into the pale of the readable, and, more important, the rereadable, for as James devastatingly remarks: "All the world can read George Sand once and not find it in the least hard. But it is not easy to return to her. . . . George Sand invites reperusal less than any other mind of equal eminence."[61] Once again Taine points the way—in an essay on Sand, he characterized idealist prose in ways that interestingly renew earlier normative idealist aesthetics:

> It is an ideal world and to maintain the illusion, the writer erases, attenuates, and often sketches a general outline, instead of depicting an individual figure. He does not emphasize the detail, he scarcely indicates it in passing, he avoids going into it; he follows the great poetic line of the passion he pleads or the situation he describes, without stopping over the irregularities that would break the harmony. This summary way of painting is the property of all idealist art.[62]

In this postrealist definition of idealism, idealism appears as a signifying practice of lack.[63] Whereas prerealist idealism, by which I mean the idealism promoted and practiced before the emergence of the specifically nineteenth-century literary movement known as *realism*, prescribed idealization as selection—the construction of the ideal with ideal parts abstracted from imperfect wholes—Sandian idealism is an art of deliberate erasure. For Sand was keenly aware of the link between details and realism, defining realism as a "science of details."[64] To be erased, passed over lightly, the detail must first be present; it is a case of emphasis subtracted. The *idealist effect* is produced by the evacuation of those same superfluous details that create the illusion of the real (Barthes), notably the fetishistic details so essential to mainstream realism (see Introduction). In this sense, we can reverse the quotation earlier from Harry Levin and say that, in the case of Sand, idealism presupposes a realism to be corrected. To read idealist fiction necessarily entails a painful renunciation of the perverse pleasure of the detail and the illusion of referential plenitude it provides. Other renunciations, similarly painful (at least in my own experience), follow, for just as the idealist text eschews the redundant descriptive detail of the object world, it refuses the seductive hermeneutic code that propels the classical realist text forward even as it undoes conventions of characterization.

The difficulties posed by the modern idealist novel are not, of course, unique to Sand—except in so far as her sex exacerbates them. They are notably intrinsic, for example, in nineteenth-century German fiction. The great tradition of realist fiction so grandly embodied elsewhere in Europe is, as is well known, strikingly absent in the history of German prose fiction. In his chapter devoted to German literature, "Miller the Musician," Auerbach speculates at some length on the reasons why a "contemporary realism" (as opposed to the realism bound up with historicism) failed to develop in Germany despite what he calls a "favorable aesthetic situation":

> Contemporary conditions in Germany did not easily lend themselves to broad realistic treatment. The social picture was heterogeneous; the general life was conducted in the confused setting of a host of "historical territories," units which had come into existence through dynastic and political contingencies. In each of them the oppressive and at times choking atmosphere was counterbalanced by a certain pious submission and the sense of historical solidity, all of which was more conducive to speculation, introspection, contemplation, and the development of local idiosyncrasies than to coming to grips with the practical and the real in a spirit of determination and with an awareness of greater contexts and more extensive territories.[65]

Whether or not one accepts Auerbach's definition of realism and his explanation for "the problem of nineteenth-century German realism" (as Swales put it), the connection he makes between representational modes and sociopolitical circumstances has interesting implications for our study of Sand. How did Sand's politics inflect her idealism and vice versa: Is there, for example, any connection between Sand's regionalism and her idealism? Is idealism the representational mode of choice for an aristocrat with popular blood and populist leanings?

III

If in Balzac's formulation realism is but a subcategory of idealism, albeit the most prestigious, Sand's idealism must nonetheless be understood as a response to what was to become known as Balzacian realism. For if idealism is not (any more than its opposite, detailism) an essentially female representational mode, the practice of an aesthetics of idealism was unquestionably for Sand a strategy for bodying forth her difference, and that difference is in part sexual. Feminist critics or gynocritics have traditionally emphasized transhistorical, transnational, transclass, etc., specificities of women's writing, but I would argue that female specificity in writing is (also) contextual, local, a microspecificity that shifts opportunistically in response to changing macrohistorical and literary historical circumstances. Writing in her autobiography of her literary beginnings, Sand made it quite clear that, in her view, to begin writing was to take one's place on a scene of competing representational modes (all represented by men):

> In that era, they were doing the oddest things in literature. The eccentricities of young Victor Hugo's genius had intoxicated the youth, who were bored by the old refrains of the Restoration. They no longer found Chateaubriand sufficiently romantic; the new master was just barely romantic enough for the ferocious appetites he had unleashed. The little rebels in his own school . . . wished to outdo him.[66]

Sand's choice of idealism was surely overdetermined, but what is significant is that it was a choice, albeit a difficult one. In what follows I want to focus on two texts that allow us to glimpse some of her earliest attempts at articulating her distinctive problematic.

In one of Sand's first novellas, *La Marquise* (1832), the realism/idealism opposition is manifested in the form of an erotic cleavage, and because this eroticization of the opposition informs many of Sand's novels, especially those centered on female doubles, I want to begin by considering this fiction, one of its most telling exemplars. Now we well know that according to Freud one of the most prevalent forms of degradation in male erotic life is the split between two types of women, those men respect but do not desire and, conversely, those men desire but do not respect. It is, however, possible to convert the undesired, that is, idealized, female sexual object (the mother, Madonna, or angel) into a desired one (the whore or harlot) by a process of lowering, or deidealization. This split has in Freud no equivalent in the female psyche; what impedes female desire, to the extent that such a thing exists at all, is familiarity, not respect. Hence the cure for women's lack or loss of desire is not, as it is for men who suffer from this syndrome, degrading the object, but in some sense enhancing it through secrecy and illicitness. What is astonishing about *La Marquise* is that in it Sand combines both male and female scenarios. But that in itself would not warrant its analysis here; what makes *La Marquise* a crucial text from the perspective of fictional idealism is that in it we can see just how erotics is bound up with aesthetics, just how, in other words, *idealization of the love object is inseparable from the promotion of idealist aesthetics.*

Presented as a kind of counter to a Balzacian "étude de moeurs" or "étude de femmes," *La Marquise* is the story of an anonymous and aged marquise as told to a nameless, faceless, and youthful male narrator, who addresses the reader in the following defiantly anti-Balzacian terms: "The Marquise of R . . . was not very witty, though it's a literary cliché that all old women must sparkle with wit"; "I beg you not to expect to find in her story the serious study of the customs of a period."[67]

Widowed at an early age after being married off to an old libertine, the marquise conceives a deep-seated aversion to both men and marriage. Indeed, by its critique of the barbarous system of the (convent) education and exchange of women, the marquise's story fits well within the inaugural Sandian cycle of feminist fiction. An element foregrounded in this early text but which will slowly be muted and then transmuted in the later texts in the cycle is, however, the equal contempt the marquise has for women, for femininity. What is problematic for the marquise is not so much the institution of marriage as the complex gender ideology that it participates in. Being a woman in the particular class and society to which she belongs is not a mere matter of having or not having certain sexual organs but of taking or not taking a male lover. So, in order to play her feminine role in society and to avoid being ostracized as a pariah who contests gender arrangements, the marquise takes as a lover that most "material" of men, "poor Larrieux" (p. 54) and keeps him for sixty years. Larrieux is the degraded love object par excellence: "He was . . . always busy satisfying some appetite" (p. 54), recalls the unsentimental marquise. Not only is Larrieux a *degraded object*, he is also a *degrading subject*, for he, too, functions in the bifurcated system of desire that inexorably severs friendship from sexuality: "He would say jokingly that it was impossible to have friendly feelings for a beautiful woman" (p. 55). And the marquise is beautiful.

But if the marquise is both degraded and degrading, she is also idealizing and idealized. Against her affair with Larrieux is set her Platonic love for Lélio, an actor. Sand here rewrites a familiar nineteenth-century script: the love of the actress that Ross Chambers has studied in the works of Nerval (*Sylvie*), Baudelaire (*La Fanfarlo*), Villiers de l'Isle-Adam (*L'Eve future*), and Jules Verne (*Le Château des Carpathes*).[68] The actress functions in this scenario as "woman freed of all her links with the natural" (p. 8), that is, the ideal woman, the woman-as-ideal (whose ultimate incarnation is a machine). The horror of physis, which is always at some level a horror of sexuality, is however not, as Sand here demonstrates, an exclusively male prerogative. Yet the *love of the actor* is as rare a theme in nineteenth-century literature as the *love of the actress*" is a common one, and it cannot be taken as merely its feminine equivalent. What the feminization of this all-too-familiar scenario allows us to see is that *for women the idealization of the love object is rooted in a horror of nature and sexuality but, more importantly, in a refusal of the constructions of gender.* What the marquise denies by her unconsummated love for the actor Lélio is the patriarchal structure and the place it assigns her.

How does this denial function? And more to the point, how does it function within the text to legitimate Sand's idealist aesthetics? The object of the marquise's idolatry is more than just an actor—he is an actor with a special talent for playing Corneille, the paradigm of idealism in classical French drama. "He was better at acting Corneille than Racine."[69] The man the marquise loves is not the man Lélio, as she discovers on seeing him off stage, out of costume, and speaking in his own raspy voice, but Corneille's heroic Rodrigue: "For me Lélio was but the shadow of the Cid, but the representative of the antique and chivalric love now ridiculed in France" (p. 74). But the love of the ideal, as we shall see repeatedly in what follows, always serves narcissistic ends; what the marquise loves is the image of herself that is refracted through this love: "I was a sensation in the salons, and when I climbed back into my carriage, I looked complacently at the woman who loved Lélio and who could make herself loved by him. Till then the only pleasure I had found in being beautiful consisted in the jealousy I aroused. . . . But from the moment I loved, I began to enjoy my beauty for myself" (p. 66).

In loving Lélio-Rodrigue she becomes a woman and accepts her own degraded femininity; loving Lélio is a balm on her narcissistic wound at being feminized. Her passion for the theater, she says, "made me woman" (p. 63). And yet if by loving the ideal she becomes the woman she was not before (and will cease to be when she grows old), she does so by taking into herself the heroic manhood of the Cornelian hero: "It was not him I loved, but the hero of ancient times he knew how to represent; these types of frankness, loyalty, and tenderness forever lost, relived in him, and I found myself with and through him carried backward to an era of now-forgotten virtues" (p. 74). The ideal of which the marquise is enamored is rather like the ideal of Mathilde de la Mole in *Le Rouge et le Noir* (*The Red and the Black*): a phallic chivalric ideal lost in the degraded Restauration society but surviving in literature or on the stage. Thus, at the outset, Sand's idealism appears to be both reactionary and revolutionary, simultaneously steeped in nostalgia and yet iconoclastic. As a mode of representation, idealism is identified with classical models; as a politics, it is identified with a vanished aristocratic (not to say feudal) order; yet, as an erotics, it involves a radical interrogation of present-day gender roles, a form of feminist critique.

Traces of the difficult emergence of Sandian idealism from the matrix of Balzacian realism can be made out even more clearly in *Indiana*, the very novel Sand was working on at the moment of her conversations with Balzac. *Indiana* is the story of Indiana (originally Noémi!), a young Creole woman from the island of Mauritius, who is unhappily married to Colonel Delmare, a disgruntled and tyrannical veteran of the Napoleonic wars. The opening scene is set in their small château on the outskirts of Paris, where a quiet family evening bringing together Indiana, Delmare, Sir Ralph Brown, Indiana's cousin and protector, and Indiana's dog Ophelia (!) is interrupted by the dramatic arrival of a neighbor, the seductive Raymon de Ramière, who is having a dalliance with Indiana's maid Noun. Inevitably the innocent and romantic Indiana falls in love with the eloquent seducer, a thorough cad and opportunist who abandons the maid for the mistress, causing the maid to drown herself, and then forgets the mistress to marry an heiress. Indiana is, however, saved from the ultimate fall and a subsequent suicide attempt by her ever-devoted cousin. Having survived a mutual suicide pact, Indiana—now widowed—and Ralph retire to a hidden valley (Bernica) on their native island and live there in tropical happiness ever after.

The celebrated double response of Sand's mentor Latouche to his star pupil's first solo novelistic venture accurately reflects the text's straddling of representational modes. After quickly scanning the opening pages of *Indiana*, Latouche is said to have exclaimed: "Come now, this is a pastiche, School of Balzac! Pastiche, what do you mean by it?"[70] However, having spent the night reading the entire novel, the very next morning Latouche saluted Sand's achievement in the following terms: "Your book is a masterpiece. I stayed up all night to read it. . . . No woman alive can sustain the insolence of a comparison with you. You are destined for a success like those of Lamartine. . . . Balzac and Mérimée lie dead under *Indiana*."[71]

The emergence of Sand's distinctive writing mode from that of her genial friend takes two forms: first, the movement from the conventionally realistic inaugural section to the controversial epilogue that so spectacularly exceeds the bounds of bourgeois realism;[72] second, the elimination in the 1833 edition of the interventions in the original 1832 edition designed to persuade the reader of the narrator's allegiance to the main tenets of the realist credo and his rejection of competing novelistic trends:

> The current fashion is to depict a fictional hero so ideal, so superior to the common run that he only yawns where other enjoy themselves. . . . These heroes bore you, I'm sure, because they are not like you, and that in the long run lifting your head up to watch them float above you makes you dizzy. I place mine firmly on the ground and living the same life as you do.[73]

And yet, the double-edged irony of this passage suggests that even within these digressions designed to guarantee the author's realist credentials and hence his legitimacy, another aesthetic is being promoted.

In what sense then can we speak of *Indiana* as an idealist novel? Indeed is it one at all? No less a Sand scholar than Pierre Salomon, author of a general introduction to Sand's life and works and editor of several of her novels, states categorically that *Indiana* is not an idealist novel, basing his determination on the deidealized representations of the male figures, notably Raymon, the vile seducer allegedly modeled on Sand's lover, Aurélien de Sèze: "If sometimes George Sand appears to be an idealist writer, it is certainly not here. The analysis is cruel, and one may well wonder at so much harshness directed against a man once beloved."[74] If, however, we recall Sand's own definition of idealism in the novel, it becomes immediately apparent that the ideal in this novel resides in the figure of its heroine and not its hero, for it is Indiana whose passionate love story exhibits the implausible extremes Sand identifies as constitutive of the fictional ideal. And yet, as useful as is Sand's explicitation of her idealizing techniques, it does not fully account for the idealism in *Indiana*. To do so we must bring into play Taine's theory of the biaxiality of the ideal in art, for what sets Indiana apart from other sadomasochistic female protagonists in nineteenth-century French fiction, notably Emma Bovary, her most illustrious descendant, is that in her story the quest for the love ideal is inseparable from an aspiration toward an ideal world. And it is in this respect that *Indiana* represents a decisive progression in relation to *La Marquise*. For all her reading of silly women's novels—that is, romances—when Indiana fantasizes, it is not, as Emma later will, about the beautiful people and Paris but rather about freedom for herself and for all her fellow slaves. Her dream of being freed from patriarchal bondage is inseparable from a dream of emancipating the victims of colonialism:

> A day will come when everything in my life will be changed, when I shall do good to others, when someone will love me, when I shall give my whole heart to the man who gives me his; meanwhile, I will suffer in silence and keep my love as a reward for him who shall set me free.[75]

And when Indiana and Sir Ralph retire to Bernica, this double fantasy is translated into reality, as the devoted couple devote their resources to buying the freedom of old and infirm black slaves, much to the local colonialists' dismay.

In keeping with Taine's theory, idealism in Sand's inaugural novel consists then in a distinctive concatenation of the erotic and the moral, not to mention the political. Moreover, and this returns us to the question of the gender specificities of idealism, Sand's feminist idealism bespeaks a yearning to be delivered both from the base desire for carnal possession characteristic of male sexuality and the injustices of a man-made system of laws that enables the enslavement of both women and blacks. And in this sense we must recall that the idealism/realism split is figured here erotically as well as aesthetically and politically. The splitting of the male object that we studied earlier in *La Marquise* is recoded here in the more familiar couple of the ideal upper-class (virginal) woman and her pleasure-loving lower-class other, Indiana and Noun.

Balzac's feminizing of positive idealization, though wrong-headed, is finally not entirely wrong: idealism, as appropriated by Sand, signified her refusal to reproduce mimetically and hence to legitimate a social order inimical to the disenfranchised, among them women. Idealism for Sand is finally the only alternative representational mode available to those who do not enjoy the privileges of subjecthood in the real. Or, more accurately, the turn away from realism to idealism involves an exploration of and experimentation with a number of genres (allegory, utopia, pastoral, and even autobiography) that are all closely associated with the ideal in its multiple meanings, though not all necessarily compatible with feminism in its equally diverse acceptations. To recanonize Sand thus requires nothing less than a reconsideration of realism as it constructs and supports the phallo- and ethnocentric social order we so often confuse with reality. Finally, to recanonize Sand will call for the elaboration of a poetics of the ethical.

Idealism

and Its

Discontents

Lélia *and the Failures of Allegory*

> Allegories are always ethical.
> Paul de Man,
> *Allegories of Reading*

In retreat from the sexual arena that has been for her the site of extreme sensual frustration and affective deprivation, Lélia seeks refuge in the solitude of "a large, abandoned monastery, half-destroyed by the battles of the revolution."[1] There she attempts to achieve tranquility through an ascetic regime of "resignation and regularity" (p. 114/179). But, as she watches the obligatory romantic sunset, it becomes apparent that her efforts to tame her demons have resulted in failure:

Sometimes I watched the sunset from the height of a half-demolished tower. The part that still stood was encircled by the monstrous sculptures which formerly adorned Catholic places of worship. Beneath me these *bizarre allegories* stretched their heads, blackened by time. They seemed to stretch toward the plain and silently to watch the flow of waves, centuries, and generations. These fantastic scaly serpents, these lizards with their hideous bodies, these chimeras full of anguish, all these emblems of sin, illusion, and suffering, lived a life that was inert and indestructible. . . . While I contemplated these bodies engulfed in masses of stone, which the hand of neither man nor time had been able to dislodge, I identified myself with these images of eternal struggle between suffering and necessity, between rage and impotence. (pp. 116–17/181–82; emphasis added)

Torn between rage and a quite literal sexual impotence, Lélia, a passionate woman of stone, looks at the "monstrous sculptures" and sees her own torments reflected in these representations. The word she uses to describe this process is "identified." Now, normally when we speak of identification in literary criticism, we refer to a relationship of perceived similarity between a reader and a character in a novel, play, or film; identification is an extreme (and little-understood) form of reader or spectator response. The identification of Lélia with the monstrous sculptures is, however, of a different order: what we have is a case of intratextual identification, a fictional character who identifies not, as we might expect, with another fictional protagonist but with fictive sculptures. The relationship of perceived similarity between Lélia and the gargoyles could be described as metaphorical (as well, of course, as metonymic, since the figures with which she identifies are contiguous to her person). But these figures are themselves caught up in another relationship of metaphoricity, *allegory*. The figures Lélia identifies with are emblems for the abstract notions "sin, illusion, and suffering." Metaphor on metaphor—Lélia, by means of her identification with the gargoyles, is also a "bizarre allegory." What is a bizarre allegory? Are all allegories bizarre? In what sense can we speak of Sand's scandalous novel *Lélia* as an allegory and, more especially, one that does not conform to the rules of the genre? Is the scandal of *Lélia* a scandal of genre rather than of gender? Or are the two interrelated in some manner that remains to be determined? And what is the relationship of allegorization to idealism?

I

On several occasions, Sand recognized that her unclassifiable novel-poem of 1833 was a problematic piece of writing. Speaking of *Lélia* in *Histoire de ma vie* (*Story of My Life*), Sand wrote: "It is, I believe, a book less usual from an artistic point of view."[2] In the preface to the revised 1839 *Lélia*, Sand commented on the aspects of her work that make it anomalous; for her that *bizarrerie* has everything to do with the work's partially allegorical nature:

> *Lélia* was and remains in my mind a poetic essay, a fantastical novel, where the characters are neither completely real, as the exclusive aficionados of analyses of manners wanted, nor completely allegorical, according to the judgment of some synthetic minds.[3]

Initially what makes *Lélia* a bizarre, not to say a failed, allegory is that in it Sand fails to respect the strict generic boundaries that separate poetry from fiction, the didactic from the fanciful, and, above all, allegorical from realist fiction. On the one hand, the main protagonists, Lélia, Sténio, Magnus, and Trenmor, and, to a lesser extent, Pulchérie, all function as disembodied embodiments of abstractions, variously named by Sand and others. Read as allegory, *Lélia*, through the conflictual relationship of Lélia and Sténio, stages the duel to the death between doubt and poetry, skepticism and credulity, experience and innocence. At the same time, read within a realist horizon of expectations, *Lélia* is the story of its female protagonist whose graphic confession of sexual impotence and bleak howl of metaphysical despair—as told to her sister Pulchérie in the pivotal third part—constitute the major scandal of the work. And one must choose between these two reading strategies, because reading for the plot is not an option available in this, Sand's most iconoclastic, work, a narratologist's nightmare, what with its unpredictable shifts from epistolarity to high romantic nature description, its jarring use of flashbacks, its deliberate refusal of standard emplotment, its almost parodic enlistment of romantic topoi (reformed convicts, deserted monasteries, masked balls, orgies, mad priests).[4]

Now, the rules that regulate poetic production dictate that the generic boundaries separating the metaphysical allegory from the all-too-physical love story not be crossed, lest a monster on the order of the hideous gargoyles we have just seen be produced. The description of the tormented gargoyles assumes in this perspective a somewhat different significance from that mentioned earlier: what they embody is not the tension between conflicting forces as much as hybridity, an impure doubling or internal rift. The image of the monstrous hybrid is precisely what arises in Sainte-Beuve's perceptive and influential 1833 critique of *Lélia*. Not surprisingly, given his stated aesthetic preferences, Sainte-Beuve speaks as an "amateur exclusif d'analyse de moeurs." Thus, after a sympathetic, indeed highly laudatory account of the novel, Sainte-Beuve qualifies his praise with this all-important reservation: "Since the raw material of *Lélia* is totally real and has its analogues in the society in which we live, I could not help but regret that in spite of the prestigious brilliance of this new form the author did not confine himself within the bounds of the novel of verisimilitude."[5] Sainte-Beuve faults Sand for not having respected the law of adequation binding realistic content to a realistic form. The result of this perverse inadequation is an aesthetic monstrosity, characters frozen somewhere between verisimilitude and symbolism: "In moving to the state of *ideal representation or symbol*, the characters or the scenes, whose starting point was, so to speak, earthbound, could not but take on at the undecidable moment of their metamorphosis a mixed and fantastic character that does not satisfy" (p. 593; emphasis added).

For Sainte-Beuve, the realistic and the idealistic aspects of the work are not coextensive; indeed, by invoking the notion of metamorphosis, he stresses the temporal priority of the realistic raw material or content over its subsequent idealizing transformations. The real is foundational: the ideal, a graft that does not completely take.[6] Inside *Lélia*, buried beneath the text's scintillating new forms, there is a realistic novel struggling to get out. For Sainte-Beuve, Sand's allegory fails because of an indeterminacy, an undecidability that threatens the secure boundaries between representational modes. Had Sand confined herself to the realist mode more adequate to her shocking tale of sexual dysfunction, there would, according to Sainte-Beuve, have been no problem, and the novel would have been an unqualified success.

But Sainte-Beuve does not speak here of allegory, rather (and somewhat hesitantly) of "ideal representation or symbol," and this terminology adds a further complication for, as we know, in romantic aesthetics there is a persistent effort to disentangle allegory and symbol, always to the advantage of the more prestigious symbol. As Tzvetan Todorov puts it, the opposition between symbol and allegory was "invented" by the Romantics precisely because the two modes tended to collapse onto each other.[7] Thus in Sand's 1839 preface, already quoted above, she seems to speak indifferently of allegory and of symbol.

While it is important to register the terminological distinction and slippages in Sainte-Beuve and Sand's writings, it is even more important to note how they are amplified by such astute modern readers as Béatrice Didier, who makes a great point in her extended preface to her edition of the 1839 *Lélia* of opposing the symbolic reading to an allegorical one, even if this means introducing new slippages, such as that among myth, symbol, and epic: "Overburdened with symbols, the characters are not for all that philosophical abstractions. Symbolic, they are not allegorical. They belong to the world of myth. They are in an epic register."[8] Didier's concern here is to ward off what she views as the inherently reductive and impoverishing allegorical reading, which cannot take into account the dense layering of meanings that distinguishes Sand's characters: "What constitutes the richness, the complexity of these characters? It is that they answer to the multiple rifts that are piled one on top of the other. They represent at the same time ideas, situation, ages of life. And that is all to the good, because that is how they escape reductiveness" (p. 31). However well-intentioned, Didier's characteristic gesture of banishing all nonrealistic readings of Sand (see the section on *Le Meunier* in chapter 3 of this volume)—epic and realism are, after all, never far apart in the theory of the novel—is not as innocuous as it might seem, because it serves less to ensure an adequate reading of *Lélia* than to rescue *Lélia* from an idealist interpretation. To my mind, it only confirms the necessity of reading *Lélia* as allegory, albeit failed—because failed.[9]

II

If both Sand and Sainte-Beuve agree that the allegory is flawed in *Lélia* because of an undecidability or oscillation that violates the laws of generic purity, Sand in her preface suggests a second and perhaps more telling reason for the problematic nature of her text. According to Sand, the

critical flaw in her work arises from her fascination with the character
of Lélia:

> As for Lélia I must admit that this figure appeared to me through a
> fiction more gripping than those that surround her. . . .
>   This predilection for the proud and suffering character of Lélia drove
> me to commit a serious artistic error: giving her a completely impossible
> existence, which, because of the semireality of the other characters, seems
> shockingly real, by dint of wanting to be abstract and symbolic.[10]

For Sand, the central artistic flaw of *Lélia* is not, as it is for Sainte-Beuve
and other critics, its general generic indeterminacy but rather the disparity
between the realism of the central protagonist and the semireality of the
other characters. To complicate matters even further, Sand claims that
Lélia's excessive reality is the perverse effect of an effort at abstraction
and symbolism. Thus in the novel the mad priest Magnus describes Lélia
as double; the rift that runs through the text separating Lélia from the
other characters also separates her from herself: "I saw Lélia as double
and complete, woman and idea, hope and reality, body and soul, gift
and promise" (p. 52/81).

What makes this autocriticism curious is that in Sand's own theory
of the novel the disparity between the central protagonist and the secondary characters is, as we have seen in chapter 1, foreseen and endowed
with legitimacy:

> According to this theory, the novel should be a poetic, as well as an
> analytical work. It must have characters and situations that are true to
> life—even based on real life—that form a grouping around a type whose
> function is to embody the sentiment or main idea of the book.[11]

That feeling is generally love, a love that must according to Sand be
idealized even to the point of implausibility. The strategy here is clear:
the realism of the secondary characters is needed to ground the idealized
central figure. But in *Lélia,* where the exigencies of realism do not obtain,
it is the reverse that occurs: Lélia, who embodies a deidealized love,
absorbs all reality, thereby reinforcing the irrealism of the secondary
characters.

Two interrelated questions then arise: First, why did Sand eschew the
realistic representational mode more adequate to her subject matter, ac-

cording to Sainte-Beuve? Second, why did Sand fail to sustain the allegorical impulse of her work? The answer to the first question is already contained in chapter 1 of this book: Sand's deliberate irrealism in *Lélia* is consonant with her stated espousal of a poetics of idealism. Sand's "theory of the novel" is, as she developed it in a number of prefaces, as well as in *Histoire de ma vie*, a theory of idealism. *Lélia*, coming on the heels of the still largely conventionally mimetic *Indiana* and *Valentine*, is a work of rupture that signals Sand's aesthetic coming of age. According to the advertising copy Gustave Planche prepared for the *Revue des Deux Mondes*, *Lélia* was to inaugurate a literary revolution directed against the primacy of the visible, which is to say realism: "*Lélia*, we are sure of it, will start a shining revolution in contemporary literature and will deliver the final blow to purely *visible* poetry."[12] Idealism, notably the ethical idealism[13] that Sand espoused, could not be accommodated within the bounds of realism. At the same time, as Paul de Man remarks in a difficult but suggestive passage of his reading of Rousseau's *Julie*, "allegories are always ethical."[14] However, and this is the crucial point I want to develop, *allegory and idealization are in turn also incompatible*. At first this proposition may seem counterintuitive, since there is a well-founded, widespread tendency to associate allegory with the ideal. Just why they cannot in fact coexist—at least not for very long—is the subject of the chapter of Julia Kristeva's *Tales of Love* entitled "The Troubadours: From 'Great Courtly Romance' to Allegorical Narrative" (pp. 280–96).

At the outset, according to Kristeva, courtly love is expressed in the form of song; it is pure affect, pure intensity, pure incantation: "The song is not a metaphor but, as the most direct inscription of jouissance, it is already a transference, a longing of affect for the absolute meaning that shies away" (p. 282). And yet, of course, the courtly love song does also ostensibly tell a story, that of a man's love for an unattainable and powerful Lady. The courtly love song thus operates on two levels, has two messages:

> One should, in short, always split the courtly message into an M1, made up of literal signification and having the Lady as referential object; and an M2, referring to joy alone and whose sign is the *song*. (pp. 287–88)

Now in time—this "revolutionary" process culminates in the fourteenth century—the narrative level, at first only a pretext for the song, overtook the incantatory level. Thus, though allegory is the mode most adequate to the courtly love song, with its strong idealizing tendencies, at the same time it is the one that spells its demise:

> Through the same motion in which the song lost its Dantean dignity . . . the courtly utterance became more literal. The metaphors that moulded courtly code became lexicalized, hence commonplace. It was *allegory's* turn to express the representability of courtly utterance. *Allegory*, however, the personification of the semantic and subjective tension specific to metaphor, became its grave. (p. 288)

There is, in other words, an irreducible and finally fatal tension between the idealizing impulse common to courtly love songs and the narrative pull of allegory, between the incantatory and the realistic:

> As figure of speech, allegory preserves an allusion of a world of abstract values (Danger, Virtue, etc.) but loses the ambiguity specific to play and joy, it conceptualizes and clarifies; along with it, the *narrative* establishes itself. . . . The narrative no longer is an intrinsic, immanent, sacred invocation of joy and *joi*, it becomes psychological. (pp. 288–89)

The circle is vicious: the idealization (of woman) implicit in the courtly love model of desire—a model that is very much at work in *Lélia* (as it is throughout Sand's erotic fictions)—leads away from incantation to allegory, which in turn collapses into linear narrative and psychological realism. In this view of things, allegory is a transitional mode, not the end point. "Allegory is precisely located along the stress line between lyrical utterance, of which song is the culmination, and narrative utterance" (p. 294). The actual end point of the decline of incantation into allegory and then psychological or didactic narrative is satire, which marks the true death of idealization, which will make a joyless comeback under romanticism:

> With woman turned into an object of carnival or satire, this signals the end of a given mode of idealization that the secular West had acquired with the troubadours and trouveres. The struggle against God and the progress of realism, along with that of science, include on the negative side some deficiency of the idealizing possibility. (p. 296)

What I want to suggest, following Kristeva, is that the failure of allegory in Sand is the inevitable by-product of her idealist aesthetic: *Allegory is the mode toward which idealism constantly strains; at the same time, it is idealism's undoing. In allegory idealism turns against itself, or, to paraphrase Kristeva, allegory is the grave of idealism.*

But the failure of allegory in *Lélia* is not merely or simply a failure of idealism. Or, to put the matter another way, the failure of idealism in *Lélia* is also a failure of idealization and one that occurs on more than one level. It is perhaps no accident that it is the figure of Lélia, the female protagonist, that Sand singles out as excessively, stubbornly realistic. Whereas Sand seems to have had no trouble sustaining her allegorization of the male figures, Sténio, Trenmor, and Magnus, she was by her own admission and despite her best efforts at abstraction and symbolism incapable of preventing the figure of Lélia from assuming a "shocking" reality. The spectacular and exceptional *deallegorization* of Lélia raises the question of the relationship between the generic scandal of *Lélia* and the scandal of Lélia's sexuality. Is there something about Lélia's story that contains within it the seeds of her fall from allegorical abstraction into psychological realism, when it is not, in Sainte-Beuve's terms, the other way around?

Lélia, as Mireille Bossis has written, suffers from "ideality,"[15] the true *mal du siècle*. Desperately seeking a god to replace the dead god of religion, Lélia deifies the men she loves, making of them metaphysical idols, only to be repeatedly disappointed, not to say disgusted, by the evidence of their all-too-human reality as it is revealed at the moment of the sexual encounter. As Lélia explains to her young lover Sténio:

> We refuse God the emotion of adoration, an emotion which was put in us to return to God alone. We transfer it to an incomplete, feeble human being who becomes the god of our idolatrous cult. . . .
>
> Today, with poetic souls, the feeling of adoration even enters physical love. Strange error of a greedy, impotent generation! When the divine veil falls and the human being reveals himself, puny and imperfect, behind those clouds of incense and the halo of love, we are frightened by our illusion. We blush, overturn the idol, and trample it beneath our feet. (pp. 36–37/56–57)

In some sense we might speak of *Lélia* as a pathologized version of *La Marquise*: whereas in *La Marquise* the lovers' mutual idealization is preserved by abstinence, by the sublimation of their desires, in *Lélia* idealization succumbs to consummation. In the act of love the idealized phallus—if that is not a pleonasm, since the phallus is always an idealization—is revealed to be the real penis, because the idealizing woman's adoration is addressed to the transcendent possessor of the phallus and not to the merely anatomically correct male. Indeed, as we have already seen in *La Marquise*, idealizing the heroic male is for a woman under patriarchy the only means to appropriate phallic attributes; *for women, idealizing Eros has compensatory functions within a regime of sexual inequality*. As Lélia explains to Pulchérie:

> With my illusion I had been as happy as characters of my temperament can be. I enjoyed the expansion of my mind and feelings. I felt intoxicated with truly divine ecstasies. . . . Calm only made me fearful. . . . I demanded obstacles, fatigues, devouring jealousies to repress, cruel ingratitudes to pardon, great works to pursue, great misfortunes to endure. This was a glorious career. Had I been a man I would have loved combat, the odor of blood, the pressures of danger. Perhaps in my youth I might have sought to reign by intelligence and to dominate others by powerful speeches. As a woman I had only one noble destiny on earth, which was to love. I loved *valiantly*. (pp. 109–10/170)

Read at this level, it would appear that Sand aligns the realism/idealism opposition with sexual difference, in that the feminine idealization or religion of love is set against the coarseness of masculine sexuality, which, because it is the intimate expression of man's violent nature, borders on rape:

> Sometimes in my sleep, prey to those rich ecstasies that devour ascetic minds, I felt myself carried away with him on clouds by balmy breezes. Then I swam on waves of pleasure, and passing my arms languidly around his neck, I would fall on his breast murmuring vague words. But he awoke. In place of that angel who had rocked me in the wind with his wings, I found this man as brutal as a wild beast, and I would flee with horror. But he would pursue me. He didn't want to have been awakened from his sleep for no reason, and he savored his pleasure on the bosom of a woman who was fainting and half dead. (p. 113/175)

According to Bossis's very interesting psychoanalytic interpretation of Lélia's pathology, what is in fact at stake is not so much the disparity between a feminized transcendent ideal and a masculinized gross real as that between a narcissistic denial of alterity and the insuperable and unbearable evidence of sexual difference—that is, of difference *tout court*. Because Lélia's pathology is not restricted to Sand's female protagonists but also affects male protagonists, notably the eponymous hero of *Jacques*, Bossis rejects the notion that Lélia's horror of the sexual act has anything to do with an incongruity between the sexes; rather, she argues, it has everything to do with denying sexual difference altogether. The anti-ideal here is not gross reality but the reality of difference, whether sexual or generational. The only way to maintain the ideal in this perspective is through the fantasied reconfiguration of the family where incest is somehow legitimated by a quasi-divine, asexual father, in this instance, Trenmor.

Bossis's interpretation is very insightful and does much to demystify *Lélia*, but it is also problematic, and this for a number of reasons. First, if one refers back to Janine Chasseguet-Smirgel's book on the "malady of the ideal," on which Bossis draws to formulate her diagnosis, one discovers that the denial of sexual/generational difference she detects in Lélia is in Chasseguet-Smirgel's system a feature of fetishism, that is, the male perversion par excellence.[16] For Chasseguet-Smirgel, the feminine equivalent to the male pervert's refusal to idealize the father, his fantasy of taking his place, is the daughter's fantasy of having a child without the intervention of a male:

> The companion to the boy's perverse deception regarding the difference between the sexes and between the generations, which installs him as mother's partner, would be, in the girl's case, the denial that the child needs to have a father. In other words she would deny all that period of development from the loss of the primary narcissistic state to the onset of the oedipal phase. (p. 35)

Indeed one of the most important arguments Chasseguet-Smirgel makes throughout involves the preoedipal nature of the *maladie d'idéalité* (malady of the ideal): to suffer from this illness is ardently to crave a return to the primary fusion between the ideal and the self, a return to origins, to the womb. It follows that for Chasseguet-Smirgel the ego ideal and the superego must not be confused, for one is bound up with the preoedipal, the other a pure product of the oedipal, one is maternal, the other paternal.

The question of fetishism is not simple when it comes to Lélia, who presents herself as a viriloid female dandy, a sort of phallic woman—which again raises the question of a female fetishism. We could refine Bossis's application of Chasseguet-Smirgel's theories to Sand and say that, to the extent that *Lélia* is an instance of female fetishism, that is, of a feminine denial of sexual difference, Bossis's analysis does apply. Or, rather, if fetishism is a denial of difference, and only a denial of difference, then Lélia, denying difference, is a fetishist. But of course the whole point about fetishism is that it oscillates between denial and recognition, so *Lélia* is an instance of female fetishism precisely because it, too, oscillates. This brings me to the second and related reason why Bossis's interpretation is problematic. Finally, it reduplicates its own analysis by eliding sexual difference, by refusing to take into account the political dimension of Sand's novel, which was only amplified in the revised and much more overtly feminist 1839 version. Though of course both male and female romantics suffered from the "malady of the ideal" that Bossis adroitly and tactfully diagnoses, what the failure of allegory in *Lélia* shows is that masculine and feminine idealization have different destinies in a patriarchal society. If Sand cannot sustain the allegorization of Lélia, it is because at the precise moment when she is writing there is a fundamental incompatibility between allegory and women's writing.

But before going on to discuss the relationship of women and allegory (as objects and subjects) one might well ask, what of Pulchérie?[17] Lélia is not, after all, the only female protagonist in the novel, perhaps not even the only female idealist, so the question arises: Is the allegorization of Pulchérie sustained where Lélia's is not? My sense is that the case of Pulchérie is inseparable from that of Lélia, with whom she proclaims her identity: "I am Lélia herself" (p. 146/220). Doubling—even when, as here, the doubles occupy incommensurate fictional spaces—determines a binding homology between characters. Though the specificities of Pulchérie's life and the particularities of her psyche do not receive the elaboration lavished on Lélia's, one scene, the great primal scene of sexual differentiation by the river, memorably binds Pulchérie to Lélia's sexual hyperreality. In this scene, where desire for the other is shown to spring directly and immediately from the mapping of sexual difference onto sexual identity—seeing Lélia as masculine, Pulchérie abandons her earlier self-directed narcissistic eroticism for heterosexual anaclitic love—Pulchérie ceases to be a type, the courtesan, an allegory of *jouissance*, to become an individual female subject coming under the sway of the phallus under highly specific psychological conditions. Like that of Lélia, the allegorization of Pulchérie collapses under the pressure of the vicissitudes of female sexuality under patriarchy.

III

It is a widely known fact that allegory, especially in the visual arts and especially in the nineteenth century, exhibits a particular fondness for the female form: "Almost all allegories, in language as in pictorial representation, are women."[18] As Marina Warner has documented in her book *Monuments and Maidens*, civic and Christian virtues are conventionally allegorized as feminine: both Charity and the Republic have a woman's features and a woman's body. But if women have been since antiquity the chief subjects of allegory, the question might well be asked: What happens when women become artists themselves, producers of works of art in their own right? Do they, too, produce female allegories? This is precisely the question Warner sets out to answer in the chapter of her book entitled "Lady Wisdom." According to Warner, the answer is unhesitatingly yes. Women writers and artists from the twelfth-century mystic Hildegard of Bingen to our near contemporary, the Mexican painter Frida Kahlo, have enlisted the female form, indeed in the case of Kahlo, her own body, in the service of allegory.

No essential incompatibility exists between female artifacts and female allegory, and yet, as Warner argues, the use of allegory by women is inflected by history. Whereas in the Middle Ages, despite the misogyny of church teachings, the allegorical image and the idea it represented enjoyed a positive affinity, "in the ensuing centuries, the misogynistic strain began to cleave image and reality, and the disjunction between women and the positive ideas they traditionally represented in allegory was increasingly stressed."[19] Lélia is not, of course, a conventional allegory—doubt, for example, is hardly a *positive* idea—and yet one cannot help thinking that writing in 1833 what amounted to a feminist protest against women's grim post-Napoleonic estate, there was no way that Sand could sustain her female allegory. The incompatibility *Lélia* points to is finally not between *women's writing* and allegory but between *feminist writing* and *female allegory.*[20] Given the status of women in nineteenth-century France, the story of Lélia, the allegory of doubt, could not help exceeding the compass of allegory and shift into the more adequate mode of psychological realism. No French feminist artist in the early 1830s could have, as Delacroix did, represented Liberty in the guise of a woman, however deidealized. Indeed as Marcia Pointon has shown, even in Delacroix's pointedly allegorical representation the foregrounded female figure slips and slides like Lélia and Pulchérie between the "axes of real and allegorical": "Liberty is simultaneously real woman and allegorical female."[21] Despite Delacroix's best efforts and numerous subsequent appropriations of the image, Liberty refuses—like the real women who actually participated as historical agents in the Revolution of 1830—to be reduced to stable iconic status, to be fixed in allegory. The failure of allegory in *Lélia* as in *Liberty on the barricades* may well go hand in hand with the rebirth of French feminism in the wake of the Revolution of 1830.

Sand, Feminism, and the Ideology of Gender: *Lettres à Marcie*

FEMINISME: n.m. (1837; du lat. *femina*) 1. Doctrine qui préconise l'extension des droits, du rôle de la femme dans la société. *Le féminisme politique des suffragettes.* 2. *Méd.* Aspect d'un individu mâle qui présente certains caractères secondaires du sexe féminin.
FEMINISTE: *adj.* (1872; du précéd.). Qui a rapport au féminisme (1.). *Propagande féministe.*—*Subst.* Partisan du féminisme. *Un, une féministe.*   Petit Robert

The episode is well known. In 1848, at the height of preelection fever, a group of feminists gathered at the Club de la Rue Taranne proposed the candidacy of George Sand to the National Assembly. Two days after the publication of that motion in *La Voix des Femmes* (April 6, 1848), George Sand sent a letter to the editors of *La Réforme* and *La Vraie République,* in which she curtly shoots down this ill-timed nomination:

Sir: [Paris, April 8, 1848]

A newspaper edited by some women has proclaimed my candidacy to the National Assembly. If this jest did not injure my pride, by attributing to me a ridiculous presumption, I would let it pass, like all those of which all of us in this world can become the object. But my silence might lead people to believe that I support the principles of which this newspaper would like to become the mouthpiece. Please receive and be kind enough to make known the following declaration:

1) I hope that no elector will want to lose his vote by having the foolish notion of writing my name on his ballot;

2) I do not have the honor of knowing a single one of the women who form clubs and edit newspapers;

3) The articles that might be signed with my name or my initials in these newspapers are not by me;

I ask these ladies to forgive me for taking these precautions against their zeal, for they have surely treated me with much goodwill.

I do not claim to protest in advance against the ideas these ladies or any other ladies will want to discuss among themselves; freedom of opinion applies equally to both sexes, but I cannot condone being taken without my consent as the standard bearer of a female circle with which I have never had the slightest relation either pleasant or unpleasant.

With my distinguished salutations,

George Sand[22]

Neither the tone nor the tenor of this text is designed to make Sand a heroine in the eyes of historians of French feminism, and it singularly complicates the task of all those—both men and women—who insist on enlisting Sand as a feminist and making of her an ancestress of the contemporary women's movement. In fact, opposite this disturbing, not to say frankly antifeminist text, we could place other texts that are equally well known and clearly feminist, where Sand defends the equality of women before the law, clamors for the rights of women to divorce and to be educated, and castigates the patriarchal order and the unjust condition of women. Or, to complicate (or simplify) matters, we could consider a text such as the letter to the members of the Central Committee, written shortly after the letter to the editors of *La Réforme* and *La Vraie République* and for similar reasons—the committee had also nominated Sand for office. In this letter, which provides a sort of gloss

Au Bureau du Charivari R. du Croissant 16   Imp. d'Aubert & Cie

Je me fiche bien de votre Mme SAND ...EU qui empêche les femmes de raccommoder les
pantalons et qui est cause que les dessous de pied sont décousus !... Il faut rétablir le divorce...
ou supprimer cet auteur là !

on the first, Sand proclaims her lack of solidarity with those who champion women's liberation in both the public and the sexual arena (e.g., the disciples of Saint-Simon, Enfantin, and Fourier) while ringingly endorsing liberation through the restoration to women of the civil rights of which marriage deprives them, through, in short, the reform of marriage laws.[23] The very fact that the bourgeois feminists gathered at the Club de la Rue Taranne could have misunderstood the nature of Sand's involvement, the extent of her *representativity* clearly demonstrates how difficult it is to classify Sand when it comes to what she calls, "the women's cause."

In fact, considering the enormity of the stakes, Sand's feminism is the pons asinorum of Sand studies. It would not be exaggerated to say that, sooner or later, all those interested in Sand are led to wonder about her feminism and to take a position pro or con. Sand's feminism is an obligatory and unavoidable theme of reflection for all Sand scholars. Certainly it is impossible to investigate Sand's idealist politics without addressing the question of her feminism, for manifestly, as we have already observed throughout what precedes, her idealist politics is rooted in a refusal of the gender arrangements both reflected and constructed by romanticism and realism.

That this question is a commonplace of Sand studies does not mean that the terms of the debate have not evolved over the years. If there are those who continue year in, year out to approach the question without demonstrating the slightest knowledge of modern feminism, as though

---

FIGURE 5.

Honoré Daumier, *Moeurs Conjugales no. 6.* Bibliothèque Nationale. In an interesting twist on the widespread association of Sand and divorce law reform, the author is here held responsible by an irate husband for his bookish wife's failure to meet her wifely duties: while she lolls about reading fiction by the likes of Sand, his pants (!) go unmended. Is it the mere fact of reading Sand's novels that is threatening to the patriarchal conjugal order or is it the novels' subversive message that must be contained? Though a republican, a devotee of the idealist symbol, Don Quixote, Daumier was a relentless mocker of women's social, political, and intellectual aspirations: the *Moeurs conjugales* series was produced from 1839 to 1842 and published in the *Charivari;* after 1848 Daumier published (also in the *Charivari*) a series entitled *les Divorceuses,* soon followed by *les Femmes socialistes.*

it were sufficient to rely on common sense and some personal or journalistic knowledge of feminism, there are others for whom speaking of Sand's feminism is, as it should be, simply another way of speaking of feminism itself.

Thus during the seventies, at the moment when the women's liberation movement was reborn from its ashes (as well as the ashes of May 1968), when, following either parallel or convergent tracks, both French and Anglo-American feminist thought were spectacularly productive, the tone, vocabulary, and even area of inquiry shift in the debate on Sand's feminism. Indeed, as soon as one considers the subject, a new difficulty arises: the problem of the evidence. On what grounds can one make a judgment: Sand's life and/or work? The fictions and/or the letters? The social and political essays?[24] Of course, there is no reason not to take all of these practices into account, to accord equal attention to the biographical elements and the fictional texts, but in actual fact, critics tend to privilege either the life or the work. The text I want to discuss constitutes a challenge to these distinctions, in that it is an epistolary novel, a fictional text that is also a novel of ideas or, as Sand puts it in her preface, "a sort of novel without events":[25] *Lettres à Marcie* (Letters to Marcie).

It is highly significant that when in the seventies American academic critics borne by the women's movement, as well as by the theoretical renewal of French neofeminism, took on the topic of Sand's feminism, they accorded special status to the fictional texts. Because their approaches seem to me exemplary, I will cite two examples of this new Sand criticism: the articles of Leslie Rabine and Eileen Boyd Sivert.

In an essay that has lost none of its currency, "Sand and the Myth of Femininity," Leslie Rabine judges Sand's feminism harshly. Not entirely excluding biography, Rabine relies essentially on a reading of *Indiana* to evaluate Sand's feminism. This choice is highly predictable in that *Indiana* is a novel that calls into question, in Sand's own words, the "unjust" and "barbarous" "laws which still govern woman's existence in wedlock, in the family and in society."[26] Nevertheless, according to Rabine, it would be a mistake to confuse the critique of marriage Sand makes in her novel with a fundamental questioning of the modes of representation of women and femininity produced by the patriarchal imaginary:

> While *Indiana* appears to contest the myth of Woman as Passive Object of Male Desire and Possession, in this novel the concepts of women's freedom and of the liberated woman are themselves mythified and incorporated into the traditional established conception of womanhood.[27]

What makes Sand a bad feminist, still according to Rabine, is her way of subscribing on the plane of fiction to masculine modes of representing desire, indeed to a conception of the subject that makes subjectivity and especially desiring subjectivity the exclusive prerogative of the masculine subject: "George Sand in this novel, reproduces the myth of Woman as Lack and Absence" (p. 13).

The great merit of Rabine's article is that rather than glossing over the contradictions in the novel, it attempts to contain them by showing how within the framework of the novel Sand herself reduces and neutralizes them:

> The message of the novel is perhaps stronger in that it is contradictory. It does not simply reproduce the stereotypes but merges feminine aspirations for freedom into them. Indiana does revolt. . . . But she runs away to Raymon only when she does it as a "sacrifice," and when "she does not in any way go to him in search of happiness." Thus Indiana's revolt is contained in her resignation. . . . Thus her independence is contained in her dependence on a man, and the novel itself must rely on a fantasy ending to save Indiana from the habitual fate of women. (p. 14)

Finally, by likening Noun's fate to that of French women in 1830, Rabine faults Sand for founding her exceptional status as a woman writer on the inferiority of other women: "She made the freedom of one woman separate from the freedom of other women" (p. 15).

Up to a certain point, Eileen Boyd Sivert shares Rabine's point of view, especially—and one can see that she, too, relies on Irigaray and Kristeva—as regards the difficulty, not to say the impossibility, of representing a female protagonist as a fully desiring subject as long as one borrows the dominant linguistic codes. But Sivert effects a significant displacement, or slippage, in relation to Rabine. To begin with, her privileged text is not *Indiana* but *Lélia*, a text that, as we have seen, escapes entirely the narrative schemas of nascent realism, which reduces all of women's adventures to one, marriage. But beyond the starting point of her discussion, Sivert's point of view, too, is radically different.

For Sivert, Sand's feminism is situated on the level of the search for a language adequate to sexual difference, to femininity. "It is in writing that we must look for an opening," she writes.[28] Sivert emphasizes the open form of the text, Sand's attempt, via her character, to find her voice, her place, her position outside of the beaten paths of male discourse, to transform her exile from the order of masculine representation into the royal way to writing otherwise. For her—and Cixous's influence is clear here—*Lélia* is an example of *écriture féminine*. Sand/Lélia's feminism is equivalent both to a desiring subjectivity and a women's writing: "Sand's discourse, which offers so many ways of approaching woman's story, does not enclose or smother, it is strikingly open, loose, plural" (p. 64).

At the dawn of the nineties, the question of Sand's feminism remains very much alive and even acquires a certain urgency, in that feminist criticism is in crisis and its operating concepts—such as that of "gender"—which enabled this form of criticism to renew the reading of literary texts and other symbolic productions, are now being interrogated.[29]

Before going on to *Lettres à Marcie*, we can already draw three conclusions of somewhat different orders based on what precedes. First, and this seems obvious, one cannot talk about Sand's feminism without starting from a definition of feminism, without making explicit the presuppositions of the discussion. That is what most of those who have dealt with this subject end up recognizing:

> Is it true that she was a feminist? Not if that word is given the meaning it acquired towards the end of the nineteenth century. George Sand never demanded, nor wanted, political equality for women.[30]

> If one defines feminism in such a way as to limit it to such traits as a scorn of domestic work, and a preference for sisterhood, organization, and politics, then one can maintain that in no way was George Sand a feminist.[31]

> Can one say that Sand is fundamentally feminist? I doubt it. . . . What makes Sand feminist are her personal audacities and her rebellion against the conjugal yoke and stupid bourgeois education: but she is not feminist in the modern sense of the word.[32]

> In Sand's case we must agree on the meaning to give to the term "feminist" since, as soon as she takes a position with regard to concrete claims

of contemporary feminists, her attitude becomes so complicated as to seem paradoxical.[33]

If feminism is defined as any doctrine which advances women's positions, Sand might be seen as a feminist.[34]

This entails in turn a second conclusion: If the case of Sand speaks to us, it is because it has the value of a paradigm; the contradictions Sand and her readers grapple with pose clearly the problem of feminism and perhaps especially feminism in France, for one must not under any circumstances lose sight of Sand's specific historical or national contexts. The issue is understanding why in France exceptional women who have contested their periods' injustices and prejudices regarding the condition of women have in general preferred not to participate in a collective struggle for women's rights and have so often refused to renounce their "difference." Sand is a screen onto which are projected the conflicts that oppose Marxist and psychoanalytic feminists, bourgeois individualistic and collectivist feminists, Lacanian and Althusserian feminists.

My third conclusion, which seems at first glance to contradict the first but in fact flows from it, is that if the debate is so unsatisfying, if the question remains forever open, it is perhaps because it is not well posed, that is, what one refuses to see is that what is problematic is the very term *feminist*. It is a striking feature of the citations above that all rely on a "modern" (equal rights) definition of feminism to dispute Sand's credentials as a feminist. Only Sand's personal politics (or an indiscriminate definition of feminism) might be seen as qualifying her as a true feminist. Instead of asking ourselves whether Sand is a feminist, or indeed whether she is a good or a bad one, one must ask if a definition of feminism exists that can account for practices and convictions that are totally heterogeneous and sometimes irreconcilable (except by fetishistic oscillations of a strategic order). By posing the question in this manner, one is led to consider the hypothesis according to which, in the end, Sand is exemplarily feminist—if for the sake of convenience we wish to preserve this troubling term—because of her contradictions and not despite them. In this case I would propose a definition of feminism that makes of it a sum of contradictions, the nodal point where dissatisfactions with contemporary society and the place it assigns women, claims for equality, claims for singular or plural differences, assertions of an essential and transhistorical female nature, and denunciations of a subaltern condition stemming from specifically historical and contingent factors clash and intertwine. In the broadest definition of the term, then, feminism would comprise elements of conservatism and contestation, of maternalism and antimaternalism, of familialism and antifamilialism, of separatism and assimilationism. The apparently irreconcilable debate that currently opposes essentialists and constructionists is false, in that neither of the warring forces has an exclusive hold on the truth. *Feminism is the debate itself*. If Sand is a feminist, it is in the sense that she bodies forth and articulates these contradictions and not to the extent that she resolves them in a more or less satisfactory fashion. To conclude these preliminary conclusions, I would like to propose that the best way to approach Sand's feminism today is through neither her novels nor her biography but rather through those writings I would term theoretical. It is time to read Sand as a theoretician of sexual difference.

The distinction is crucial. It isn't a matter of re-marking yet another binary opposition that so many have worked so hard to undo, of reinstituting a hierarchy between theory and practice, but of situating Sand's disparate writings on women's fate (in the form of letters, novels, essays) in the context of current theoretical work on sexual difference. In this perspective, as I've already indicated, *Lettres à Marcie* constitute a major document.

Lettres à Marcie presents itself as a correspondence between a (presumably male) "friend" and a young woman who, not having a dowry, cannot marry and thus considers other possible ways of living: free love, romantic voyage, the active life, the convent. The friend eliminates them one by one to exalt the superiority of the female maternal vocation, which is somewhat paradoxical given his correspondent's situation.

Lettres à Marcie was originally written as a serial novel for the newspaper *Le Monde* published by l'abbé Lamennais, whom Macherey terms, "the great heresiarch of the 1840s."[35] When Lamennais made some cuts in the third letter without consulting her, Sand informed him respectfully but firmly that if she were not free to speak about what she wanted, she would be obliged to abandon the project and interrupt the writing of the *Lettres*. In particular, she asked the abbé if he would have any objection to her speaking of divorce in a subsequent letter: "To tell you in a word all my audacities [*hardiesses*], they would involve asking for Divorce in marriage. Despite all my efforts to find a remedy for the bloody injustices, the endless miseries, the passions without remedy that trouble the union of the sexes, I don't see any other solution than the freedom to break and reform the conjugal bond."[36] When Lamennais was reticent, she continued for a while to produce copy but ended up abandoning the text in midstream. It was then published in a state of incompletion, which was unusual for the author.

Rarely has a text of Sand's been marked by more uncertainties, more doubts as to its legitimacy. Obviously Sand was not comfortable in the role of theoretician of sexual difference. As she admitted to Lamennais, theorizing the role of women represented for her a challenge:

> What's strangest about this is that I who have written my whole life on this subject [the actual fate of women], I hardly know what to think, and not having ever summarized myself, not having ever concluded anything but in the vaguest terms, I find myself today concluding from inspiration without really knowing where it's coming from, without being able not to draw the conclusions I do and finding in me I don't know what certainty, which is perhaps the voice of truth or perhaps the impertinent voice of pride.(3:712)

Indeed, one issue at stake throughout this text is precisely whether women can function in the loftiest spheres of thought, in the realm of abstraction. From the outset, Sand declares in her preface that *Lettres* is "an unfinished essay . . . an incomplete fragment and without any philosophical value whatsoever" (p. 165). But further on, the friend addresses Marcie—whose letters we don't have (these letters read as a sort of anti–*Letters of a Portuguese Nun*)—in these terms: "Women, you say, are not and cannot be philosophers. If you take the word philosophy in its primitive meaning, love of wisdom, I think you can, you must cultivate philosophy" (p. 227). In fact, the whole beginning of the sixth and last letter, to which I will return below, is devoted to the question of woman and philosophy. In the end, one of the great questions posed by *Lettres à Marcie* concerns woman's (proper) relationship to philosophy, to theoretical activity.[37] And the nature of that relationship depends on the meaning one gives to *philosophy*.

At first glance, Sand's theoretical work seems to revolve around the great paradigm of feminism, the opposition of equality and difference. But, as Joan Scott has masterfully demonstrated, this opposition is false in that any notion of equality implies that of difference, the recognition

that everyone is not identical; as Sand remarks—and Scott echoes her—
"equality . . . is not similarity";[38] "the alternative to the binary construction of sexual difference is not sameness, identity or androgyny."[39]
But there ends the agreement between Sand and Scott. Whereas Scott's
deconstruction works to replace the necessary but tacit recognition of
difference in any political conception of equality by that of the multiple
differences among women, Sand attempts to show that *difference* and
equality are not incompatible. In other words, each one deconstructs the
opposition, but where Sand seeks to reconcile the two terms, Scott displaces them by a third that comes somehow to encompass them both:

> Equality, as I told you earlier, is not identity [*similitude*]. Equal merit
> does not mean that one is fit for the same jobs, and to deny man's
> superiority, it would have sufficed to entrust him with the domestic duties
> of woman. To deny the *identity* of woman's faculties with those of man,
> it would similarly suffice to entrust her with virile public functions; but
> if woman is not destined to go beyond private life that is not to say that
> she does not have the same degree or the same excellence of faculties
> applicable to the life she is assigned.[40]

> Placing equality and difference in antithetical relationship has, then, a
> double effect. It denies the way in which difference has long figured in
> political notions of equality and it suggests that sameness is the only
> ground on which equality can be claimed. It thus puts feminists in an
> impossible position, for as long as we argue within the terms of discourse
> set up by this opposition we grant the current conservative premise that
> since women cannot be identical to men in all respects, they cannot expect
> to be equal to them. The only alternative, it seems to me, is to refuse to
> oppose equality to difference and insist continually on differences . . .
> differences as the very meaning of equality itself.[41]

The difference—or the difference of differences—between Sand and Scott
is instantly apparent and brings out clearly what is for Sand the true
aporia: the opposition between public and private; in other words, the
great Enlightenment opposition ratified by the French Revolution that
structures Sand's thought, her theorization of sexual difference.[42] What
is not so much the unthought as the unthinkable for Sand is the transgression by woman (as well as by man) of the bar that separates the two
spheres. For Sand, the separation of the spheres is sacred, inscribed in
nature, and must be maintained, for social order depends on it. This

brings us back in a sense to our starting point: Sand's consistent refusal (whether it be a question of the National Assembly or the French Academy) to take her place on the public scene. To speak of Sand's feminism must be to consider this opposition and the way it functions in her thought system.[43] What one quickly recognizes is that for Sand, if this opposition is essential, transhistorical, it is nonetheless inscribed in a historical continuum to whose repercussions it is subject. In *Lettres à Marcie*, according to a story the friend recounts at the end of the last letter, just before he hastily concludes this interrupted correspondence, the taboo that affects the educated woman, the bluestocking, is a specifically modern fact:

> The prejudice that denies women serious intellectual occupations is of quite recent vintage. Antiquity and the Middle Ages do not to my knowledge offer us any examples of aversions and systems of abuse against those women who pursue the arts and sciences. (p. 231)

Such a time would have been a golden age for woman, and that age coincided with a period in which man was mobilized by war: called on to leave home, man is only too happy to have a companion who is capable of running the *oikos*.

> Social troubles, here the crusades, there the wars of schisms, take man far from the hearth and leave at the head of the family a woman invested with an uncontested authority; if her responsibilities [*attributions*] are considerable, if her role is important in the society, the education she may have acquired is a real advantage for the fortune and dignity of her husband. (pp. 232–33)

According to this curious version of women's history, the separation of spheres is not, as it is in supposedly scientific accounts, a product of the industrial revolution, urbanization, and the rise of capitalism; rather, it is a traditional arrangement that worked well as long as man devoted himself to extradomestic aggressive activities and left woman in charge at home. What marked the decline of the condition of women is the end of wars of religion, crusades, schisms, and man's return to the hearth, in short the "enervation of the manly character" (p. 232). The modern era must invent a new relationship between the sexes that corresponds to the end or more precisely, the "suspension" of wars yet perpetuates the empowerment of women inherent in the old order.

It might appear at first glance that with this fable Sand does little more than to reinscribe from a feminist perspective the ideas of Rousseau in the *Nouvelle Héloïse*, but without calling into question Rousseau's fundamental assumptions: the separation of spheres on which the social order depends is founded on the hyperbolization of masculine and feminine roles, the consolidation of masculinity and femininity. But, on closer inspection, it would seem that in fact Sand's ideal is quite different and would be on the order of a matriarchy, a division that would do without a masculine presence altogether and leave women in full command. In a paradox familiar to historians of women during the first half of the twentieth century, according to Sand, political and economic disorders—the state of war as well as the regime of scarcity—ensure the social order by enhancing female power; conversion to a peacetime economy necessitates a special vigilance so that women do not lose the power and privileges that accrue to them in men's absence.

How then, Sand asks herself in 1837, can one maintain the separation of spheres, now that the men have come home, that is, (re)invested the private and domestic sphere previously reserved for woman? This original way of posing the question sheds an unaccustomed light on postrevolutionary society. For what the version of events given here by Sand allows us to observe is that if, as Michelle Perrot writes, "the nineteenth century is the golden age of the private,"[44] that happy state did not include women, the supposed queens of the private. The accentuation of the separation of the so-called masculine and feminine spheres, and especially the hypertrophy of the private in bourgeois European societies in the nineteenth century, did not benefit women because according to Sand, while they were kept at a distance from the public arena, men were everywhere the masters, occupying simultaneously all the places, all the positions. Restoring the division of labor of an earlier era wracked by wars and all manner of civil disorder would guarantee for women a space of their own.

If Sand could neither imagine nor admit—at least in the immediate— the breakdown of the separation of spheres, if she could not find words harsh enough to condemn those women who claimed "the same attributes" as men, to wit "speech at the forum, [but] the helmet and the sword, the right to condemn to death" (pp. 201–2), in short, political, military, and juridical power, it is because, like all French theorists of difference, she is more utopianist than feminist—or, more precisely, a utopian feminist (as one speaks of a utopian socialist). On this point, I am in complete agreement with the conclusions drawn by Kristina Wingard Vareille when she summarizes her analysis of Sand's feminism:

> Far from confirming and consolidating an unjust system by aspiring to be a part of it, women must then preciously cling to their marginality, which thus becomes the visible sign of an inevitable change, the index of the necessity of creating a society founded on new principles. It's as though by refusing to endorse the most apparently radical claims of contemporary feminists, Sand was intent, on the level of mythical imagination if not that of rational reflection, on ensuring for female marginality a function of radical interrogation of existing society.[45]

Vareille's analysis of Sand's feminism would apply just as well to that of her contemporary heirs, Cixous and Irigaray, who (just like Sand) reject the egalitarian/reformist model of feminism, indeed feminism itself, in the name of a mythical feminine that might constitute a reserve of alternate and superior moral values. This comparison is meant less to demonstrate the persistent utopian temptation of French feminists—with which I have great sympathy—than to emphasize the logic that necessarily links the theory of the separation of spheres to utopian feminism. The theory of the separation of spheres reinforces utopian feminism, to the extent that it enables one to imagine a protected locus where the Ideal prevails. No feminist utopia, at least not in France, does not on some level imply the separation of spheres and does not take over the separation of society set into place by the liberal system produced by the Enlightenment.[46] French neofeminists have always been intent on marking their refusal of feminism in the restricted sense of the word as an avatar of the (humanist) thought of the Enlightenment; but insofar as they have subreptitiously and unknowingly reinscribed the division of the socio-symbolic space set into place by that system of thought, insofar as they are always tempted to seek refuge in their "private garden,"[47] they remain prisoners of the very system they denounce. By going back to the sources of French feminism, one sees that in the future the daughters of George, herself a daughter of Jean-Jacques, will have their hands full getting rid of the problematic legacy of the French Revolution and going beyond the private/public split, all the while maintaining their hope of a new revolution.[48]

CHAPTER THREE

The

Politics of

Idealism

La vraie force du socialisme, qui le rend redoutable, et dont nous ne saurions triompher qu'en lui opposant une force de la même nature, c'est d'être un idéalisme.
Ferdinand Brunetière, *La Renaissance de l'idéalisme*

Intelligent idealism is closer to intelligent materialism than is unintelligent materialism.   Lenin

Utopia is a transparent synonym for socialism itself, and the enemies of Utopia sooner or later turn out to be the enemies of socialism.   Fredric Jameson, *The Ideologies of Theory*

The notion that idealism constitutes a powerful counterdiscourse in mid–nineteenth-century French fiction may strike some Marxist critics as hopelessly naive. Are not the politics of idealism well known, is not idealism the reactionary ideology rampant among the romantic humanists of the nineteenth century (including George Sand and George Eliot, Victor Hugo and Charles Dickens) and always lurking even or especially among the Marxist theoreticians of the twentieth? Thus, in his celebrated polemic with Lukács, Brecht speaks of the "utopian idealism which still lurks in Lukács' essays."[1] And, in a revealing commentary on this aspect of the Brecht-Lukács debate, Fredric Jameson suggests that it be viewed "as a therapeutic warning against the permanent temptation of idealism present in any ideological analysis as such."[2] If Marxist critics are so obsessed with rooting out idealism wherever it springs up, it is precisely because Marxist analysis itself produces idealism as an inevitable by-product, an undisposable waste.

> There would then be *two* idealisms: one the common-or-garden variety to be found in religion, metaphysics, or literalism, the other a repressed and unconscious danger of idealism within Marxism itself, inherent in the very ideal of science itself in a world so deeply marked by the division of mental and manual labor. To that danger the intellectual and the scientist can never be sufficiently alerted.[3]

If idealism inheres in all epistemological investigation, Marxist or otherwise, it veritably haunts Marxist aesthetics, producing what Hans Robert Jauss has called "The Idealist Embarrassment" of materialist aesthetics. "To reduce matters to a provocative formula," writes Jauss, "the state of this discussion might be epitomized by the question whether a materialist aesthetic must not admit that it cannot get along without a central core of idealism."[4] This core of idealism is the troublesome legacy bequeathed by the posthumously published aesthetic writings of the young Marx, which are steeped in admiration for the Greek ideal in art.

My concern throughout what follows will be not be with the complexities and perplexities of Marxist aesthetics, however; rather, I will focus on the first and banal form of idealism mentioned by Jameson, the everyday mode whose familiarity and omnipresence has rendered it self-evident, transparent, and analytically boring. A striking feature of much current critical discourse, whether (post)-Marxist or poststructuralist, is that when it deploys the terms *idealist* and *idealism* as part of its anti-idealist reflection, the terms are almost never defined, the dangers of idealism, rarely if ever spelled out. At the risk of being accused of "literalism" (whatever Jameson means by that term), I want to preface my discussion of Sand's idealist political fiction by a brief recall of some of the main arguments against idealism.

The Politics of Idealism

What in a Marxist perspective are the chief counts against idealism?[5] Let me by way of a first approximation propose the following quartet: idealism as an *ideology* signifies the denial of material conditions of production; idealism as a *philosophy* signifies the belief in the omnipotence of individual consciousness; idealism as an *aesthetics* signifies the espousal of an elitist approach to art; idealism as a *system of values* signifies a nostalgia for a preindustrial model of organic communitas. This deliberately schematic set of propositions may or may not adequately represent the Marxist case against idealism as it shifts across disciplines and conceptual fields; it is itself, however, an idealization, an abstract. What one finds if one sets out to locate *actual* critiques of idealism in contemporary theoretical writing is a hybrid discourse that attests to the current interpenetration and thus inseparability of critiques of idealism deriving from two distinct and in many instances rival sources, traditional Marxism *and* seventies poststructuralism. It would appear, in fact, that over the past two decades the two have merged almost seamlessly to produce an anti-idealist discourse that draws its unquestionably impressive power from its positing of idealism as the binary opposite of *both* materialism and constructionism. A particularly well-done characteristic conflation of the Marxist and poststructuralist critiques of idealism can be found in the introductory chapter of Rosalind Coward and John Ellis's *Language and Materialism*:

> Idealism depends on notions of "human essence" which somehow transcend and operate (indeed, cause) the social system, and are not constructed in this system. The idealist "deformation of thought" mobilizes notions of "mankind" and the "human" as the specific language-using entity. They underlie the idea of identities which pre-exist the individual's entry into social relations. Idealism has, in other words, an idea of identity which is in complete opposition to the materialist tenet of the subject resulting from its construction in sociality.[6]

Once identified with essentialism (when it is not, as it is elsewhere, with empiricism[7] or, still more recently, conventionalism[8]), idealism is swept away and at least temporarily lost as a serious topic for discussion. What is worse, and however paradoxical this may appear, it would now seem that taken to an extreme, the constructionist, antiessentialist argument (especially made by such influential Foucault-inspired theoreticians such as Mouffe and Laclau and Butler), with its single-minded emphasis on the primacy of the discursive over the material and the referential culminates in a new (linguistic and philosophical) idealism, which Neil Lazarus characterizes as follows: "Idealism here consists in the relentless reduction of the social to discourse in that term's conventional usage—as talk, conversation, treatise, etc.—in the dematerialization of the social that follows necessarily from the construction of its various instances, one and all, in analogy to language" (p. 124). This dressing-up of idealism in postmodernist garb leads in turn to a (post-Marxist) Marxist revival of anti-idealism and reinvestment of realism.[9] Because idealism today is either unavowed (by postmodernist thinkers who do not speak openly as latter-day idealists) or disavowed (by poststructuralist thinkers who do not always speak openly as latter-day Marxists), idealism remains in much contemporary theoretical writing an unthought.

Though I have no wish to reduce Marxist literary criticism to a monolithic entity, I think it fair to say that, especially in the long shadow cast by Lukács, Marxist literary criticism is often a theory of the realist novel, of the great European tradition in which Sand has no part. The idealist trends that do manifest themselves in the works of the great realists such as Eliot, the only woman writer admitted into this pantheon, can only be viewed in this perspective as unfortunate though perhaps inescapable marks of bourgeois ideology. They are, at any rate, disqualified as objects of serious study, let alone elaborate theorization. In this sense, given the conservative function of the canon, the hegemony of realism in the French literary canon is perfectly consonant with Marxist criteria of literary value.

The conjoined triumph of realism and demonization of idealism in the dominant tradition of Marxist aesthetics leaves the ideological critic with only blunt instruments for studying the literary production of perhaps the foremost self-described communist novelist in nineteenth-century French literature—none other than George Sand. And, of course, the case of George Sand is not unique, since as we have already noted, idealizing trends are to be found in virtually all major nineteenth-century authors who placed themselves, however awkwardly, on the side of "the people," the "progressives." Whatever label one attaches to Sand's politics, whatever judgment one renders on her political activities—and some (especially by Marxist feminists) have been harsh—her major political novels merit critical consideration precisely for the same reasons that they have been, with some exceptions, ignored: their very humanism, indeed their idealism.

Le Compagnon du tour de France (1840)

"Only writers with an ambivalent class-relation to the [Victorian] society could, it seemed, be open to the contradictions from which major literary talent was produced," writes Terry Eagleton in *Criticism and Ideology*.[10] Though one might want to question this foolproof recipe for literary greatness, the applicability of this law to the case of George Sand is unquestionable. The product of a unique alliance between a mother issued from the lowest popular classes and a father born into an illegitimate but distinguished branch of the aristocracy, no major nineteenth-century French writer was more oddly and uncomfortably inserted into the class structure than was Sand, and the issue of class difference was to mark her writings as forcefully as that of gender difference, though it is the more colorful embodiments of her gender ambivalence that popular legend has retained. Of course, there is no separating Sand's oscillations between male and female subject positions from her imaginative attempts to suture the split between maternal and paternal class inscriptions. And yet it can also be said that whereas in the feminist fiction of the thirties, which culminate in the *Lélia* of 1839, gender is foregrounded, in the socialist idealist[11] fiction of the forties, gender is subsumed to class. Thus, in the predominantly feminist novels, marriage is viewed as the prime means of legitimating the unequal allocation of power between men and women, while in the predominantly socialist novels, marriage is transvalued into the privileged mechanism for transcending class differences.[12]

The centrality of the institution of marriage in the modern European novel, from LaFayette's *La Princesse de Clèves* to Joyce's *Ulysses*, is a critical commonplace. It is after all through the exchange of women between men and the legitimate transmission of the father's name and property that marriage serves to ensure that patriarchy endures and class differences are held in place. Because of its centrality, however, marriage is particularly vulnerable to all manner of dysfunction and blockage, and the nineteenth-century French novel rings the changes on the spectacular failure of the marriage system in a society where women are deprived of their subjectivity and of their fundamental legal and political rights. Hence the fascination with adultery (*Madame Bovary*) so brilliantly studied by Tony Tanner in *Adultery in the Novel*, hence the recurrent theme (*Eugénie Grandet, Le Malheur d'Henriette Guérard*) of the recalcitrant daughter who refuses to be properly exchanged. In her early feminist fiction, notably *Indiana* and *Valentine*, Sand emphasizes perhaps the most significant form of resistance to the implacable determinations of the marriage plot, the daughter's no, her refusal to consummate the marriage into which she is forced to enter. Given in exchange by her violent father to her violent older husband, Indiana remains implausibly chaste. Married off by her mother—an interesting exception to the rule of male-to male-exchange that can be explained by the imperatives of the aristocracy—to a dissolute aristocrat with gambling debts, Valentine is too drugged on her wedding night for the marriage to be consummated, and the next day her husband leaves for his diplomatic posting in far-off Moscow, leaving his wife *virgo intacta*. The rejection of marriage culminates in *Lélia*, which is written outside of the conjoined conventions of mimetic realism and the marriage plot. In the second, more overtly feminist *Lélia* of 1839, Lélia withdraws altogether from society into the cultural space Catholic societies specifically allocate female dropouts from the exchange system and/or the erotic marketplace, the convent.

Somewhere around 1839, the year of the revised *Lélia* (but also of the curious dialogic novel *Gabriel*, which contains one of Sand's most sustained meditations on gender and its constructions), Sand seems to have hit the wall of her feminist anger, and though questions pertaining to the condition of women and gender identity continue to inform her writing, they are no longer charged with the affective intensities they mobilized in her first decade as a writer.[13] A possibly aberrant but no less telling sign of the changes in her thinking is her portrayal of the character Mme Cardonnet in *Le Péché de Monsieur Antoine* (The sin of Monsieur Antoine, 1846). The oppressed wife of the Grandet-like figure of Victor Cardonnet, she is blamed for abjectly colluding in her own victimization:

> Attending to all the details of housekeeping had become for her more than a voluntary and honest occupation. It had been made for her such a serious and sacred law that a Roman matron could have at the most been compared to her for the childish solemnness of her domestic labor.

> She offered the strange anachronism of a contemporary woman who while capable of reasoning and feeling, had made an insane effort over herself to regress several thousands of years to resemble one of those women of antiquity who prided themselves on proclaiming the inferiority of their sex.[14]

Though feminist in its assertion of equality and progress, this passage represents a shocking regression in comparison with *Indiana*, *Valentine*, and *Lélia*, in that it places the burden of guilt for wifely misery squarely on the wife's shoulders. What is significant about this passage is not so much that it does not issue in a contestation of male privilege—elsewhere in the novel the system of patriarchal-capitalist values represented by Cardonnet is amply criticized—but that it carefully seals off the institution of marriage from the threat constituted by a particular instance of failure. Instead of directly calling into question the entire power/gender system in which it is implicated, the Cardonnets' bad marriage (unlike the failed marriages of Indiana and Valentine) is charged to an individual case of female pathology, and its disruptive potential deftly defused.

If Sand resorted to such a classical stratagem to preserve the institution of marriage from a systemic critique, it is because for her the stakes were high. Drawing on the resources provided by the popular idealist genres at work in her fiction—fairy tale, comedy, pastoral—Sand looked to marriage to resolve the increasingly intolerable tension between the rich and the poor in her class society. Sand's sudden investment of marriage with a positive ideological function gives the measure, I think, of her growing panic in the face of social rifts that strike at her very being. The urgency that marks her socialist trilogy draws its affective impetus from a veritable ontological crisis, for given Sand's parentage, the fissures in the body politic duplicate those that divide her against herself.

But perhaps I have overstated the contradictions between Sand's anti- and promarriage positions, for it might well be argued that the marriage she promotes is not the same as the one she decries: the latter is the marriage of *realism*, the former that of *romance*.[15] In Sand, socialist idealism entails the idealization of marriage—which is not to say that in her socialist idealist novels one type of marriage has entirely supplanted the other. On the contrary; much of the interest in these texts arises from the interplay between the two conjugal regimes. Furthermore, the elaboration of the romantic cross-class marriage scenario is gradual.

No marriages conclude *Le Compagnon du tour de France* (The companion of the tour of France, 1840), indeed there is no closure, no final resolution, only deferral, as the central cross-class couple, Pierre Huguenin and Yseult de Villepreux, decide that neither they nor the world are ready for the transgression of the taboo on cross-class marriage. Yseult's father/grandfather—a sort of doubled instantiation of the symbolic order—must come to terms with Yseult's choice, and Pierre must devise a way of reconciling his ideals with wealth. In one of the numerous and interestingly always gendered addresses to the reader that stud this text, Sand promises a sequel that would ultimately decide what is left undecided at the end of volume 1 of the *Bildung* of Pierre Huguenin:

> I do not give his conclusions to you as the last decisions of wisdom, friend reader. If the youth of Pierre Huguenin, the companion of the tour of France, has interested you some little, his manhood, with which I intend to entertain you in another romance, will interest you still more, I hope; and you will see that several times in his succeeding years he doubted of what he had done, and conscientiously interrogated himself.[16]

This sequel was never written, though Sand later claimed that *La Ville noire*, a belated utopian novel (1861), was that sequel, despite the fact that the characters are not the same, and the setting is totally different!

Let us look more closely at *Le Compagnon* to try to understand the reasons for the unwritability of its sequel, that is, the unrepresentability of the union of its highly idealized main protagonists, Pierre Huguenin, the Christ-like "proletarian philosopher" (p. 123/147; translation modified), and Yseult de Villepreux, the bookish daughter/granddaughter of the count whose chapel Pierre's father has been commissioned to restore. Newly returned from his tour of France—the novel owes much to the account of the *compagnonage* initiatory rites and secret societies provided by Agricol Perdiguier—Pierre is actually in charge of the project. In the course of his work, he enters into a platonic relationship with Yseult, who lends him books and shares his dreams for the future. Though much of the novel is given over to several interwoven subplots—the reciprocal violence between rival secret societies (the Gavots and the Dévorants), the political plotting of various secondary characters (the novel takes place in 1823), the parallel and passionate love affair between Pierre's friend Amaury and Josephine, Yseult's cousin—the focus remains clearly on the exemplary central couple.

Though both figures are highly idealized, the modes of idealization applied to each character vary: one does not idealize a worker in the same terms as one idealizes a lady. *Idealization is not a uniform or always identical technique of embellishment;* it is instead a meliorative mode carefully calibrated to take into account a character's specific traits, notably his or her class, as well as, of course, gender. Or, to put the matter another way: *Idealization, as what we might call an interventionist discursive mode, functions within the context of preexistent models of representations as a counterdiscourse; it implies a norm, a stereotype.* At best it works within the constraints of ideology as a contestatory, and even, in this instance, revolutionary strategy; at worst, it subtly underwrites dominant forms of oppression and reinforces existing inequities and prejudices.[17] Thus, the idealized figure of the worker makes sense only when it is viewed as a denaturalization of the worker type as an ignorant, brutish *untermensch*, just as the idealized figure of the aristocratic woman signifies by its difference from reigning representations of the lady as frivolous and vain.[18]

The first and by far the most important difference between the two idealizing practices is that one—the idealization of the worker—produced a shock effect among Sand's contemporaries that the other, to which it is nevertheless related by Sand, did not. What Sand's retrospective "Notice" written in 1851 makes clear is that in the early 1840s in France, an unwritten law enjoined against idealizing a member of the working class:

> I wrote the novel of *Le Compagnon du tour de France* with sincerely progressive ideas. In trying to represent as advanced a type of worker as exists in our times, it was quite impossible for me not to give him ideas about present-day society and aspirations toward a future society. Nevertheless, some classes cried: Impossible, you exaggerate. I was accused of flattering the people and of wanting to embellish them. Well, why not? Why, admitting my type was too idealized, did I not have the right to do for men of the people what I had been allowed to do for those of the other classes? Why not sketch out the most sympathetic and the most serious portrait possible so that all good and intelligent workers would have the desire to resemble him?[19]

Over a century of intense idealization of worker figures—under the auspices first of realism-naturalism, then, more recently, of various forms of socialist realism—have blunted the thrust of Sand's scandalizing idealized portrayal of her worker-philosopher. What is more, repelled by the seemingly inert didacticism of the "positive hero" type that is so central to socialist realism and to the critical analyses it has inspired,[20] the postmodern reader, whatever her politics, has difficulty working up much interest in his representation. Overcoming, then, my own jaded responses to this figure, I want to examine in some detail the conditions of his admissibility to representation at the very moment when the ancient rules regulating the proper relationship between class and representation were at last succumbing to the pressures of modern industrial societies. This representational shift—to which more than one nineteenth-century author has laid claim—can be interpreted variously as a victory for the symbolically and politically disenfranchised or, more cynically, as a triumph for the rising forces of capitalism. The first interpretation is that of the progressivist, humanist Sand, who writes further in her "Notice": "A worker is a man like any other, a gentleman just like any other gentleman, and I am very surprised that this still surprises anyone."[21] The second is that of the suspicious contemporary ideological critic who would argue that promotion of the manual worker to representational status works in the end not so much to enfranchise the model worker as to insert him more securely in the capitalist system (when it is not, of course, the communist system).

Two passages drawn from the second chapter of the novel will allow us to observe proletarian idealization in France *in statu nascendi*:

> Pierre Huguenin, the master joiner's son, was the handsomest youth for twenty leagues around. His features had the nobleness and regularity of statuary; he was large and well made in person; his feet, hands, and head were very small, which is remarkable in a man of the people, and very compatible with great muscular strength in handsome races; finally his large blue eyes, shaded by black eyelashes, and the delicate coloring of his cheeks, gave a gentle and pensive expression to that head which would not have been unworthy of Michael Angelo's chisel. (p. 15/47)

> The curate, who assisted the old joiner to read his letters, made him remark, not without pleasure, that his son's handwriting became more and more fine and flowing, that he expressed himself in chosen terms, and that there was in his style a measure, a nobleness, and even an eloquence, which already raised him above himself and all the old workmen of the country whom he called his equals. (p. 18/50)

Though Sand's idealist *parti-pris* is unique, one understands clearly on reading these passages why so often in the nineteenth-century French novel the worker figure is a *déclassé*. *Not only is idealization not incompatible with the representation of the worker, it is its very condition.* It is only by emphasizing Pierre's sublime sculptural beauty—throughout the novel, Michelangelo and Raphael are invoked as the guarantors of the proletarian sublime—the nobility of his traits and his style, in short, his difference from and superiority to the common worker that Sand affords him entry onto the scene of representation. Aestheticized, asepticized, Pierre is a hybrid of the popular and the aristocratic.

Pierre's legitimizing "nobility" is, however, not merely corporeal. It is also and perhaps more importantly intellectual, even literary. For the nineteenth-century writer invested with the mission of lifting the masses out of their ignorance and obscurity, literacy and even literariness are the chief attributes of the idealized worker. Pierre's superiority to his fellow craftsmen consists in his ability to manipulate both the scriptural and semantic codes of the symbolic. Not only is the hand that defines this manual laborer unusually dainty, it also produces a fine hand. But there is more: the very terms that Sand uses to characterize the felicities of Pierre's epistolary style might be, indeed have been, applied to describe Sand's prose, with its distinctive (and often derided) *flow* (Proust speaks of "le flot puissant" [the mighty torrent] of Sand's prose, in the celebrated *scène du baiser* where his mother reads him *François le champi*). What this homology between author and character points to is the secondary benefit of the idealization of the worker, the legitimation of the writer's redemptive imperative. By blurring the differences between the upwardly mobile worker and the socially conscious writer, the writer succeeds in advancing her own claims to moral leadership while pressing the working class's claims to self-representation.

Though, as we shall see in a moment, the modalities differ, the stakes of idealizing the aristocratic heiress are finally the same as those of idealizing the proletarian prophet: grounding authorial authority. *If there is a law of idealization, it is that idealization is always inscribed in a specular economy, where the benefits of the process redound to the idealizer; there is no such thing as disinterested idealization.* Just as idealizing Pierre's epistolary prowess serves to enhance the author's moral authority, idealizing Yseult's intellectual attainments serves to justify the author's very right to wield a pen. For, if Pierre's intellectual achievements place him beyond his station, Yseult's place her beyond her gender: "Yseult, who was much interested in the reading and analytic compilation of works quite serious for her sex and age, remained a part of the day in her study" (p. 191/209). The idealized figure of Yseult is part of the same didactic humanist agenda as is Pierre's; both serve to combat the mutually reinforcing evils of class and gender prejudice in the liberating arena of education. As Sand states in her "Notice":

> It is not necessary to have graduated to be as educated as all the bachelors of arts in the world. It is not at school that one learns religion and morality, since all you learn there are Greek and Latin. One acquires there very slowly a certain learning that a worker, just as a woman, can acquire later and faster with intelligence and will. Finally the vaunted inferiorities of race and sex are prejudices that do not even have the excuse today of being upheld in good faith, and to combat them anymore would be very childish at this moment in time. (p. 32)

Despite Sand's smooth, doubly stated homology between worker and woman, class (*race*) and gender (*sexe*), it is clear that in this "postfeminist" novel, the issue of women's equal access to knowledge and power is subsumed to that of the worker.[22] Not surprisingly it is the idealization of the worker and not that of the woman that provoked protest and aroused criticism; by 1840 the figure of the bluestocking, even idealized, was not shocking—it has become a cliché. What is more troubling about Sand's homology is that it operates by holding apart class and gender, by glossing over their interweaving in the constitution of the subject. It is because both characters are doubly determined— Yseult is both a woman and a member of the privileged class, Pierre is both a man and a member of the proletariat—that their ultimate union is indefinitely deferred. In the end, class difference overrides sexual difference. Indeed, as though to maximize the distance that separates the ideal pair, Sand endows Yseult with the most prestigious paternity imaginable in nineteenth-century France. According to a rumor the narrator coyly refuses to discredit, Yseult is no less than Caesar's daughter, an illegitimate offspring of the emperor Napoléon himself. What follows is a dialogue between Pierre and his informant:

> "What have you to tell me then?"
> "Something very particular. Do you know whose daughter people say she is?"

"I do not know."
"The emperor Napoleon's, neither more nor less."
"How could that be?"
"Very naturally. Her father, the old count's son, married a young lady attached to the empress Josephine's household; so that the first child of that marriage, if the chronicle is to be believed, might be born a little earlier than was correct, and could have in the lines of her profile a softened resemblance to the Corsican eagle." (pp. 226–27/241)

The Napoleonic motif is reinforced by the insistence of the signifier *Josephine* in the novel, for Josephine is the name of the antiheroine, whose prosaic affair with Amaury (le Corinthien) is counterpoised to Pierre and Yseult's poetic idyll. The erotic quartet is, as is well known, a fundamental component of the Sandian plot, from the Goetheian *Jacques* through the rustic *Maîtres sonneurs*; what is perhaps less well understood is the function it serves, enabling Sand to distinguish two erotic regimes, the realist and the idealist, and to play off what Béatrice Didier nicely terms the "utopian couple" against the "reality couple."[23]

In what does the realist regime consist? It is essentially the regime Flaubert will later and indelibly make synonymous with the name *Madame Bovary*. A by-product of the bourgeois exchange of women, it is rooted in fiction. Though bearing the title *Marquise*, Josephine, we soon learn, is a member of the aristocracy only by marriage, a marriage cynically engineered by her ambitious parents and to which the silly Josephine consents:

> The Clicots knew very well beforehand that the marquis was neither handsome, nor young, nor amiable; that his morals were as much disordered as his fortune; in a word, that his wife would have no chance of happiness, nor of real consideration; but an alliance with *the family* . . . had turned their heads, and the little Clicot was consoled for everything by the title of marchioness. (p. 163/183–84)

Separated from her ne'er-do-well husband, who has squandered her dowry, Josephine returns to live with her family in straitened circumstances. Forced to take up again a prosaic life in a grim factory town after having lived the high life in Paris, Josephine takes to novel reading as a form of escape and compensation:

> Banished suddenly to a smoky and bad-smelling factory, surrounded by workmen or superintendents, of better intentions than manners, hearing only of wools, trades, wages, dyes, prices current, and stocks, she had no other resource against despair but to read novels in the evening, and sleep a part of the day. . . . In her solitude she created for herself wonderful adventures and conquests; but compelled to fall back into reality, she was only the more to be pitied. (pp. 163–64/183)

When Josephine goes to live at the Villepreux manor and meets the handsome, artistically talented carpenter Amaury, she is ready to move on to the next stage of female reader response, the acting out of fiction-induced fantasies:

> The poor Josephine, having read many romances . . . experienced an irresistible desire to bring into her own life a romance of which she should be the heroine; and the hero was found. He was there, young, handsome as a demi-god, intelligent, and pure, more than any of those who have a right of citizenship in the most proper romances. Only he was a journeyman joiner, which was contrary to all received usage, I confess; but he was crowned, besides his beautiful hair, with the glory of an artist. (pp. 194–95/212)

At this point in our analysis we can observe a first and crucial difference between Sand's and Flaubert's handling of the theme of the dangers of (mis)reading: in Sand's pre-1848 novels, the problematic mediation of desire by fiction is deliberately and scrupulously inserted into a class-conscious social universe, whereas in *Madame Bovary*, though the aristocracy continues to exert a powerful erotic fascination over the petit-bourgeois heroine, desire is, as we well know, largely a category of metaphysics.

What then does Josephine read? Whose novels does she feel the irresistible need to stage, to enact? What is the role of class differences in these novels? The only novels whose author is specified in *Le Compagnon* are those by Sir Walter Scott, whom Sand calls the "king of novel-writers" (p. 205/222). As though to confirm the inseparability of Balzacian realism and Sandian idealism, both flow from the same intertext:[24]

> Those novels, in spite of their exquisite and adorable chastity, are quite as dangerous for young heads, quite as subversive of the old social order, as novels must be which are romantic and read with avidity by all classes of society. It is therefore to Sir Walter Scott that must be attributed the

disorder which had become organized, if we may so speak, in the brain of Josephine. She dreamed that she was a lady of the fifteenth or sixteenth century who was to be pursued by a young artisan, the foundling of some great family, soon to rush forward in the career of talent and glory, and to recover his titles or attain them by his merit and reputation. (pp. 205–6/222)

Sand's parodic account of the standard plot of Scott's novels is informed by her critique of his fictional politics. For all his praiseworthy "instinctive" love of the people, Scott stops short of a truly subversive representation of cross-class romance, one that did not confer in extremis nobility on the upstart young lover, thereby negating by its reassuring closure the very force of its initial situation:

> Faithful to his aristocratic prejudices, and too English to be bold to the end, he never fails to discover for his noble vagabonds an illustrious family, a rich inheritance, or to make them ascend, step by step, the ladder of honors and fortune, in order to place them at the feet of their ladies, without exposing the latter to a misalliance by a pure love-marriage. (p. 205/222)

Sand's wager is to surpass her privileged intertext by carrying the initial class asymmetry to its logical conclusion without capitulating to the pressures of prejudice, class and/or national, without resorting to what Leroy-Ladurie calls the "the tricks, the feeble little tricks" that enabled pre-1850 popular novelists to effect class conciliation through marriage.[25] That Sand was only partially successful in her attempt to differentiate herself from Scott gives the measure of the force of the taboo on cross-class marriage in nineteenth-century society—or, rather, in its fictional representations.

However disappointing Scott's (and Sand's) ultimate failure of nerve, his novels are, as Sand conceded, sufficiently revolutionary to appeal to a wide spectrum of readers and to lend themselves to a full range of interpretations. Thus Amaury comes upon a novel of Scott's that the marquise has forgotten in the manor's garden. Knowing Pierre's love of all manner of books, Amaury brings him his find, and together the two craftsmen devour the novel in one sitting. So enthralled are they by their reading that they borrow the second volume from the bookseller in the neighboring town. But though both young men share the same copy of the novel, the novel they read is not the same, and that difference in their reading is from my perspective central: "This reading produced upon them an effect equally deep but different. Pierre saw in it the fanciful idealization of woman; the Corinthian there saw the possible realization of his own destiny, not as the unknown heir of some great fortune, but as the predestined conqueror of glory in art" (p. 206/223). *Idealism is not just in the novel but in the reader as well.* Pierre, who embodies the ideal, reads as an idealist, while Amaury, who operates at a lower ethical level, reads as a realist, in the most literal sense of the word, and here he joins Josephine, the ambitious daydreamer par excellence. What interests me here is the way in which each form of reading corresponds to a distinct libidinal economy, what I've been calling the romantic and the realist. Unlike Flaubert—and this is Sand's second difference from her great friend of later years—Sand does not reduce all meaning to the always-doomed pursuit of a trivial illusion; for her, all fictions are not veils masking an invariably sordid reality. The difference between Pierre and Amaury (as well as between Yseult and Josephine) is not that one identifies and the other doesn't, not that one seeks to realize what he reads and the other doesn't but rather that the love story one reads and lives is ideal and the one the other lives and reads is not. And what makes Yseult and Pierre's love story ideal is not that it is as "exquisitely and adorably chaste" as those imagined by Scott but that it is bound up with and ennobled by their communitarian politics. *The opposition between idealism and realism in sexuality is the difference between altruistic and egoistic love.* In the context of a chapter dealing with Josephine and Amaury's passionate physical affair, Sand articulates with a rare degree of explicitness her credo of erotic value:

> Certainly, this feeling had in itself nothing culpable or insensate. But it soon had the fate of all the intoxications into which a man plunges without an ideal of virtue or of religion. We have all indeed the right to be happy, to aspire to works of genius and the suffrages of mankind. We are allowed to be proud of the object of our love, and to count upon the victories of our intelligent will. But this is not all the life of man; and, if the love of self is not closely bound to the love of our kind, this ambition, which might have triumphed over all obstacles in the state of devotedness, suffers, becomes embittered, and threatens to fall at every step, when it remains in the state of selfishness. Love, which extends this selfishness to two beings melted into one alone, is not enough to legitimatize it. It is

beautiful and divine as a means, as a help, and as an aegis: it is poor and miserable as an object and an only end. (p. 294/303)

On one level, it might be said that there is nothing surprising or, rather, new about Sand's condemnation of the lovers' "égoïsme à deux." The moralizing tone of Sand's impassioned denunciation is in keeping with the critique of selfish individualism that accompanies the rise of capitalism in fiction, philosophy, and political theory. But to stop there would be to read Sand out of context, to forget the French literary scene of the 1840s, to deny Sand's specificity, no matter how problematic. However devastatingly Balzac and Stendhal's fiction may contribute to the critique of self-seeking individualism, of the contamination of love by ambition, they imagine no acceptable alternative regime, no space outside the marketplace of unbound appetites that is not a regressive preoedipal space connoted as maternal, presided over by an idealized, all-forgiving, long-suffering figure of the mother. As though to deny the politicization of affect in postrevolutionary France, love under realism is excessively and, increasingly, desperately privatized. The idealist novel— whether it be by Hugo, Sand, or even that arch anti-idealist, Zola— represents an attempt to turn to account the *real*, effective interleaving of the private and the public, the individual and the collective, by projecting a passage between the most intimate erotic transactions and the most divisive political struggles. It represents, in other words, a rejection of the private solution to social conflict or, better, a recognition of its impossibility. In its paroxysmic form—and the analogies between the situation in France in the 1840s and that in the United States and Europe in the 1960s will not be lost on those of us who came of age in the heady sixties—idealist Eros is conterminous with revolutionary fervor:

Pierre was intoxicated, out of his senses. The fever which burned in Yseult's veins passed into his. Both believed themselves transported by faith alone, and that they had at this moment no other bond than that of virtue. Still it was love which had assumed this form, and undertaken to kindle in them the flame of revolutionary enthusiasm. (p. 286/296)

It is, of course, precisely because such hopes of harnessing erotic energy to the chariot of state appear to us naive and deluded, if generous, that such fictions are inevitably dismissed as "hopelessly idealistic" and in common parlance idealism is always qualified as hopeless. My concern here is not to adjudicate between the claims of realism and idealism; I simply want to show how in Sand's most overtly political fictions idealism is promoted as an erotic and ultimately conjugal mode superior to realism—*the politics of idealism is a sexual politics*. The question then becomes: How does Sand in her subsequent political novels of the 1840s work out the passage between love and cross-class marriage that she fails to find in *Le Compagnon*? (How) does she imaginatively effect the conciliation of the classes toward which *Le Compagnon* so ardently strains but in the end fails to achieve?

Le Meunier d'Angibault (1845)

An important five-year interval separates *Le Meunier d'Angibault* from *Le Compagnon du tour de France*, years marked by the publication of several major works, notably *Consuelo* (1842–43), *La Comtesse de Rudolstadt* (1844–45), and the mythic *Jeanne* (1844). Although all these novels feature cross-class pairings and are suffused with idealistic politics, they are not part of the triptych that constitutes my text, which belongs generically to what the Germans call "Sozialroman."[26] The *Consuelo–Comtesse de Rudolstadt* saga is set in eighteenth-century Venice and Austria, while *Jeanne*, though set in the Berry of the 1820s, is steeped in Celtic mythology. In short, what these novels lack is the paradoxical realist underpinning necessary to Sand's political fiction. In this sense Sand's political fictions are antithetical to utopias, at least in their conventional, etymological forms. They are sited in landscapes of verisimilitude and set more or less in the historical present.[27] And none more so than *Le Meunier*, whose opening scene places the action audaciously close to the present of enunciation—"This was going on very recently, perhaps last year"[28]—and whose original title was to be *Au jour d'aujourd'hui*, echoing the refrain of Bricolin, the villain in the novel. The temporal proximity of the events produces a reality effect that serves to offset and ground its manifest implausibilities; at the same time, the association of the immediately contemporaneous with the insistently deidealized figure of Bricolin, the designated representative of the newly rich peasantry, suggests that presentness in Sand is taxed with all the grimness of the real.

Chapter 1 of *Le Meunier* stages a late-night tryst between two Parisian lovers: the rich and lovely Marcelle de Blanchmont and her unprepossessing, impecunious student lover, Henri Lémor. Recently widowed, Marcelle offers her hand to Henri only to be refused for reasons of political principles, prompting her to exclaim bitterly: "—Is it possible, Henri that you are so attached to your utopias? What! Even love cannot conquer them? Ah! How little you love, you men! she added with a deep sigh. When it is not vice that desiccates your soul, it is virtue, and anyhow, cowardly or sublime, you love only yourselves" (p. 32). Unlike Yseult— also the proposer in *Le Compagnon*—who fully understands the reasons for Pierre's refusal, Marcelle uncomprehendingly disparages Henri's political ideals, even going so far as to align them with male egotism, a frequent target of Sand's feminist animus.

But what really distinguishes *Le Meunier* from *Le Compagnon* is that in the interval—and though five years separate their publications, it can be said that one picks up where the other leaves off—class differences have hardened into a seemingly impenetrable wall: "Everything about your position and mine," Henri tells Marcelle, "is an insurmountable obstacle" (p. 33). The optimism that animates *Le Compagnon* has given way to a sense of crisis, a pessimistic anticipation of "a great struggle that is more or less near" (p. 36), though just how close this great struggle was neither Sand nor her most ardent socialist comrades could foresee. But, finally, the most significant difference between the sublime high idealism of *Le Compagnon* and the somewhat degraded, hence more pleasing idealism of *Le Meunier* is that at the outset Marcelle denies any possible intersection between her private fantasy of a blissful, legitimate union with her social inferior and the ominously impending social cataclysm whose advancing storm system she acutely perceives. On the contrary: initially her *ressentiment* is directed against the class struggle itself, as though it were an external force threatening her personal pursuit of happiness. Stunned by Henri's refusal, by the end of chapter 1 Marcelle emerges from the imaginary of aristocratic privilege to begin to understand one of the major laws of the social symbolic order: there is no secure boundary between the public and the private, no subject position outside of or beyond class, no realm of intrapersonal relations that is not traversed by the axis of class difference:

> This struggle between feelings and ideas is henceforth deeply engaged. As though emerging from a dream Marcelle saw herself suddenly plunged into it in the midst of her illusions. The moral and intellectual war was declared between the classes, each imbued with conflicting beliefs and passions, and Marcelle found a sort of irreconcilable enemy in the man who adored her. (p. 37)

Marcelle's awakening, her abrupt plunge into a disenchanted world cause her to revise her familiar surroundings in terms of material value and to question the social inequities they both produce and support. For the first time, Marcelle recognizes that she lives in the phantasmagoric world of commodities and that in that world women are both the chief objects and subjects of exchange and desire:

> She awoke completely at dawn, and, casting a dreamy look over the furnishings of her apartment, she was for the first time struck by the useless and costly luxury deployed about her. Satin wall coverings, overstuffed and oversized furniture, thousands of ruinous refinements and shiny bibelots, in short the whole lot of gilt, porcelain, sculpted wood, and useless objects that today clutter the home of an elegant woman. "I would really like to know," she thought to herself, "why we have such contempt for kept women. They get people to give them things we can give ourselves. . . . They have the same tastes as we do, and it is to seem as rich and happy as we are that they degrade themselves. . . . And if one wished to compare our indissoluble marriages with their transitory unions, would one find more disinterestedness among the young women of our class?" (pp. 38–39)

The equation of marriage and prostitution is a founding axiom of Sand's (and her contemporaries') feminist writings; what is radically new here is the linking of "femmes honnêtes" and fallen women via their common socially constructed consumerism. In the shiny new world of nascent capitalism, consumption becomes the great equalizer, not to say the implacable leveler.

The loss of illusions—an emergence from the imaginary into the symbolic simultaneous with an awakening into the world of merchandise— is the great formative or, better, normative subjective experience of the nineteenth-century French fictional protagonist. Whether epiphanic as in the case of Sand's Marcelle or Balzac's Lucien de Rubempré or endlessly drawn out, as in the case of Flaubert's Frédéric Moreau, it is an obsessively recurring scenario, a topos. It is no accident that on more than one occasion the rude awakening of the deluded protagonist (often a man from the provinces) occurs in a sordid hotel room, the *commonplace* par excellence (even more so when that room is located in a so aptly named "hotel de passe," but even when it is not, the brothel remains the subliminal model of the hotel). Some years before the suicidal hero of Flaubert's early novella *Novembre* discovers the deceit of romanticism in this privileged urban locus of initiation,[29] Indiana loses her last shred of false hope in a seedy Parisian hotel room. From the moment of Indiana's ironically ill-timed return to France—she arrives in Bordeaux in the midst of the July revolution and just as Raymon de Ramière has decided in what can only be read as a pointed political allegory to marry Laure de Nangy, heiress to an immense industrial fortune—she is subjected to a series of depersonalizing losses that culminate in that hotel room. The first loss involves her identification papers: wandering dazedly about the city in the throes of the revolution, Indiana learns that the Bourbon monarchy has fallen and, in what we have by now learned to recognize as a major aspect of Sand's imaginary, hyperbolically personalizes the effects of the revolution: "In the whole revolution she was personally interested in but one fact; in all France she knew but one man. She fell into a swoon, and came to herself in a hospital—several days later."[30] As though in punishment for her excessive personalization of History, Indiana is quite literally stripped of her identity. Having no papers on her when she falls into a swoon, she appears "on the books there [at the hospital] and also on the police books under the designation *unknown*" (p. 274/293). Though she does not end up like Balzac's Colonel Chabert, that astonishing victim of History, as a mere cipher in the disciplinary system, she does endure in the course of her hospitalization an equally devastating and significant loss, one that assaults her gendered being, the loss of her beautiful black hair, fetishized earlier in the novel by Raymon in a ghoulish scene I have analyzed elsewhere:[31]

> But, when she was ready to arrange her hair, she sought in vain the long and magnificent tresses she had once had; during her illness they had

fallen under the nurse's shears. She noticed it then for the first time, her all-engrossing thoughts had diverted her mind so completely from small things. (pp. 293–94/275)

Castration is always retroactive, caught up in the dizzying temporality of the Lacanian psychic registers, where the imaginary can only be glimpsed in the rearview mirror of the symbolic.[32] Before the ultimate humiliation and depersonalization of her visit to Raymon—she throws herself at his feet only to learn that he is married—Indiana is blithely unaware of her grim surroundings. It is only *after* the coachman deposits "Madame" at her hotel following her disastrous encounter with Raymon and his new wife that Sand situates the extraordinary intervention by the narrator that only an unwary reader would dismiss as mere pathos. For the first time the reader sees the romantic subject—and not just a neutral, supposedly universal subject, but a subject gendered in lack, a woman—in the cold light of the symbolic. The anonymous and tawdry furnished room, antechamber to the dirt and indifference of the metropolis, is the "défilé," that dark and narrow passage through which the subject must pass as she accedes to the common language. In the hotel room even proper names become just ordinary signs, caught up in a system of traces inscribed on a tarnished mirror. After much hesitation, I reproduce this remarkable passage in its entirety, refusing to cut the "tresse" of the text, to wield the scissors of critical castration:

> I do not know that there is anything more horrible on earth than life in a furnished lodging-house in Paris, especially when it is situated, as this one was, in a dark, narrow street, and only a dull, hazy light crawls regretfully, as it were, over the smoky ceilings and soiled windows. And then there is something chilly and repellent in the sight of the furniture to which you are unaccustomed and to which your idle glance turns in vain for a memory, a touch of sympathy. All those objects which belong, so to speak, to no one, because they belong to all comers; that room where no one has left any trace of his passage save now and then a strange name, found on a card in the mirror-frame; that mercenary roof, which has sheltered so many poor travellers, so many lonely strangers, with hospitality for none; which looks with indifference upon so many human agitations and can describe none of them: the discordant, never-ending noise from the street, which does not even allow you to sleep and thus escape grief or ennui: all these are causes of disgust and irritation even

to one who does not bring to the horrible place such a frame of mind as Madame Delmare's. You ill-starred provincial, who have left your fields, your blue sky, your verdure, your house and your family, to come and shut yourself up in this dungeon of the mind and the heart—see Paris, lovely Paris, which in your dreams has seemed to you such a marvel of beauty! see it stretch away yonder, black with mud and rainy, as noisy and pestilent and rapid as a torrent of slime! There is the perpetual revel, always brilliant and perfumed, which was promised you; there are the intoxicating pleasures, the wonderful surprises, the treasures of sight and taste and hearing which were to contend for the possession of your passions and faculties, which are of limited capacity and powerless to enjoy them all at once! See, yonder, the affable, winning, hospitable Parisian, as he was described to you, always in a hurry, always careworn! Tired out before you have seen the whole of this ever-moving population, this inextricable labyrinth, you take refuge, overwhelmed with dismay, in the cheerful precincts of a furnished lodging-house, where, after hastily installing you, the only servant of a house that is often of immense size leaves you to die in peace, if fatigue or sorrow deprive you of the strength to attend to the thousand necessities of life.

But to be a woman and to find oneself in such a place, spurned by everybody, three thousand leagues from all human affection; to be without money, which is much worse than being abandoned in a vast desert without water; to have in one's past not a single happy memory that is not poisoned or withered, in the whole future not a single hope to divert one's thoughts from the emptiness of the present, is the last degree of misery and hopelessness. And so Madame Delmare, making no attempt to contend against a destiny that was fulfilled, against a broken, ruined life, submitted to the gnawings of hunger, fever and sorrow without uttering a complaint, without shedding a tear, without making an effort to die an hour earlier, to suffer an hour less. (pp. 281–2/299–300; emphasis added)

It is a long way from Indiana's nervous breakdown in a Parisian "hôtel garni" to Marcelle's dreamy awakening in her Parisian "hôtel particulier." Driven, like so many Balzacian protagonists mired in the imaginary by a powerful death drive, Indiana undergoes yet another near or quasi-death in the hotel room that she leaves only after Ralph, her cousin-brother-father-lover, has enticed her with the promise of a double suicide in the valley of Bernica on the "île Bourbon," the very site of their presexual idyll. Miraculously and implausibly saved as they are about to jump over the precipice into the waterfalls, Indiana and Ralph survive only to live on in a curious liminal state symbolizing an uneasy compromise between life and death, the imaginary and the symbolic, the personal and the political, the ideal and the real. Everything about the couple bears the mark of indeterminacy: Indiana's existence ("her existence was still a problematical matter to many of the people," p. 317/334), her guilt or innocence ("that woman was either very guilty or very unfortunate," p. 320/337), Ralph's intellect as well as his guilt or innocence (p. 318–19/334–35). It is of course true that this indeterminacy is an effect of a narrative strategy of external focalization that deliberately deprives the reader of any direct access to Indiana's feelings and allows only a glimpse of Ralph's. Devoting their lives and their revenues to buying infirm blacks out of slavery, Indiana and Ralph seem to fulfill Sand's ideal of the erotic. But do they? Their antislavery politics remain purely local, more philanthropic than revolutionary; they live exiled from the polis, in virtual autarky; and, finally and perhaps most disturbing, it is not at all clear that they are married or even lovers. Based on her close and remarkably thorough reading of the novel, Vareille makes a convincing case for Indiana's sexual blossoming in the utopian setting of Bernica but concedes the "discretion" of the emphasis on her sexualization.[33] Ultimately the question of Indiana's virginity remains quite deliberately, it would appear, undecided. Even if we do follow Vareille in her analysis, I would argue along with other commentators that the absence of any children is symptomatic of a disturbance in the couple's sexuality.[34] This raises several questions to which I cannot yet respond: Can ideal Eros deploy itself fully anywhere outside of utopia? Is communistic love compatible with adult, genital, that is, normative sexuality? Or does it participate in the pervasive desexualization of the Sandian heroine?

Marcelle's trajectory is altogether more euphoric and less marked by uncertainty than is Indiana's. Having in a moment of insight become aware of her class privilege and of the obstacle it constitutes to the pursuit of happiness, Marcelle does not relinquish the pursuit but instead plunges into it determinedly. Just as Ralph proposes a suicide pact to Indiana, Marcelle proposes a sort of marriage pact to Henri. If after a year apart devoted to enhancing her worthiness, to becoming in the apt vocabulary of folktale analysis a fully "qualified" heroine—of the three novels under investigation the *Meunier* is by far the closest to a folktale—Henri sees no further objection to their union, they will marry. Here again we find Sand confronted by what we might call the "Scott problem": how to engineer a marriage between an upper-class woman and a lower-class man without resorting to a providential last-minute elevation of the man to the woman's social and, more importantly in this instance, economic level. *Le Compagnon* ends in an impasse as a result of Sand's/Pierre's refusal to compromise. In *Le Meunier*, Sand/Marcelle devises an ingenious alternative solution, which in fact only serves to emphasize the intractability of the problem. Since Henri cannot be elevated without violating Sand's law of the genre, then Marcelle will have to be lowered for there to be any sort of conventional resolution to their story, and since we are in both a folk and a comedic mode, conventional closure must prevail. Thus Marcelle decides to spend her mythical year of qualification rusticating on her country estate. Her plan succeeds beyond her wildest dreams when, upon reaching Blanchemont, she discovers that she is for all practical purposes ruined as a result of her profligate late husband's improvidence, a piece of news Marcelle announces in a letter to Henri in the following terms: "How wonderful! how delightful! I am ruined" (p. 118). That Sand means us to laugh at Marcelle's naive quickie solution to the complex and menacing class struggle is indicated by the positioning and idealization of the miller of the title, Grand-Louis.

Earlier we noted that idealization is not a uniform technique in that the specific features idealized vary according to a character's class and gender. Now we must refine that observation further: even within a single class and gender, idealization does not function in cookie-cutter fashion. In *Le Compagnon* and *Le Meunier*, for example, though physical beauty and eloquence are the chief attributes of the idealized man of the people, there is a crucial difference between the idealized artisan and the idealized miller: what is idealized in Pierre is in the final analysis his idealism itself, whereas what is idealized in Grand-Louis is his common sense, his ability to disengage goodness from foolishness.

> The specimen of the province that appeared before Marcelle at that moment was five feet eight inches tall, a remarkable height in a country where the men are generally shorter rather than tall. He was proportionately robust, well built, at ease, and with a remarkable face. The girls

> where he came from called him the handsome miller, and this epithet was as well deserved as the other. . . . His features were regular and broadly hewn like his limbs, his eyes were black and well shaped, his teeth, dazzling, and his long and wavy sandy blond hair tightly curled like that of a very strong man framed a wide and well-filled forehead that promised more finesse and good sense than poetic ideal. (pp. 41–42)

Whereas in *Le Compagnon* idealism is compounded by idealization, producing a sort of idealism to the second power, in *Le Meunier* idealization is uncoupled from and even, in the case of its main protagonist, counterpoised to idealism, with the result that both are diminished. For, as Taine rightly understood, the distinctiveness of Sand's idealist poetics resides in the linkage of idealization and idealism. As the example of *Le Meunier* demonstrates, *in the nineteenth-century novel idealization without idealism is always in danger of lapsing into a modified bourgeois apologetics, and, conversely, idealism without idealization is never far from being discredited as just another utopian socialism.*

The cleavage I have detected at work in *Le Meunier* between idealism and idealization is yet another of the rifts in this curiously forked text. From the outset the novel was perceived as divided against itself. In a letter of July 1845 Sand defends herself against her publisher Véron—who had initially contracted to publish the novel then refused to honor his commitment for political reasons—in the following terms: "When M. Véron faulted me for having promised him a novel of manners and given him a novel of ideas, I could not and will never understand the distinction."[35] Just as Sainte-Beuve could not come to grips with the tension between *Lélia*'s realist and allegorical dimensions, critics of *Le Meunier* have since its publication struggled with what they view as its most salient aesthetic transgression: its intermingling of realism and idealism. What is ultimately most significant is not, however, the critics' dismay in the face of the text's hybridization of supposedly incompatible modes; it is their insistence on valorizing the text's realism. Thus, in an important early review, Eugène Pellatan praises the novel's realistic depictions of the country scenes, while excusing the idealism on the grounds that it is philosophy for women: "[The novel] converts above all through feeling; it is a philosophical treatise for women (*sic!*). If it does not provide the reasons for solutions, it provides the enthusiasm. It places before us an ideal which guides us across mountains and rivers to the cradle of nascent truth."[36] And though Béatrice Didier and Marielle Caors, the prefacers of the two recent critical editions of the novel, neither reject idealism outright nor associate it with the feminine, both in different ways seek to minimize its significance, to contain its effects. Caors states at the outset of her preface that she has no intention at this late date to prove "that this novel fuses social concerns with the evocation of the peasant world," that it is both a socialist and a country novel. Rather she wants to "show how it evokes them and to what extent."[37] And yet, several pages later she writes:

> Obviously, it [the novel] is socialist and its first "fathers" are Louis Blanc and Pierre Leroux. *But* we must not neglect the contribution of a geographic real that provides a framework, everyday life, and secondary characters. For it's the constant shock that allows one to oppose ideals and reality and to show precisely that *George Sand is capable of restraining her idealism*, of perceiving the limits of her ideals, thanks to an uninterrupted contact with the reality of the Berry. (p. 14; emphasis added)

Caors's language is eloquent. Though throughout her fine preface she mimes the oscillation she sees at work in Sand's fiction between the ideal and the real, giving both their due, the thrust of her analysis is clearly to convince the reader that this roman à thèse is safely anchored in the real, indeed the most scrupulous geographical realism, and that Sand is capable of curbing her idealist impulses.

Didier proceeds exactly the same way, writing boldly in the concluding paragraph of her preface: "George does not flee reality; she plunges into it."[38]

The felt urgency to demonstrate *Le Meunier*'s realism does more than provide yet another confirmation of the legitimating function of realism in the French canon (and beyond), it bespeaks a crucial anxiety provoked by interpretations of the novel that reduce it to its "ideas," to its socialist political message, the familiar anxiety about the contamination of the pure and above all vivid realm of fiction by the dead hand of ideology—for, in this instance, idealism is seen as synonymous with ideology.[39]

It is at this point that the distinction I introduced earlier between idealization and idealism opens up another strategy for dealing with this text, one of Sand's most intriguing problem novels. By separating the work of idealization from the workings of idealism it is possible to address the workings of ideology as it operates at all levels of the novel, for, of course, ideology is not strictly and safely limited to the expressed political ideals of the characters, though it is also and no less present there. To put the matter somewhat differently, while I agree with those critics who equate idealism and ideology—it would be difficult to do otherwise—I would question their assumption that detailed descriptions of sordid reality are the necessary antidote to ideological pollution, for as we shall see by looking at two realistic descriptions by Sand in the novel, *idealization is not incompatible with realism if by realism we understand the mimesis of prosaic reality.*

Let us begin by looking at a passage to gladden the heart of the reader addicted to Balzacian description. It is the unusually fierce description of the farm belonging to the repository of all evil in the novel, the grasping figure of Bricolin:

> Nothing sadder and less pleasing than this rich peasants' dwelling. The new castle is but a large peasants' house built some fifty years ago with the remains of the fortifications. But the solid walls recently replastered and the loud red tiled roof were signs of recent repairs. This external rejuvenation clashed with the age of the other farm buildings and the striking filth of the yard. These dark buildings, showing traces of an earlier architecture, but solid and well kept-up, formed a single corps of stables and granges that were the farmers' pride and the envy of all the local farmworkers. But this enclosure, so useful for the farm industry, and so convenient for the installation of cattle and the crops, hemmed the eyes and thoughts into a space that was gloomy, prosaic, and repulsively dirty. (p. 68)

In terms of the novel's politics of location, the so-called new castle ("château neuf"), a monument to agrarian capitalism, stands as the antithesis of the paradisiacal mill, which in its pristine beauty prefigures the utopian commune to which the novel gestures in closing. The Bricolins' farm is the site of a bourgeois order of interest and accumulation ruthlessly indifferent to human happiness, as we shall see in a moment, and, what is more, unredeemed by any social ideal: "No social idea, no progressive feeling sustains them [country bourgeois]" (p. 75). Let us note that what is condemned in the type represented by Bricolin (as in the case of Grandet, for example, who represents a precapitalist mode of miserliness) is not so much the accumulation of money as the absence of any higher imperative—religious or social—any future orientation that would somehow justify the acquisition of wealth and lift the petty-bourgeois peasant out of the present. Inasmuch as the novel turns on the issue of the proper distribution of wealth, on rethinking and rewriting the "inheritance plot" in light of socialist and even communist ideals, the terms of Sand's critique of the rising peasant bourgeoisie are significant. *Idealism in the context of a rising capitalist society functions as redemptive*, for as we shall see in the final novel in the triptych, *Le Péché de Monsieur Antoine*, great wealth (rather than great need) is the necessary precondition for a new and more just social order.

But let us turn to the second passage I mentioned earlier, for in contrast to both the radically deidealized home of the Bricolins and the conventional neopastoralism of the mill stands a third site that in some sense mediates between the two binary opposites. It is in this description that interfuses the prosaically detailed reality dear to realism with the spiritual elevation dear to idealism that Sand's ideology is perhaps most interestingly and complexly configured. Passages such as these—and they are rare—communicate the most clearly the ideological charge of idealization, for idealization, especially of a scene of abject poverty such as that represented here, is the most insidious of gestures on the part of the idealist writer. The topos of the spotless cottage or slum that recurs in so many neo- or counterpastoral, sentimental, and/or naturalist representations reveals that *in Sand's social fiction, idealization is a double-edged instrument, now providing inspirational models for social change (as in* Le Compagnon*), now providing demobilizing representations of seemingly naturalized deprivation (as in* Le Meunier*)*.

The passage describes the cottage where Louis arranges a secret meeting for Marcelle and the notary he has found to help her save her fortune. It belongs to Piaulette, the wife of a sickly day laborer:

> After having crossed one of those small peasants' gardens, so poorly kept and consequently so pretty, so lush, and so green, sliding through the hedge she entered into the courtyard of one of the poorest huts in the Vallée-Noire. This courtyard was twenty by six feet long. It was bordered on one side by the small house, on the other by the garden, at each end by thatch-covered wooden sheds that housed several hens, two sheep, and a goat. This represents the entire wealth of a man who earns his bread from day to day and possesses nothing, not even the miserable house he inhabits and the narrow patch of land he works; this man is the true

country proletarian. The inside of the house was as miserable as the entry. Marcelle was touched to see the extreme cleanliness with which the courageous woman struggled there against the horror of the misery. The uneven and rough floor was spotless; the two or three poor pieces of furniture were as bright and shiny as though they had been varnished; the small set of earthenware dishes on wooden shelves against the wall were washed and arranged with great care. Among most of the peasants in the Vallée-Noire, the most abject, the most complete poverty lies discreetly and nobly hidden behind these conscientious habits of order and cleanliness. There, rustic poverty is touching and tender. One would happily live with these indigents. They do not fill us with disgust, but with interest and a sort of respect. It would take so little of the rich man's excess to put an end to the bitterness of their life, hidden beneath this apparent poetic calm! (pp. 204–5)

Such a powerful authorial intervention stands out in a novel marked, like all of Sand's social novels, by a noticeable muting of the narrative voice so intrusively present in her earlier fiction. But what in fact is the author saying? And to whom? One cannot read a passage such as this without raising the issue of Sand's addressees, for what I have identified above as the ambivalence of idealization is intimately bound up with Sand's deliberately doubled structure of address. Whereas what was most striking about the double structure of address in *Le Compagnon* was its splitting along gender lines, what emerges most forcefully here is the splitting of the intended reader, or narratee, along the fault lines of class cleavages. As Karlheinrich Biermann points out in his study of Sand's (and others) social fiction, the question of the intended addressee lies at the heart of Sand's controversial revolutionary literary politics and her critical reception. As Sand explains in the general preface to the 1851 complete edition of her works, her choice of format (including illustrations) was dictated by her desire to produce good-quality, modestly priced books that would be accessible to her target popular audience: "What has concerned me most is the desire to make available to the poor classes those works of which a great part was composed for them."[40] And according to the testimony of Agricol Perdiguier, the model for the "compagnon," she did succeed in reaching her intended readers. Regarding the *Compagnon*, he wrote her: "The workers are beginning to know and love you; for some time now I am almost a book jobber, I place numerous copies of *Le Compagnon du Tour de France*, but scarcely has one read this first part that one eagerly asks for the next instalment."[41] Or, in a similar vein, as late as 1851, the locksmith-poet Gilland wrote Sand: "Up until now only the bourgeoisie read your novels, they and we, bookish workers, but today the light will reach down to the masses and warm them like the sun's rays."[42] But this popular success did not endear her to her bourgeois audience, as exemplified by Lerminier, the critic for the *Revue des Deux Mondes*, who wrote with evident disapproval of Sand's social fiction:

> Then we saw the author . . . by one of the most unfortunate whims to ever mislead a writer, turn his back on elite society, on the world whose approval he had sought and often earned. . . . Mme Sand imagined that she should no longer write for the people, but for the proletariat. . . . There was no hesitating; one had to change audiences, readerships, and, all banners unfurled, Mme Sand enters not the camp of the classical or romantic, but the camp of proletarian literature.[43]

We come here to what may well be the heart of the mystery we have sought to unravel throughout this study: What happened to George Sand? Obviously, the reasons for Sand's decanonization are multiple and mutually reinforcing, and both the gendering of her idealist aesthetics and her politics are major determinants of her devalorization. But as feminists, we must recognize that there may be instances where transgressions of gender boundaries are far less threatening to the status quo than are other forms of transgressions and hence that Sand's peculiar place in literary history may have as much if not more to do with her transgression of the barrier that separated literature addressed to an elite audience from that addressed to the lower classes at a particularly critical juncture in class relations in France.

In one of his most chillingly prescient pronouncements, Balzac, the principal beneficiary of Sand's demotion, is quoted as saying after the publication of *Le Compagnon*: "George Sand is not wanted anywhere: *Le Compagnon* has done her in."[44] Though Balzac's *schadenfreude* was a bit premature and Sand did recover from the strong criticisms leveled at her social fiction by the bourgeois press, going on to recapture her bourgeois audience, she did so at a price—that of abandoning her project of taking her idealist works to the popular reader, of returning to the fold of a bourgeois reading public. What is striking about her most enduringly popular (counter)-triptych of "romans champêtres" is that their intended audience is so explicitly the bourgeois Parisian audience she had turned away from with the socialist novels of the early forties. Feminist criticism may have to recognize that in certain instances of canonical marginalization the sex of the author and the gendering of her literary practice ultimately matter less than the class of her intended audience. As Rey Chow has recently written in a very different context:

> Feminism's most significant contribution to the academic institution does not lie in an exclusive focus on women's problems. Rather, it lies in the way it alerts us to barbarism and mutilation that go on in other spheres of knowledge production. As feminism consolidates its place in the reinterpretation of knowledge in all . . . fields, there persist other types of problems which feminists need to recognize and confront—by forsaking arguments for the rights of women as their primary goal.[45]

If we return now to our passage, we see the delicacy of Sand's mode of double address and how easily she could have ended up falling between two stools, alienating one audience while failing to capture the other. As she wrote in 1844 to Véron in response to his request that she moderate her critique of the propertied class: "I would rather be killed than abandon the cause of the poor who do not read me to please the rich who read me a little."[46] Or as she put it in an 1851 letter, at a moment of extreme disillusionment: "I injured the bourgeoisie that read me, rather than educating the people who could not read me."[47]

Indeed, the passage might serve as a perfect demonstration of how such a double misfire of what Caors calls, following Cabet, the "double didacticism" of Sand's social fiction might work.[48] On the one hand, it contains a scarcely veiled sermon to the rich to divest themselves of their superfluous riches; on the other, it instructs the poor to imitate the exemplary dignity of the humblest of the Berrichon agrarian proletariat. But the passage is undercut by a terrible irony: even as the author ran the risk of alienating the overprivileged members of the class to which she belongs—and we know from Véron's refusal to publish the novel as contracted that she did do just that—she risked not even reaching the class she sought to redeem, because *they could not read*. Left alone for a moment in the darkened windowless room of the cottage, Marcelle completes the process of disillusionment begun in her bedroom:

When Marcelle had thus enclosed herself, she found herself engulfed by darkness, and then she wondered what life was like for people who because they were too poor to afford a candle were obliged in winter to go to bed as soon as night fell, or to spend the day in the gloom to fend off the cold. I said and thought I was ruined, she thought to herself, because I was forced to leave my gilt, padded apartment covered with silk; but how many degrees of the ladder of social lives must one descend before reaching this life of the poor that differs so little from that of animals. . . . How does this unfortunate family spend the long winter evenings? Talking? (p. 207)

When Sand idealizes the man or, as in this instance, the woman of the people, she is at best both providing the members of the infantlike lower classes with the idealized specular selves with which they must identify in their struggle for equality and reassuring an anxious upper class that it has nothing to fear from the "classes laborieuses." Thus, writing to the worker-poet Poncy in September 1844, she called for a poeticization of individual crafts because such poetry would serve the double purpose she assigned to writing: "It would be to teach the rich to respect the worker, the poor worker to respect himself."[49] But in the passage quoted earlier, something else is going on: the idealization of the proud poor woman, her conformism to bourgeois standards of cleanliness, is amputated of one addressee, the poor one. What is finally troubling about the passage is not so much its humanitarian cri de coeur as its enabling exclusion of one of its intended recipients, its assertion of complicity with the privileged narratee. It is no accident that this key chapter culminates in Lémor's granting Marcelle the right to keep her money, indeed affirming her sacred duty to her son not to divest herself of her inheritance, as he did earlier when he distributed the money he had inherited from his father to those he had exploited. "Keep your wealth" (p. 210), cries Lémor in what can only be interpreted as the ultimate cri de coeur in this novel that constantly treads the line between legitimating and delegitimating social inequities.

The divisions in the political and cultural context in which *Le Meunier* appears are then so deep as to be irresolvable. The two couples separated by their differing fortune—Marcelle and Henri and the Meunier and Rose, Bricolin's youngest daughter—do finally overcome the various obstacles to their union, but only thanks to a series of highly implausible events that work to erase their differences and place them more nearly on an equal financial footing. The novel ends with the promise of two marriages and, what is more, of a future communal life in which what we might call the basic paradigm of property and class division in Sand, "le mien et le tien," will be replaced by a utopian commune in which the foursome will share everything. Are these then the conciliatory marriages toward which *Le Compagnon* strained but could not represent? Is this then an instance of the vaunted "fusion des classes" that is said to characterize Sand's social fiction? Biermann rightly points out that the supposed cross-class fusion in Sand is nothing but a myth fabricated by Lanson and uncritically reinscribed by subsequent readers and that this "cliché" of Sand criticism has had "fatal consequences" for Sand's critical reception: "It [the myth] served to render harmless the advanced position that the author had advocated in her social novels, to prepare her complete works for the consumption of the bourgeois reading public in the guise of a beautiful idyll."[50]

To verify the accuracy of Biermann's reading, let us look more closely at the final page, indeed the final sentence, of the novel, where the various strands of the plot are knotted together. Responding to a question from Edouard, Marcelle's son, the meunier says: "I caught in the clearest waters a little angel who brought me luck" (p. 270). Edouard is the veritable "ange" of Angibault. In his frail person is embodied the utopian social order to which this novel points, and that order does involve a "fusion"— not between the haves and the have-nots but between the knowers and the know-nots. "Why" asks Marcelle as she imagines a future where Edouard will be instructed by Henri and apprenticed to the miller, "would one not be both a hardworking worker and an educated man" (p. 270). The ultimate idealist longing is to overcome the barrier between the intellectual who produces idealism and the manual laborer—that is, in some sense, the very division between those who work with their hands and those who do not. In short, *the ultimate and to date always fantasmatic form of idealism is a dream of the end of idealism itself*, in both its everyday and its more specifically Marxist meaning.

Curiously, in *Le Meunier*, this form of idealism is figured as exclusively male: Edouard and also Henri and Louis are imagined as its prime agents and beneficiaries. At first glance this may seem strange since here, as in *Lettres à Marcie*, *Le Compagnon*, and elsewhere, Sand asserts the capacity of women for social and political theorizing. In contradistinction to a powerful philosophical tradition, precisely the German idealism represented by Hegel, which posits women as congenitally incapable of abstraction, Sand makes a strong case for women's access to the most prestigious forms of idealism. Women, in *Le Meunier*, are not consigned merely to the devalorized and hence feminine form of idealism, a prettifying idealization; they are idealists in the noblest sense of the word:

> There is nothing in the loftiest spheres of thought that is foreign to the women of our time. Depending on the range of their intelligences, without risking affectation or ridicule, all can henceforth read every day in all forms of writing—journal or novel, philosophy, politics or poetry, official discourse or intimate conversation—the great book of contemporary life that is sad, diffuse, contradictory, and yet profound and meaningful. (p. 36)

Why is it then that men are assigned the role of vanguard in the reconciliation of the manual worker and the intellectual? Is it because, in a paradoxical inversion, for Sand it is manual and not intellectual labor that is off limits for women, that is, upper-class women? Of course, female characters in Sand work with their hands, but they are almost always at the lowest end of the economic scale or inept. The reason for this gendered division of revolutionary labor has nothing to do with whether women can perform manual tasks and everything to do with the fact that Sand's allegiance to bourgeois values is, as we have seen, located precisely in her subscription to the separation of spheres, in her gender ideology.

For if the issue of property and its proper distribution is the overt theme of the novel, issues of gender and the proper exchange of women are also and simultaneously central concerns. There is a strong feminist protest in this novel—much more so than in *Le Compagnon*—since the tyranny exerted by the "paysan parvenu" over his daughters is the chief symptom of the new bourgeois avariciousness and dehumanization. It is interesting in this respect to compare the vicissitudes of the oedipal configuration as it is played out in the three texts discussed in this chapter, for, as we shall see when we turn to *Le Péché de Monsieur Antoine*, Sand's triptych culminates in an extraordinary fusion of oedipal rivalry, patriarchal sexual transgression, and luminous utopianism. In the representation of the relations between father and son (the rivalry between Pierre and his father) as well as between (grand)father and daughter in *Le Com-*

pagnon, the paternal figures are portrayed as more venerated and vulnerable than threatening. In *Le Meunier*, there is a marked change as exploitation is insistently masculinized or, rather, patriarchalized: first, in the fleeting figure of Henri's father, whose crimes of economic exploitation Henri seeks to repair, and second and more spectacularly, in the repulsive figure of Bricolin, the alcoholic, abusive father who does not hesitate to sacrifice his daughters' personal happiness to his relentless upward mobility.

The novel is haunted by the figure of Bricolin's older daughter, known as la Bricoline, who went mad when the man her father forbade her to marry because he was too poor goes off and dies in Algeria. A sort of cross between Charlotte Brontë's Bertha Mason and Balzac's Eugénie Grandet, Sand's madwoman in the garden eloquently testifies to the perversion of the bourgeois family by the materialist drives of rising capitalism. In her state of abject mental and physical degradation, la Bricoline is clearly intended as a figure of immense pathos, a living testimony to the evils of patriarchal bourgeois capitalism; she is "this mute victim of her parents' greed" (p. 198). But the abject is always also, not to say primarily, an object of revulsion, a projection of those dreaded forces that one would expel from one's psyche. La Bricoline is a martyr to bourgeois patriarchy but also, much more disturbingly, the embodiment of a form of femininity rejected by Sand, in keeping with the principle enunciated by Cora Kaplan: "If texts by women reveal a 'hidden' sympathy between women [in this instance Marcelle and Rose] . . . they equally express positive femininity through hostile and denigrating representations of women."[51]

Now, it is one of the clichés of Sand studies to write of her doubles, especially female, and to observe that these female doubles tend to follow the split observable in male representations of the female as either virgin or whore. The negativized femininity in these instances is always sexualized. The case of la Bricoline presents, however, a crucial variant to this familiar scenario, for la Bricoline is no Noun, no Pulchérie; far from being a pleasure-seeking fallen women, she is a frustrated virgin, and far from being a member of the racial underclass, she is Rose's sister, another privileged bourgeois self. As such, the character of la Bricoline calls into question both the ahistorical, mythico-Freudian reading that has generally prevailed in studies of Sand's female doubles (my own included) and the assumptions that underlie Kaplan's Marxist readings of the degraded female subjectivities represented in nineteenth-century British fiction, for in both Marxist and postcolonialist feminist criticism, the woman who grounds the middle-class white woman's subjectivity is always a member of a subaltern economic or racial group (or both). Kaplan's notion of the doubled discourse of bourgeois women authors, representing working-class women "on one page as oppressed workers, on another as lascivious servants who initiate and infect their bourgeois female charges,"[52] has unquestionable relevance to Sand, especially the early feminist Sand of *Indiana*. Yet, if one is at all serious about recognizing alterities and differences, one cannot grant *British* nineteenth-century fiction—which is unqualifiedly always referred to as nineteenth-century fiction *tout court* by its most politically aware critics—the status of paradigm even within the European sphere. What ever happened to French, not to mention Russian, nineteenth-century fiction? At least in her idealist social novels, and despite their double structure of address, Sand reserves her animus for bourgeois women. As we have seen in *Le Compagnon*, her idealization of la Savinienne as a Raphaelesque Madonna-like figure deliberately and consistently plays off against the stereotype of the sexually loose and maternally inadequate working-class woman. Perhaps most significant is a detail regarding the genesis of the novel: originally Josephine, who represents the devalorized form of femininity, was to be Yseult's chambermaid, but in the end Sand decided to endow her instead with the emerging stereotypical traits of the bourgeois woman—narcissism, romanticism, adulterousness. All this being said, what Kaplan shows is that the Manichaean splitting of the feminine is an intrinsic part of the gender ideology so many nineteenth-century feminist writers inherited from Rousseau and the French Revolution.

As Linda Orr has astutely pointed out, *Le Meunier* is one of those nineteenth-century French novels that can and should be read as allegories of the mimetically unrepresentable events of the French Revolution: "In George Sand's *Le Meunier d'Angibault*, the Revolution lurks beneath the mystery of every character's madness and ends up working itself out again, metaphorical Bastille and all."[53] The fire la Bricoline starts at the château (old and new) and in which she perishes is, as both Didier and Caors note, linked in the thematic repertory of the elements to the fire the "Chauffards" applied to the soles of her grandfather's feet to make him reveal the hiding place of his and his master's gold during the days of the Terror. Associated with physical torture on the one hand and wanton destruction of property on the other, the French Revolution is hardly viewed here as the motor of progress. But there is more. In the figure of la Bricoline is inscribed another sinister legacy of the Revolution and the philosophical tradition underpinning it: on the one hand, the eighteenth-century view most significantly associated with Rousseau of female subjectivity as defective in regard to reason: on the other hand, the feminist response to that view, most memorably articulated by Mary Wollstonecraft in *A Vindication of the Rights of Women* but broadly disseminated throughout nineteenth-century radical feminist writings, including Sand's. Rejecting Rousseau's naturalization of "the disorder of woman,"[54] his feminist daughters responded by a form of constructionism. If, they argued, woman is socially constructed through her readings and education as a slave of love—and, as we have seen above, Sand is merciless in her condemnation of female reader response, her repudiation of feminized romances—woman can be "liberated" "from the sensual into the rational" only through a renunciation of passion. Thus Kaplan, drawing on work by Nancy Cott, remarks: "Through the assertion that women were not innately or excessively sexual, that on the contrary their 'feelings' were largely filial or maternal, the imputation of a degraded subjectivity could be resisted."[55] Viewed in this unromantic perspective, it becomes clear that the madwoman in the garden represents less an object of sympathy than a danger that must be contained and ultimately destroyed. Hence the concern in *Le Meunier* with isolating the madwoman so that her madness will not infect her sister—she, too, a reader of novels. As the doctor remarks: "Madness, even if it is not hereditary, is contagious" (p. 224). The notion that passionate female sexuality must be excised from Sand's fictional universe may seem strange, for one of the reasons for Sand's immense popularity with the Victorians was precisely what they viewed as her typically French portrayal of unconstrained erotic passion. And yet viewed in the perspective of the ideology of gender Sand inherited from the Enlightenment, this popularity may have been based on a misunderstanding. Sand's fundamental allegiance is, as we have seen, to the same split female subjectivity as that devised by her British contemporaries. Indeed one might argue that she went even further than they, by living out this split in a series of love affairs sublimated into pseudomaternal relationships.

The exile from Sand's utopia of the woman mad for love, whose entire being is consumed by an unquenchable passion, corresponds, however, not only to a desexualization of woman; it also goes hand in hand with the exclusion of women from the active life. In exchange for renouncing her supposedly hyperactive sexuality, the upper-class female protagonist in the nineteenth-century novel can aspire to the highest reaches of abstract thought, but confined to the gynaeceum of the newly emergent sexually segregated social order by her exclusively altruistic love, she is barred from any activity that does not emanate from her idealized femininity. The utopian Sandian heroine may minister to the sick and the needy, instruct the ignorant, and of course magnificently fulfill her duties as wife and mother, in short, perform all the occupations of the bourgeois housewife, but she cannot reconcile them in her person with the fully embodied activities of the worker. The social contract of Sand's utopia is imagined as masculine: fraternal in *Le Meunier*, paternal in *Le Péché de Monsieur Antoine*.

Le Péché de Monsieur Antoine (1846)

Of all the differences between the realist and the idealist novel, perhaps none has been more instrumental in ensuring the triumph of the former over the latter than the absence in the idealist mode of the suspense Barthes identified some years ago as an essential element of realist plotting under the heading "the hermeneutic code."[56] Part of the reason for what Henry James described as the luminousness of Sand's fiction is that it generally unfolds under a regime of transparency, of immediacy that contrasts starkly with the "mystères" mode popularized by one of Sand's main rivals for the feuilleton public, Eugène Sue, and widely practiced by Balzac and Zola (author of *Les Mystères de Marseilles*), among others. *Idealism is by definition antienigmatic and, by extension, antioedipal* in that, as Barthes makes clear, the presumably universal model for the hermeneutic code is Oedipus.

But, one may object, what of the oedipal dramas in Sand's fictions? What of Henri Lémor's hatred of his father? What of the struggle to the death between Bricolin and la Bricoline? How can I speak of antioedipal fiction in these instances? Worse yet for my argument, there are mysteries in both *Le Meunier* and *Le Compagnon*, some of which are never cleared up: Who is Yseult's real father? What ever happened to the gold stolen from Bricolin and Blanchemont senior? I could respond to all of these questions by conceding that no novel is purely idealistic; idealism, as I have argued throughout, is less antithetical to realism than dependent on it, coextensive with it. Idealism sublates realism rather then canceling it. And that response is ultimately correct, but for complex reasons that will become much clearer in a moment. These family secrets and dramas are fragments of the realist narrative modes at work in Sand's idealist fiction, but they are only fragments. They do not orient one's reading; no readerly expectation is either frustrated by the lack of resolution of the question of Yseult's paternity or satisfied by the clearing up of the mystery of the ''Chauffards'' and the beggar Cadoche's wealth. However, the situation in *Le Péché de Monsieur Antoine* is quite different, and it is to this text and its difference from the other novels in the series that I now turn.

What is Monsieur Antoine's sin? From the title forward, we are plunged into a mystery that will be carefully maintained and slowly lifted throughout the novel. At first we are given only the merest hints: we know that he is a fallen aristocrat gone proletarian who lives with his daughter, whose mother is probably not Janille, the loyal servant who has raised her, though that possibility—with all its implications of cross-class fusion—is kept alive as long as possible; we know further that there has been a dramatic falling-out between Monsieur Antoine and his aristocratic neighbor, the marquis de Boisguilbault. Boisguilbault himself is a zombielike fantastical figure who lives in a fairy-tale castle complete with a single deaf retainer whose secret Emile, the young protagonist, is determined to uncover. In time the mystery is solved, and we discover that Monsieur Antoine's sin was the very bourgeois sin of adultery: Gilberte, his daughter, is the product of his affair with Boisguilbault's wife, long since dead. In fact, as Latouche, one of Sand's most perceptive readers points out, there is something unsatisfying about the novel's dénouement, a residual obscurity: "The end of this novel seems to me a bit hasty. . . . In the passage on the friendship the Count has preserved for the Marquis there is a small lantern missing to illuminate it."[57] Why in this particular novel does Sand adopt such an atypical novelistic strategy, that is, the strategy of the mystery book?

The answer to this question is, I think, to be found in the writings of Ernst Bloch, the foremost Marxist theoretician of "the Utopian function" in art and literature, notably in two paired essays, both written in 1965: "A Philosophical View of the Detective Novel" and "A Philosophical View of the Novel of the Artist."[58] I want to read *Le Péché de Monsieur Antoine* in the light of these two essays as containing elements both of the detective novel, which is already quite obvious, and of the novel of the artist, which is not.

What is most distinctive about the detective novel for Bloch is that it is entirely past oriented; its "principal earmark" is a "darkness at the beginning" (p. 256). Detective fiction and its allied forms (including psychoanalytic cases) always contain a "dim focal point," to which all clues point and from which all subsequent events flow, that "shuns the light of day and lingers in the background of the story" (p. 249). The founding misdeed or crime, "usually" (but not always) a murder, must be "wrested from their pre-narrative, un-narrated state" (p. 249). Unlike the reader of other fictional texts, the detective novel reader is never a witness to the "something that happened *ante rem*" and must rely entirely on the detective to provide a reconstruction, to recover the "dark prelude, the unknown pre-history" (p. 256) from which he is barred. And the paradigm for this preliminary event shrouded in darkness is Oedipus. "Thebes is everywhere" (p. 257), even in the least oedipal of stories: "In order to develop, all plots of this type are preceded by a crime or at least a mysterious mistake that needs to be uncovered. This is the criminological knot that constitutes the Oedipal theme, the archetype for all later occurrences" (p. 258).

Clearly *Le Péché de Monsieur Antoine* is an occurrence of this oedipal theme. Monsieur Antoine's sin, the dark event that hangs over and lends interest to this novel is definitely oedipal in nature, in that the triangle constituted by Antoine, Boisguilbault, and his wife is a thinly disguised classical oedipal triangle, where Boisguilbault occupies the position of the father, Antoine, the son, and Madame Boisguilbault, the mother. As though to underscore the oedipalized nature of the narrative, there are two variations on the founding triangle: the conventional triangle of the nuclear Cardonnet family, with its heavily politicized father/son (capitalism versus socialism) rivalry and intense mother-son bond, and the unconventional triangle constituted by the pseudofamily of Janille, Antoine, and Gilberte. The superimposition of these three triangles generates further oedipal motifs: Emile's heroic quest involves uncovering the secret of Gilberte's "nom maternel" but also finding a good father to replace his cruel and unworthy one, a communist father to replace his capitalist sire. In Boisguilbault, the childless misanthrope, Emile ultimately finds that good ideological father, but along the way pseudopaternal relationships also form between Emile and Jean Jappeloup, the illiterate but brilliant woodcutter who provides moral support, and, most curiously, Monsieur Antoine, who considers both Gilberte and Emile to be his children. Not surprisingly, given the tangle of oedipal relationships operative here, the idealized couple is in fact incestuous, marking a fantasmatic solution to the problem of cross-class marriage. To put it somewhat differently, we must consider the possibility that because it is so intractable, class difference constitutes in Sand's fiction the major mechanism for preventing heterosexuality from collapsing into fraternal incest. At any rate, in the logic of this novel, it is Boisguilbault, who stands in similar though asymmetrical positions in relation to Emile, his spiritual son, and Gilberte, his wife's child, who endows the couple with the riches that magically make their fraternal union possible. *In the logic of idealism*, as we shall see even more clearly in the following chapters, *parenthood is severed from genealogy*.

To the extent that *Le Péché* is a detective story in Blochian terms—and it is—its temporality is backward-flowing, and yet, of all the novels in this triptych, it is the most future-oriented, the most utopian. *Le Compagnon* is set in the Restauration, *Le Meunier*, in the present of the enunciation of the July Monarchy. At first, *Le Péché* seems to represent a slight regression in comparison with the insistent contemporaneity of *Le Meunier*, as the initial events of the story take place "several years ago." But in many ways it picks up where *Le Meunier* leaves off and goes fast forward, to speak in terms of contemporary technology. To borrow from Hollywood, *Le Péché de Monsieur Antoine* is a nineteenth-century version of *Back to the Future*. It is interesting to note in this regard that one of the many titles Sand considered for this novel was "*Hier et demain*" (Yesterday and tomorrow).[59] The communal existence only hinted at at the end of *Le Meunier* is already in place here: whereas

Henri is about to apprentice himself to Louis as *Le Meunier* closes, Monsieur Antoine is a practicing aristocrat-carpenter. More to the point, Gilberte is as close as Sand comes to portraying an upper-class female protagonist who combines the highest intellectual attainments with at least some form of manual activity (spinning), though the taboo on women as manual wage earners remains unbroken, unbreakable. And then there is the crucial fact that, whereas in *Le Meunier* capitalism is essentially agrarian, *Le Péché* recounts the implantation of the machine of industrial capitalism in the heart of the pastoral garden: Monsieur Cardonnet is an industrial capitalist from the metropolis who plans to build a factory in the rural heart of the Berry, a factory whose precise purpose is never spelled out but whose main effects on the countryside are to generate an artificial rise in employment and to ruin the local people who depend on the hydrological power of the river Cardonnet unsuccessfully attempts to capture. (In a lovely irony, millers like the miller of Angibault are the most direct victims.) In short, *Le Péché* is a French industrial novel. But for Sand, the way of the future does not lie in the development of industry, for Sand was no Saint-Simonian (no more than she was a Fourierist); the legacy that Boisguilbault bequeaths Emile and Gilberte, his extensive estate, is to be the site of an agrarian commune, an explicitly antiurban, anti-industrial earthly paradise:

> This will be the *garden of the commune*, which is also its gynaeceum, its ballroom, and banquet hall, its theater and church: do not speak to me of those narrow spaces where stone and cement confine men and thought; do not tell me of your opulent colonnades and your magnificent court, in comparison with this natural architecture provided by the Supreme Being. (p. 374)

How then in terms of Bloch's theories can we reconcile the past orientedness of the detective novel with the future orientedness of what I will call for the moment the utopian novel? Quite simply by bringing into play Bloch's other major novelistic genre, the novel of the artist.

Already in the concluding section of the essay on the detective novel, Bloch introduces this complementary category:

> Item: something is uncanny, that is how it happens. Investigative uncovering is indeed only one aspect, aimed at the origin. Investigative edification is the other, aimed at the destination. There, the finding of

something that has been, here, the creation of something new. . . . And strangely enough: even edification appears in its own form of novel, in a form again frequently sinister, then again significantly elevated, in the so-called *novel of the artist*.[60]

What is obscured in this passage by Bloch's characteristically elliptical style are the precise modalities of the articulation of these two investigative modes, and he is quite unhelpful in speculating on the reasons for this alliance. Yet in a lovely and suggestive phrase toward the very end of the essay, he reasserts their necessary linkage: "Though the novel of the artist finds itself in the same book as the detective or detection novel, it is written on another page, which in both literature and philosophy is not even half as comprehensive—indeed, its Promethean form is presumably a thing of the future" (p. 263). The allusion to Prometheus is crucial here, for what Oedipus is to the detective novel, Prometheus is to the novel of the artist: in the classical paradigm, he is the "archetype of the artist" (p. 268). Emile is certainly not an artist—though his socialist-communist dreams are treated by his father as so much useless literature—and yet I stake my claim to viewing *Le Péché* as an artist novel in the widest sense on an incongruous yet absolutely motivated comparison between Emile and the mythical artist figure: "Lying on a boulder, he saw the vultures flying over his head and thought of Prometheus's sufferings" (p. 222). Later, Emile recounts a nightmare in which the Promethean and the oedipal motifs are joined, as his father is figured as the devouring vulture:

> Ah! I remember the dream I had the first night I spent in this part of the country. I saw my father set upon me to suffocate me! . . . It was horrible, and now this odious vision is coming true; my father has placed his knees, elbows, and feet on my breast; he wants to tear out my conscience or heart. He is digging into my entrails to find the weak spot that will give in to him. (p. 291)

Just as Bloch's "detective novel" is a capacious category, so, too, is his novel of the artist. Though most of the examples he provides are quite literally novels of the artist (e.g., *Doktor Faustus*), what characterizes these novels is less their aesthetic than their utopian dimension. The novel of the artist is the utopian novel in that it is entirely in the service of the "not-yet," entirely concerned with "*the formation of the human*" (p. 276):

> That which moves one in the novel of the artist itself, as one which ultimately, like the genuine Faust material, concerns all of mankind, even without the respective epithets, is the desire to break new ground, with knights, death, and the devil, to head for the envisioned utopian castle or to that which corresponds to its formation in shape, sound, or word. (p. 277)

Boisguilbault's projected commune is that "envisioned utopian castle." It is the radiant horizon toward which the hero's quest transports the reader, far away from the horrors of a Darwinian industrial capitalism and its ruthless exploitation of men and nature represented by the bad father, Cardonnet.

And yet, even if we take the novel of the artist in its largest sense, there are problems with this "application" of Bloch's categories to reading Sand's utopian fiction, not the least of which is the fact that, in Bloch, utopia is, as I understand it, essentially ineffable and unrepresentable. Only through cryptic "anticipatory" signs can its transcendent promise be made out. Now, the utopian impulse or function in Sand's text is neither hidden nor unconscious; we do not need to be critic-detectives skilled in the "hermeneutics of restauration"[61] to glimpse in her representation of an unredeemed present the allegorical figuras of a transformed future. To account for the utopian function in Sand's novel, we must turn to Bloch's essay from *Das Prinzip Hoffnung*, "The Conscious and Known Activity within the Not-Yet-Conscious, the Utopian Function," for it is here that he articulates, albeit in what one of his readers describes as his frequently opaque "churning discourse," the relationship he posits between the utopian function and its hierarchically arrayed "underdeveloped" forms, ranging from archetypes to allegories and symbols. According to Bloch, there exists even in cultural artifacts still mired in ideology a *surplus* that the utopian function may reclaim or, better, "refunction" so that *à la limite* no work that contains some gesturing— and, as Darko Suvin notes in a brilliant insight, utopia always operates "deictically"[62]—toward "the 'dream of the thing' " is without its utopian dimension. What Bloch's controversial theory of utopia—Suvin labels it "imperialist," and Finkelstein speaks of its "totalitarianism"—enables is a reclaiming of precisely that aspect of Sand's (or any other utopian socialist's) utopianism that is most stubbornly irrecuperable in other Marxist approaches: its idealism. For one of the stations on the way to the allegories and symbols that stand at the apex of Bloch's hierarchy of "underdeveloped" utopian forms is the ideal.

But before going on to consider Bloch's remarks on the ideal and their relevance to Sand, I want to take note of yet another of his categories of pre- or proto-utopian "embellishments" of the "status quo," the lowest of the low, what he calls the "interests." The interests correspond to the stage of rising capitalism just as ideology belongs to the stage of bourgeois hegemony. They are the lies early industrialists told themselves and others to mask the nasty truth of their selfish pursuit of wealth.

> The exploitation led by voracious dealers who were not at all burdened by bourgeois ethics could doubtlessly have gone on the same way without embellishment. The gentlemen of the East India Company did not include any kind of utopian function in their business. It would only have harmed them. But the average manufacturer in the beginning of the industrial revolution still needed and cherished the belief in the greatest possible fortune found in the largest numbers. He needed this belief as the link between his egotistic impulses and benevolent ones that he dreamt of and pretended to have. (pp. 112–13)

The struggle between Emile and his father is a struggle not between an idealist and an anti-idealist but between two forms of idealism: the interests of the industrialist father and the ideals of the utopian colonialist son. What we have in *Le Péché* is a *conflict of ideals*, a Saint-Simonian ideal of industry and productivity versus a communistic ideal of justice and equity. As Cardonnet père heaps scorn on his son's utopian daydreams, he does not relinquish to him the moral high ground; instead, in a rhetorical operation strikingly familiar to survivors of the Reagan era, he claims it for himself and for the capitalist system he defends. To distinguish the interests of the father from the ideals of the son, we must return to Bloch and his theory of the ideal.

In contradistinction to Freud—and Bloch's remarks on the ideal are part of what Jameson calls his "dialogue" with Freud—Bloch's emphasis is on the "bright aspects of the ideal," that is, its aspiration toward "lofty *perfection*."[63] "It is precisely the *intended perfection*, all of its confessed anticipation, that makes the ideal accessible to a utopian treatment" (p. 135). The refunctioning of abstract idealism is thus bound up with a recognition of what Hans Robert Jauss calls the "need" or "longing" for the perfect, an abiding human need that was met in Western culture first by religion, then by art, and that endures even in the face of the modernist repudiation of the "aesthetic totality of the perfect."[64] For Jauss the "need for the complete and the perfect [*das Volkommene*]" (p. 11) is an ontological category that precedes the need for the beautiful, so that Western civilization's earliest aesthetic images of perfection—Greek gods—are "images of inaccessible divine perfection" (p. 12). Aesthetic idealization always raises the specter of metaphysical perfection because "poetic fiction has surreptitiously slipped into the space formerly occupied by theodicy" (p. 16). Secularization and the concomitant rejection of an aesthetic ideal of beauty grounded in metaphysics have not disposed of the religious residue, because, according to Jauss, "fictionalizing things *inevitably* brings with it their idealization" (p. 24). The modernist preference for imperfect, open, and fragmented work over the perfect, closed, and complete work of premodernism does not fundamentally call into question the presumably transhistorical human need for the perfect, because it remains the "horizon of understanding" for contemporary art: "So it is that although perfection seems to lose its secular validity as an aesthetic norm, it survives by functioning heuristically" (p. 25).

Though I do not share Jauss's seemingly nostalgic concern with the epistemological break between the neoclassical aesthetics of the perfect and the modernist rejection of that ideal, I find that his essay, taken together with Bloch's (whom, interestingly, he never mentions), provides precious material for rethinking the repressed and discredited notions of the ideal, idealism, and idealization in their relation to the sacred, the numinous, the metaphysical. Sand's utopianism, like all utopianisms, bespeaks a longing, if not for a perfect, then—here I follow Suvin's amended definition of utopia—a "more perfect"[65] social universe than the alienated world the author and her characters inhabit, and that brave new universe is envisioned as an earthly paradise presided over by God. The coming of earthly paradise is prefigured by a communal meal, a sort of agape in the enchanted park that brings together in a brief moment of harmony the contesting forces present in the novel: father and son; husband and adulterer; peasant, bourgeois, and aristocrat.

It is perhaps here that the influence of Pierre Leroux is most readily apparent, for, as Jacques Rancière observes, the communal meal is Leroux's "master image," notably in his 1838 treatise, *De l'Egalité.*[66] According to Leroux, through the Eucharist Jesus extends the egalitarian banquets of antiquity to include all humanity; the sacrifice of Jesus makes accessible to all those who were excluded from the communal meals of classical antiquity, namely women and slaves, the privileges that come with sharing a meal with others. To eat together is not merely a material event; it signifies brotherhood, nationhood. By making of the banquet scene the telos of her utopian fiction, Sand espouses Leroux's philosophy of the politics of food: "For a people to be a people, there must exist among the citizenry a certain feeling of community, a certain equality, a certain fraternity; they must consider themselves to be equals, brothers, as constituting a family; and the sign of that fraternity is a shared meal."[67]

There is, however, one loser in this great scene of reconciliation and anticipation, one member of the family missing from the engagement party, and that is the bride's natural mother, the adulterous wife. Throughout the novel, the mystery of Gilberte's maternity is bound up with the portrait of a woman that the marquis keeps hidden away and veiled in a room in his chalet and that both Emile and Gilberte observe by effraction. In a striking variation on a topos of French women's writing I have studied elsewhere,[68] at the center of the utopian space (the park) there hangs the portrait of a fallen woman. We are now in a better position to understand how in the pages of this novel the detective genre and the artist novel come together and why Sand insisted on shrouding the reconciliation scene between Monsieur Antoine and the marquis in darkness. What is consummated in their unnarrated, dimly lit interview is the chilling erasure of the fallen woman, the adulterous wife, and the dead aristocratic mother that is the enabling condition for the coming utopia: "The marquise's name was never pronounced between them. It seemed as though she had never existed" (p. 370). As if to ensure the containment of the negativity represented by the portrait, the inner sanctum in which it hangs behind a green veil is sealed off: "The chalet too was opened, except for the study whose door had this time been sealed shut thanks to Jappeloup" (p. 371).

Once again Sand's social contract is fraternal. Indeed, earlier in the novel, during one of his great confrontations with his father, Emile (!)

describes his vision of the future this way: "One day on some barren and deserted heath transformed by my efforts, I will have founded a colony of free men living as brothers and loving me like a brother" (p. 146), provoking his father to mock him in the following terms: "Here's the utopia of brother Emile, Moravian brother, Quaker, neo-Christian, neo-Platonist, or what have you" (p. 146).

In a highly original article, Anne Freadman suggests that Sand's adoption of masculine dress be read as her means of claiming for herself a place in the brotherhood instituted by the French Revolution, writing:

> The exclusion of women from the ideals of humanism or Christian spirituality functions for her as a betrayal. . . . This exclusion is the same as that operated by the Republican slogan, and implicitly by the vestimentary laws and practices of the society of which she was a member. Against the moral philosophers, she argued and protested vociferously. Against the laws of dress and codes of political fraternity, she did otherwise: she simply claimed the place of a brother.[69]

French feminists in a shaky line that runs from Sand through Beauvoir and up to Antoinette Fouque have, as we have seen, struggled with the legacy of the French Revolution, alternately seeking inclusion within the Republican brotherhood, as a means of asserting their equality with men and gaining their civil rights, or striking out on their own, as a means of grounding the right to their specificity, their difference.[70] Sand's utopian fictions are to a large extent nothing but projections of the claim to fraternity into the future. But, as we have also seen, this aspiration toward a more truly inclusive fraternal order has a dark underside: in keeping with the terms of the Republican pact, for women to claim their rightful place in the fraternal society of the future, they must relinquish their erotic passions and bind up their errant desires. In the passage to the promised land, those women who remain tainted with the slave mentality of the old order must be left behind: the narcissistic female novel-reader, the love-mad woman, and the adulterous mother. From Sand to Beauvoir, the discredited forms of female subjectivity remain strikingly similar; they are all variants of the paradigm of femininity set into place by the nineteenth-century bourgeoisie and held in place by its modes of exchange (of women and/as goods). We can regret Sand and other French feminists' failure to think their way out of the heritage of the French Revolution, but we should not, I think, condemn them for it. The challenge for women, especially but not exclusively in France today, is, as Antoinette Fouque observes, to add a fourth term—which would account for sexual difference—to the revolutionary motto, to make a revolution in the symbolic that would render such mutilations, such feminist self-hatred obsolete.[71] There will be no feminist utopia until there is a place in the promised land and at the communal banquet table for the erotically unfit: the bourgeois adulteress (*Le Compagnon*), the love-mad virgin (*Le Meunier*), and the fallen aristocratic mother (*Le Péché*).

The Fraternal

Pact: *La Petite Fadette*

and *Nanon*

> Tout concourt à l'histoire, *tout est histoire*, même les romans qui
> semblent ne se rattacher en rien aux situations politiques qui
> les voient éclore.　　　　　　　　　Sand, *Histoire de ma vie*

In her 1979 essay entitled "Fraternal George Sand," Ellen Moers, pioneering American feminist critic and perceptive reader of Sand, writes: "Sand's originality—and it was this that must have attracted Dostoevski to her heroines—was to redefine fraternity from the woman's point of view, as friendship between men and women. . . . Friendship seems to me to be George Sand's greatest theme."[1]

There is much that is appealing about Moers's bold characterization of Sand's project; nevertheless, I think it stands in need of parsing, qualification, rethinking. Moers's moves are too swift, her conclusions, too optimistic. To say that "redefin[ing] fraternity from a woman's point of view" is central to Sand's idealist project is surely a brilliant insight, but to go on to say that she does so by transforming an ideal of male brotherhood into a model of heterosexual friendship is to miss what is most problematic for feminists about the concept of fraternity elaborated by modern social contract thinkers and enshrined by the French Revolution: its foundational inability to include women as fully gendered, fully embodied subjects. *The revolutionary ideal of fraternity is a classic instance of false universalism.* Speaking of what she pointedly refers to as the "fraternal social contract" that founds civil society according to the convergent fables of Rousseau (*The Social Contract*) and Freud (*Totem and Taboo*), Carol Pateman reminds us that "the contract is made by brothers, or a *fraternity*. It is no accident that fraternity appears historically hand in hand with liberty and equality, nor that it means exactly what it says: brotherhood."[2] It would appear that only by losing sight of the intractably homosocial nature of the fraternal pact can one imagine a female or feminist redefinition of fraternity. However, to say that there is no feminizing fraternity is not to say that friendship between men and women is not an ideal that Sand pursued in her writings and in her life and, as we shall see in our final chapter, most magnificently attained in her epistolary relationship with Flaubert. It is simply to take sober account of the fact that the ideal of heterosexual friendship is not the same as the ideal of fraternity or, rather, that such heterosexual friendship confirms rather than infirms the predominance of the homosocial in modern European civil society.

If Sand is not free simply to redefine fraternity as heterosexual friendship, it is because discursive constraints govern friendship as well as fraternity; there is a politics, indeed a gendered politics, of friendship. Thus, speaking of the politics of friendship, which is always bound up with the preempting of politics and the public sphere by men, Derrida draws attention to what he terms "the *double exclusion*" he sees "at work in all the great ethico-political-philosophical discourses on friendship, namely, on the one hand, the exclusion of friendship between women, and, on the other hand, the exclusion of friendship between a man and a woman." And this *double exclusion* has at least two consequences that bear directly on my reading of Sand. First: "This double exclusion of the feminine in the philosophical paradigm of friendship would thus confer on it the essential and essentially sublime figure of virile homosexuality." And second: "Within the familial schema . . . this exclusion privileges the figure of the brother, the name of the brother or the name of brother, more than that of the father—whence the necessity of connecting the political model, especially that of democracy and of the Decalogue, with the rereading of Freud's hypothesis about the alliance of brothers."[3]

Before going on to consider the place of brotherhood in Sand, however, I want first to consider that of fraternity, noting in passing that however much these two terms are indissociably linked, they are not always strictly interchangeable, and it is precisely the semantic gap (which exists in English but not in French) between the two that makes it possible to forget their mutual implication.

Two days before the April 23 elections that were to mark a critical turning point in the Revolution of 1848, George Sand wrote a letter to her son Maurice exhorting him to continue the good fight against the forces of the provincial counterrevolution. To give him courage and to remind him of the political ideal of the Revolution he had to defend, Sand described in eloquent hyperbolic terms the Fête de la Fraternité she had participated in on April 21:

> The Fête de la Fraternité was the most beautiful day in history. One *million souls*, forgetting all rancor, all differences of interest, excusing the past, not caring about the future, and embracing each other from one end of Paris to the other to the cry of *Long Live Fraternity*. It was sublime. . . .
>
> From the top of the arch of the Etoile the sky, the city, the horizons, the green countryside, the domes of the great buildings in the plain and the sunlight, what a backdrop for the most gigantic human scene that ever took place! From the Bastille, from the Observatoire to the Arch of Triumph, and beyond and below Paris, over a space of *five leagues*, four hundred thousand rifles pressed together like a wall on the march, the artillery, all the arms of the line, the militia, the suburbs, the national guard, all the costumes, the pomp of the army, all the rags of the *sacred rabble*, and the entire population of all ages and all sexes looking on, singing, shouting, applauding, joining the procession. It was really sublime.[4]

I take this experience of sublime fusion with the enthusiastic but nonviolent revolutionary urban crowd to be the most extreme realization of Sand's utopian fraternal élan, not only because on this unique occasion all potentially divisive differences—such as those between generations, sexes, and classes—were held in check by an almost cosmic celebration of union, but perhaps especially because Sand viewed this extraordinary event from the privileged vantage point of an unofficial member of the provisional government. Her standpoint was that of the pinnacle of public power, the top of the Arch of Triumph.[5] In other words, the event marked the culmination of her most significant participation in the brotherhood ushered in by the French Revolution. Sand was, as the historical record shows, a privileged though unofficial female participant in the otherwise all male group that governed France between the fall of Louis-Philippe and the bloody June days that marked the end of the initial phase of the Revolution of 1848.

It is against the background of this extraordinarily euphoric experience of fraternity—which was, of course, to varying degrees that of the famed generation of 1848, many of whose members never recovered from the dashing of their utopian dreams—that I want to address the question of brotherhood in Sand. Reading *La Petite Fadette*, Sand's preeminent fraternal fiction (there are others), as a sort of allegory of the vicissitudes of the fraternal contract, the ideal of brotherhood in postrevolutionary France, I want, following other feminist analysts, to place particular emphasis on the ways in which the fraternal social contract is a sexual contract.[6] Reading *La Petite Fadette* for and beyond sexual difference, I want to look closely at the ways the text figures the constructions of gender in Napoleonic France. Some of the questions I will address are: What then of brotherhood in Sand? Is the fraternal bond the ideal relationship Sand makes it out to be in her espousal of the revolutionary social contract and its utopian socialist rescriptings? How does gender inflect brotherhood, and how does the ideal of brotherhood affect the constructions of gender? What becomes of the female subject in the society of brothers? What becomes of the marginal male subject in the new social order legislated by Napoléon?

I

Triptychs, with the notable exception of Flaubert's *Trois Contes*, have not fared well in the hands of critics who prefer to analyze the intricacies of a single text rather than the complex interplay of three that both stand alone and share a dense network of linking characters and themes. The case of *La Petite Fadette*, the third panel of Sand's pastoral trilogy that also includes *La Mare au diable* and *François le champi* is no exception to this rule. Invariably read, when it is read at all, as an autonomous work, *Fadette* is not seen for what it in fact is: the final elaboration of material already worked through in the previous texts—the difficulties of male object choice (*La Mare au diable*) and the temptations of mother-son incest (*François le champi*). My effort to reestablish the connection between *Fadette* and the two previous pastoral tales is not intended, however, to emphasize continuity but, rather, to point up the discontinuity that irrevocably separates them. For, as Sand noted in the dialogue that serves as one of the two prefaces to *Fadette*, the writing of the trilogy was interrupted by an event so catastrophic that what was in fact a one-year hiatus in the composition of the series seemed more like ten:

> "Do you remember," he said to me, "that we came this way *a year ago*, and that we stopped here for a whole evening? For it was here that you told me the story of *François le champi* and that I advised you to write it in the same intimate style in which you told it to me."
>
> "And that I found by imitating the style of our hemp hackler. I remember, and it *seems like ten years ago*."[7]

The radical historical break that was the Revolution of 1848 introduced a cleft within the triptych, which in *Fadette* Sand attempted to suture by turning her back on history, a textual repression that I will argue was less than successful.

In the second of her two prefaces, this one written in December 1851, after yet another major watershed in French history, Louis-Napoléon's coup d'état, Sand theorizes that there are two responses to civil war: that of men of action, who are active participants in the events, and that of poets and "women of leisure" (*femmes oisives*), who watch events form the sidelines:

> For men of action who are personally involved in political events there is, in every course of action, in every situation, a feverish hope or anguish,

anger or joy, the intoxication of victory or indignation at defeat. But for the poor poet, and the woman of leisure, who watch events without having a direct and personal interest in them, whatever the outcome of the fight may be, there is a profound horror at the blood shed on both sides, and a sort of despair at the sight of this hate, of these insults, these threats, these calumnies which rise to heaven like a foul holocaust after social upheavals. (p. 7/39)

It is of course true that a poet such as Dante managed to write his *Divine Comedy* without averting his gaze from contemporary horrors. But, according to Sand, artists, reduced to the passive status of onlookers in the new historical era ushered in by 1848 (Lukács) had the duty to represent an ideal world, avoiding any *direct* allusion to the terrible events at hand. The post-1848 writer was thus placed by history in the impotent and marginal position traditionally identified with femininity, and the feminization of the writer entailed an obligatory turn away from the real and toward the ideal. The pressure of historical events served only to heighten Sand's persistent utopian tropism, her stated preference for representing ideal worlds. But Sand's recycled post-June-days-of-1848 idealism is not the same as the idealism at work in her utopian trilogy of the 1840s. More explicitly aligned with femininity, this idealism is consoling rather than mobilizing, distracting rather than hortatory, regressive rather than progressive:

> We believe that the mission of art is a mission of feeling and love, that today's novel should take the place of the parables and apologia of more simple times, and that the artist has a greater and more poetic duty than to propose some measure of prudence and conciliation to mitigate the horror inspired by his depictions. His goal should be to make lovable the objects of his care and, if need be, I would not fault him for embellishing them just a little. *Art is not the study of positive reality; it is the search for an ideal truth.*[8]

In the case of her pastoral trilogy, whose general title was to be *Les Veillées du chanvreur* (The evenings of the hemp hackler), the ideal world is a nostalgic evocation of pastoral simplicity. As if to underscore the distance that separates the reader from this lost world, the narrator adopts the persona of a mere translator, who transcribes and translates the tales told by the hemp hackler in his native dialect into the more familiar Parisian French of the narratee. The pastoral tales are thus coded as translations from a minority language into the language of the dominant culture and troped as textiles. Sand's enlistment here of two recurrent tropes in French women's writing—translation and/or weaving[9]—for the act of writing as a woman suggests that Sand's predilection for the pastoral genre draws its impetus not only from her desire to idealize, to offer a corrective to the horrors of a then-triumphant Balzacian realism, but from her sense that the tales she had to tell were so foreign and strange that they could only be told in the reassuring guise of what she referred to with mock modesty as her "bergeries," or shepherd's tales.

II

La Petite Fadette is the story of Fadette, the ugly duckling tomboy who, loved by the handsome and well-to-do peasant Landry, metamorphoses into a beautiful and good woman who has lots of children and lives happily ever after. This brief plot summary is, of course, a caricature, but only barely, of one possible reading of *La Petite Fadette*; what we might call a "first-stage" feminist reading focused on the female protagonist, her strengths, and her weaknesses.[10] Such a reading would follow the *Bildung* of the female character as she is integrated into patriarchal society and is precisely the approach that prevails in psychoanalytically based interpretations of the tale. Let me give two examples. The first occurs in Helene Deutsch's *The Psychology of Women*, where in the course of an extended analysis of Sand's "masculinity complex," Deutsch offers a reading of *Fadette* that emphasizes its autobiographical nature. Deutsch recalls one of the most traumatic episodes recounted in *Histoire de ma vie*, the occasion on which Sand's grandmother, confronted with little Aurore's desperate desire to join her mother in Paris, tells her the truth about her mother's sordid past. "My thesis," writes Deutsch, "is that George Sand's sadistic-masculine reactions to disappointment followed the pattern of her first reactions to her grandmother's destruction of her mother ideal" (about which more in the following chapter).[11] Little Fadette's experiences closely resemble little Aurore's. Just as Aurore's mother went off to Paris, leaving her daughter in the custody of her paternal grandmother, Fadette's mother abandons her and her younger brother to become a camp follower, and Fadette, raised by a cold grandmother, faces a hostile community that condemns her mother as a whore and treats her abandoned children as pariahs. In Deutsch's words: "In her novel, *La Petite Fadette* ('The Cricket'), she describes a little girl who is exactly like the little Aurore of her diaries after the disclosures made by her grandmother. Little Fadette acts like a naughty, sadistic boy" (pp. 304–5), sharing the young Sand's rebellious attitude toward society, her refusal to conform to the sugar-and-spice model of femininity, her malicious habit of taunting her persecutors and flaunting her superior command of the logos. But, Deutsch goes on to say: "Fadette grows up to be a sweet and kindly woman; sadistic aggression in her is transformed into a woman's loving passive attitude. The transformation takes place when a man's love awakens her to femininity" (p. 305).

Another psychoanalytic reading focused on the development of the female protagonist is the sympathetic feminist reading provided by Michael Danahy in his article, "Growing Up Female: George Sand's View in *La Petite Fadette*." The main theme of the tale, according to Danahy, is "the effect on a young woman growing up without the benefit of an adequate female role model."[12] Eventually, however, according to Danahy, Fadette makes it through to maturity by assuming her identification with her fallen mother, "the primary domestic role model."[13]

In both these readings, growing up means growing up female, and the difficulties Fadette encounters in her development are tied to her problematic identification with a deidealized mother who is closer to the whore than the angel. Emphasis is placed on Fadette's positive resolution of her sexual identity. In the syntagmatic logic of these readings, the central scene in the tale occurs when Landry tells Fadette that she must give up her tomboy ways and take the conventional path toward normal femininity:

> "Very well, Fanchon Fadette, since you speak so sensibly, and since, for the first time in your life, I see you gentle and docile, I'll tell you why people don't respect you in the way a girl of sixteen ought to be able to command respect. It's because you are not in the least like a girl and so like a boy in your looks and manners. . . . Well, do you think that's right and proper, at sixteen years of age, not to be in the least like a girl? You climb trees like a squirrel, and when you jump on the back of a mare, with no bridle and no saddle, you make her gallop as though the devil were on her back. It's a good thing not to be afraid of anything, and for a man it is a natural advantage. But for a woman enough is enough, and

you look as though you were trying to draw attention to yourself." (p. 91/136)

The affinity of psychoanalytic critics for this particular Sand text seems to derive from its preinscription of Freud's teleological myth of female development. Landry speaks with the assurance of a spokesman for the patriarchal order, serenely articulating the laws of the symbolic that enjoin the little girl to abandon the active mode of the phallic phase and accept the passive stance that will ensure her smooth development into femininity. But how do women readers respond to this scene? How does Sand go about making Fadette's relinquishing of her masculine attributes palatable to her female readers, who have identified, as female readers do, with the female protagonist? That women are charmed, indeed seduced by *Fadette* is attested to by Ellen Moers, who writes of Sand's peasant tales: "Here the critic of women's literature must simply abandon principle and, faced with George Sand, call the style of *La Mare au Diable* and *La Petite Fadette* plain seductive."[14] These are strong words. Though Moers does not specify exactly what principles the critic of women's writing must abandon when confronted with Sand's "delicious" peasant tales, her call for a letting-down of one's critical defenses testifies to the powerful charm exerted by the text over the resisting woman reader. What Moers does make explicit is how Sand disarms her feminist reader: by an aesthetic benefit, a stylistic felicity that overcomes all resistance, what Freud in his essay "Creative Writers and Day-Dreaming" calls an "incitement premium" or "fore-pleasure."

I would suggest that elements other than Sand's untranslatable delicious prose style work, in Teresa de Lauretis's phrase, to "seduce" the female reader of Fadette "into femininity,"[15] and that seductive supplement must now be examined. To make palatable to the resisting reader Fadette's dwindling into femininity, Sand compensates for her renunciation of the strength and mobility that are, according to the doxa, essential male prerogatives by endowing her with an undeniable individual intellectual superiority and great wealth. Thus at the close of Landry's speech in praise of sexual difference, he offers Fadette a clever inducement to give up her inappropriate behavior: " 'Think about it a little, and you'll see that if you were to be a bit more like other people they would be less resentful of the fact that you have more understanding than they have' " (p. 92/137). What Landry urges on Fadette is what we might call a trade-off: in exchange for conforming to the cultural construction of the female, Fadette will be rewarded with recognition of her *real* difference—her superior qualities of mind (for Landry is the first to recognize Fadette's quick wit, her superior command of language). Just when Fadette's intellectual gifts are valorized, the class difference that initially separates Fadette, the town marginal, from Landry, the son of prosperous peasants, is overturned when, after her grandmother's death, Fadette finds herself an immensely rich heiress, a reversal of fortune that is instrumental in overcoming the prejudices of the Landry family, especially its patriarch, Père Barbeau, against Fadette. Seduced into identifying with Fadette's exceptional masculine intelligence—in her therapeutic use of herbs, Fadette displays the methodological skills of the experimental scientist—and independent means, the female reader is lulled into forgetting that the wages of genius and wealth are the acceptance of a definition of femininity that essentializes difference and naturalizes social inequity.

III

These readings, centered on the female protagonist and grounded in the unproblematic assertion of absolute sexual difference, have at least one major drawback: they completely fail to take into account about one-half of the text. Fadette does not make her appearance until chapter 8 of the tale, and even then her presence is fitful, intermittent, like that of the firefly ("follet") with which she is associated both meto- and homonymically.[16] Despite the title that arouses and orients the reader's expectations, the tale is not focused on its eponymous heroine. *La Petite Fadette* is not centered on an individual protagonist at all but on a unique set of doubles: the male twins, Sylvinet and Landry. Indeed, originally Sand had proposed to entitle her tale *"Les Bessons,"* an archaic dialectal word used throughout the tale to signify twins. As the author of the introduction to the Garnier-Flammarion edition writes:

> In this world protected by its isolation and which remains true to the beliefs and social mores of the past, Sand has placed the story of two *bessons* and a wild young woman. Perhaps initially she had thought only

of the former. It is indeed strange to observe that she had originally chosen as her title *Les Bessons*; in fact little Fadette only appears quite late in the first outline.[17]

According to the author of this introduction, Sand's original inspiration came from a ballad by the Provençal poet Jasmin, called precisely "Les Deux Bessons." What this author fails to note is the appeal this popular theme might have had for an author whose predilection for doubles we have already noted on more than one occasion. Many recent readers of Sand's oeuvre have been struck by the proliferation of doubles in her work, doubles that tend to fall into two groups. One group consists of the female doubles, generally viewed as symptomatic of Sand's inability to overcome the traditional split (mother/whore) that governs the representation of women in male-authored fiction. The other group, another modulation of the same obsession, consists of the doubles cast as male/female alter egos (*Jacques*). *Fadette* is, however, an extreme instance of a third, more problematic group of novels featuring male doubles as brothers or half brothers (*Les Maitres mosaïstes*, *Le Marquis de Villemer*, *Les Deux Frères*). We have here something on a different order from the split female or the ambisexual couple, both of which are in some sense ordained by the dream of an impossible integration of warring sexual selves. What then is the significance of this unique pair of doubles? What is the significance of this twinning, the always uncanny repetition of the identical? What, if any, is the relationship between these pastoral brothers and the society of brothers installed by the French Revolution?

In writing a tale about male twins, knowingly or unknowingly, Sand repeats an ancient motif. Indeed, according to Bruno Bettelheim: "The motif of the two brothers is central to the oldest fairy tale, which was found in an Egyptian Papyrus of 1250 B.C. In over three thousand years since then it has taken many forms. One study enumerates 70 different versions, but probably there are many more."[18] Much of the extraordinary appeal of *Fadette* is rooted in its manipulation of material that is doubly archaic: archaic because of its venerable ancestry; archaic, too, because it focuses on one of the earliest stages of human development, individuation, the separation of the self from the Other. By making the two brothers twins Sand hyperbolizes their initial indistinguishability. The very first gesture performed by the midwife who delivers the babies, the wise Mère Sagette, is to mark the firstborn to distinguish him from his identical twin. Thus is the disaster of violence averted, for, as René Girard reminds us, the birth of twins is viewed in many primitive societies with a special horror, which has long puzzled anthropologists. In keeping with his own theory that violence is bred, paradoxically, by an excess of similarity, Girard suggests that the fear inspired by the birth of twins is due to the potentially dangerous crisis of difference their uncanny resemblance figures:

> Twins invariably share a cultural identity, and they often have a striking physical resemblance to each other. Wherever differences are lacking violence threatens. . . . It is only natural that twins should awaken fear, for they are harbingers of indiscriminate violence, the greatest menace to primitive societies.[19]

From the outset the story of the twins bodies forth the need to institute difference within sameness. We have already alluded to the distinguishing mark etched onto the elder twin's skin by the wise midwife. This diacritical gesture is immediately followed by another, indeed a doubly diacritical gesture that demonstrates the inherently differential nature of language and of subjecthood ruled by language. In being inscribed in the onomastic kinship system, the twins are twice differentiated: the one from the other and each from his godfather:

> The older one was called Sylvain, which soon became Sylvinet, to *distinguish* him from his older brother, who had acted as his godfather; and the younger one was called Landry, a name which he kept unchanged from the time of his baptism because his uncle who was his godfather, had been called Landriche since he was very young. (p. 10/42; emphasis added)

But diacritical differences on the plane of the signifier are not sufficient guarantors of peace and happiness. The midwife sternly advises the parents to separate the twins from the outset or dire consequences will ensue: "By every means you can think of, stop them getting too involved with each other . . . if you don't follow my advice you will rue the day" (p. 12/44). Predictably, given the laws of the fairy-tale genre, the parents do not heed the midwife's warnings, and the twins are suckled at the same breast and brought up as inseparable playmates. Throughout their childhood the twins are fused into a remarkably self-contained dyad that renders the grammar of possession and personal property inoperative:

> Sometimes attempts were made to give something to only one of them, when they both wanted it; but if it was something good to eat, they would immediately share it; or if it was a little toy or small knife for their use, they would use it together or take turns, without bothering about what belonged to whom. (p. 18/50)

In time, however, as they enter adolescence, practical considerations dictate the necessity for a physical separation of the two members of the dyad. It is at this critical juncture that Sand is closest to the ancient motif, for an invariant feature of the two brothers' tale is that one leaves while the other stays home, that one successfully breaks the ties that bind while the other remains fixated at the earlier stage of symbiotic bonding.

It is of particular relevance to the argument I want to make that the differentiation between the twins will at one point be coded as sexual. Sylvinet, the stay-at-home brother, is the mother's favorite because of his feminizing attachment to the domestic sphere, while Landry enjoys the father's favor because of his superior virile strength. The mother makes the sexualization of the difference between the twins quite explicit when she says to herself: "My Landry is a *real boy*, he only wants to live, move, work and move about. But this one here has *the heart of a girl*—he is so gentle and sweet that one cannot help loving him for it" (p. 25/58; translation modified, my emphasis). For all its charming naiveté this is a complex passage: on the one hand, the mother relies on preexisting notions of boyness and girlness to ground her sexual differentiation of her twin boys; on the other, her boys are boys, and sexual differentiation appears here to be merely a secondary, belated difference mapped onto anatomical sameness. Sexual difference is then arbitrary, not essential. It is applied onto sameness to institute difference where difference is lacking. It is not the founding difference of the symbolic order but merely *the difference of differences*. Indeed, invariably in Sand, distinctions between same sex doubles are isomorphous with sexual difference, as can be seen in *Lélia*, where the difference between the female doubles, Lélia, the frigid intellectual, and Pulchérie, her orgasmic courtesan sister, involves the disparity not merely in their capacity for sexual pleasure but in their very sexual inscription, Lélia being coded as masculine, Pulchérie as feminine.

In enlisting sexual difference as a privileged mode of distinguishing members of the same sex Sand is not, I hasten to point out, innovating; she is adopting a conventional mode of exposing the conventionality of gender definitions. Flaubert resorts to exactly the same means to introduce difference within sameness while at the same time subverting the sexual stereotypes of bourgeois patriarchal culture, first in *L'Education sentimentale*, where Frédéric plays woman to Deslauriers's man and, more strikingly still, in the case of his male couple of retirees, Bouvard and Pécuchet. Nevertheless, Sand's and Flaubert's deconstructions of the male/female paradigm differ, and the difference corresponds to that between masculine and feminine forms of fetishism. Whereas Flaubert consistently refuses to decide the question of sexual difference, Sand, as we observed in our first reading of *Fadette*, does on one level stop the endless oscillation of fetishism in recognition of the inexorable force of cultural constraints in transforming anatomy into destiny. However arbitrary and unnatural sexual difference is, Fadette must give up her phallic attributes if she is to pursue the positive narrative destiny of woman, that is, marriage and motherhood.

The double strands of the plot I have teased out appear at this stage to resist any attempt to weave them into a seamless text. If we read *Fadette*, as Sand explicitly instructs us to do, as the story of a female *Bildung*, sexual difference in the traditional sense of opposition is assumed as the inevitable outcome, the telos of human development. If, however, we focus on the parallel plot, the maturational progress of the male twins, the assertion of an essential sexual difference is subverted, for the twins' growing up is not bound up with assuming their designated places within the binary sexual economy but with achieving differentiation. Whereas Fadette's growth consists in identification (with her mother), the twins' consists in disidentification (with each other).

The difference that must be instituted between the two brothers in order for them to enter the symbolic is the difference between self and Other, the sundering of a symbiotic dyad. According to Lacan such a dyad is always, in the end as in the beginning, the founding dyad constituted by the mother and child in the imaginary. However, as many commentators have noted, for Lacan the imaginary is unisexual, before rather than beyond difference. And yet ever since Freud began, somewhere around 1925, to recognize that the development of the little girl could not simply be traced from the template of male development, because of the whited-out continent of the female pre-Oedipus, psychoanalysts have argued that separation from the mother represents a far more complex task for the little girl than it does for the little boy. Indeed, if there is one thread that runs through the texts bearing on feminine specificity on both sides of the Atlantic, it is the recovery and valorization of the mother-daughter bond. For Luce Irigaray, Western phallocentric conceptual systems are grounded not so much in the repression of the female as in the suppression of women's essential bond with their mothers. A feminist psychoanalyst of the object-relations school, Nancy Chodorow, approaching the question from the angle of sociology, has placed particular emphasis on the almost insuperable difficulties the girl child encounters in achieving separation from the mother under current child-rearing practices, where the primary caretaker is female. She concludes that the daughter does not ever really achieve total separation from the mother and that this continuousness with the mother is extended to her other relationships, making women more caring, more intimately connected to others than are men.

While operating with different assumptions and different agendas, both Irigaray and Chodorow locate the specifically feminine in the intimate intensities of the mother-daughter relationship. By rewriting the traditional tale of the two brothers as an exemplary tale of separation and individuation, Sand has then stamped it with a distinctive sexual mark, one I will call feminine. To put it another, more paradoxical way, it is precisely Sand's insistence on the difference *before* sexual difference, on differentiation rather than difference, that constitutes the feminine specificity of her writing in this tale (as well as in many other of her works of fiction).

IV

How then does this differentiation take place? Or rather, where? For invariably in Sand, differentiation, whether sexual or diacritical, is linked to the theme of water, to the space of a riverbank. If the Fadette plot line culminates in the scene where Landry tells Fadette she must renounce her unfeminine ways and become a woman, the "bessons" narrative I am now foregrounding culminates in the scene where Landry, archetypally, enters the woods to find his lost brother, who, angered by Landry's fancied neglect, has gone off to sulk. Just as Landry is about to give in to his despair, Fadette materializes seemingly out of nowhere—this is her first appearance in the novel, and it is as a figure of the good witch who helps the hero in his trial in the dark woods—and tells Landry where his brother is—on the other bank on the portion of the river the twins call, in their own idiolect, *la coupure*, with a small *c*: "So Landry went to the cutting, which is what he and his brother used to call this part of the field of rushes" (p. 42/79). What is striking about the scene of their reunion is that throughout it the two brothers are separated by the cutting waters and remain on opposite banks of the stream. The *coupure* figures the diacritical slash that institutes difference within sameness; topology is ontology.

From that day forward, the break between Landry and Sylvinet will widen, as Landry goes forward into the world, eagerly growing up, while Sylvinet, filled with envy and resentment of his brother's betrayal of their symbiotic pact, remains at home, clinging to his mother's apron strings, hopelessly fixated at an early stage of affective development. Sylvinet's bad feelings reach fever pitch when Landry becomes involved with Fadette, who played such a crucial part in the separation of the twins, since it was she who showed Landry the way to *la coupure*. She comes on the scene of fiction at the precise moment when the two brothers are to be definitively precipitated into difference; in a word, far from representing the feminine side of the sexual paradigm, when viewed from the perspective of the twins' story, *Fadette figures differentiation*—she is *la coupure*.[20]

In true witchlike fashion, when Fadette appears to Landry in the dark woods, in exchange for coming to his aid she extracts from him a promise: that he will do her bidding, whatever and whenever it will be. Months go by, and Landry begins to forget his Faustian contract. Then one day Fadette appears and makes known her wish: that Landry dance with her and her only at the upcoming ball. Landry is extremely troubled by this request because he had earlier promised his first dance to his sweetheart, the coquette Madelon, the opposition of the coquette to the so-called natural woman being a topos of nineteenth-century women's writing.

The male protagonist must in the course of his erotic apprenticeship transfer his affections from the conventionally attractive coquette, whose attentions gratify his narcissism, to the less conventionally pretty and often poorer love object, with whom he can have the anaclitic relationship appropriate to masculine eroticism. (This transference is explicitly thematized in the first of Sand's three pastoral *contes*, *La Mare au diable*.) Because Landry has told no one, not even or least of all Sylvinet, of his encounter with Fadette, his selection of the homely "little cricket" as a dance partner is largely viewed as incomprehensible. Sylvinet, in particular, is distressed and humiliated by his brother's bizarre and ridiculous choice and turns his hostility against Fadette.

When, as the tale draws to a close, the break between the brothers appears irreversible, the case of Sylvinet attains pathological proportions. Finally he succumbs to what we might call anachronistically a nervous breakdown, taking to his bed and refusing to get up. After all efforts to cure Sylvinet fail, Landry asks Fadette to intervene. The method Fadette adopts to cure Sylvinet is, however, neither magical nor botanical, it is psychological. In order to deliver him from his pathological hostility toward herself, his rival for his brother's affections, Fadette devises a cure that consists in talking out the feelings whose repression has caused Sylvinet to fall ill and produce somatic symptoms:

> "You are so learned, Fanchonette, you should find a way of curing him."
> "The only cure I know is reasoning," she answered, "for it is his mind which makes his body ill, and whoever can cure the one will cure the other." (p. 156/206)

Sand never stopped inventing psychoanalysis. The notion that neurosis and even the threat of psychosis can be averted only by passing through the strait gate of the symbolic is a recurrent theme in her fiction (see *Mauprat*). But precisely because Fadette is an experimental scientist, the uncanny anticipation of another scene that was to unfold in Vienna, light years away from the rustic Berry setting of the tale, is more amply developed here than elsewhere in her fiction. Rehearsing the emergence of psychoanalysis from hypnosis, Fadette's initial treatment of her patient involves laying her hands first on his hand, then on his forehead, while he is plunged in a feverish sleep. By entering as it were into direct contact with Sylvinet's unconscious, Fadette succeeds in transforming his hostility toward her into that peculiar form of dependence Freud was to call transference. When Sylvinet emerges from his fever, he asks his mother: "Where's this Fadette, then? I think she helped me. Isn't she coming back?" (p. 173/227). Fadette returns and now begins the talking cure, as she instructs her patient to respect the cardinal rule of what was to become psychoanalysis, the uncensored articulation of all thoughts: "Say it all, Sylvain, you mustn't keep anything back" (p. 174/229). The effect produced on Sylvinet by Fadette's novel treatment is spectacular, and his condition improves markedly. There is, however, one major hitch: just as in the princeps case of psychoanalysis, Anna O., in the course of the treatment an unmastered transference turns to love.

Subverted on one level, sexual difference returns at another. Just as Fadette's social integration necessitates her renunciation of masculine behavior, Sylvinet's cure entails his substitution of a heterosexual object choice for the homosexual one constituted by his brother. Thus one of the other wise women consulted by his parents in the course of his illness says in no uncertain terms: " 'There is only one thing which will save your child—to love women' " (p. 152/201). And she adds: " 'He has an overabundance of affection in him, and always having turned it on his brother he has almost forgotten his sex, and in doing so he has gone against the Lord's law, which says that a man shall cherish a woman more than father and mother, more than sisters and brothers' " (p. 152/ 201).

Before we condemn the utter conventionality of Sand's model of human desire, which is also to say of narrative closure, for the two are inseparable, we must take into account the perverse twist of the text's conclusion: when Sylvinet does make the transition to heterosexuality, he chooses what is in fact an incestuous object of desire, his brother's wife. Thus, for him, far from providing any sort of resolution, the Oedipus consummates his sexual irresolution. The happy ending of the tale is purchased at the price of Sylvinet's self-imposed exile, for fated to love forever the first woman he falls in love with, Sylvinet takes himself out of the picture of domestic bliss and goes off to serve in Napoléon's army, rising rapidly in the ranks. The escape from incest signals the fall back into or return to the history from whose bloody conflicts Sand sought to escape in her pastoral narrative. The reinscription of an absolute sexual difference signaled on the one hand by Sylvinet's love for Fadette and on the other by the apparently comedic closure of the tale—Landry's and Fadette's marriage—is undermined by the persistence of Sylvinet's unresolved sexual destiny.

Heterosexuality, and the sexual difference that grounds it, is inseparable from the incest taboo, and incest is here only averted, indefinitely deferred rather than definitively prohibited. We know that elsewhere in the triptych of which *Fadette* constitutes the third panel, in that privileged Proustian intertext, *François le champi*, incest is not only consummated, as François weds his adoptive mother, but happily so, as the mother-son pair lives as happily ever after as any other fairy-tale couple. That Sylvinet's desire cannot achieve the same happy resolution and that that impossibility drives him out of pastoral into epic suggests that in *Fadette*, that most immediately postrevolutionary of tales, a certain happy ending becomes unstuck and the fundamental unsociability of human desire cannot be accommodated within the framework of the narrative. The bloody civil war has left its mark on this tale of the impossibility of two brothers achieving happiness. The fraternal bond idealized in Sand's utopian pre-1848 fictions reveals itself to be undermined by an economy of scarcity: in the sphere of human sexual and affective fulfillment, there is simply not enough happiness to go around. If, on the one hand, as we have seen, the idealized society of brothers cannot accommodate rebel daughters such as the young Fadette; on the other, the equally idealized conjugal regime represented by Fadette and Landry constitutes a real threat for fraternal male bonding. Reading *La Petite Fadette* double reveals two unsuspected and interdependent aporias within French postrevolutionary ideologies of gender: *The homosociality of the social contract is at odds with the compulsory heterosexuality of the bourgeois marriage contract.*[21] *At the same time the compulsory heterosexuality of the fraternal social contract is at odds with the homosexuality of the brothers.* Unhappily poised between beloved brother and incestuous love object, Landry is the new male postrevolutionary subject par excellence

V

In 1872, in what is doubtless her last great work of fiction, *Nanon*, Sand returned to the question that haunts the writings of most major nineteenth-century French writers: the transformative effects of the French

Revolution on French society. *Nanon* purports to be the memoirs of a woman who, born into the most destitute of the peasant class, is enabled by the French Revolution and its breakdown of hierarchical barriers and especially redistribution of property (the famed sale of the Biens Nationaux) to acquire knowledge and with it property and personal happiness. Just as in *La Petite Fadette* 1789 is filtered through 1848—hence the emphasis on brotherhood—in *Nanon* the events of the French Revolution are filtered through the prism of the Commune, with the result that the emphasis is not placed on the ideal of brotherhood (however demystified) but on its bloody underside: 1793, the Terror, civil war. Thus though both works deal with the French Revolution, they do not in fact deal with the same moment in it; instead, they reveal a split within the Revolution that most French mythmakers—up to and including the organizers of the recent bicentennial—would like to occlude.

How do brotherhood and fraternity fare in this Sand's last and most serenely optimistic fictionalization of her utopian ideal? We might begin by making a simple observation that has far-reaching consequences: the original fraternal social cell in this novel is not a set of identical twins—that is, biologically related or hyperrelated brothers—but a fraternal order that is by its very nature nonfamilial, a social artifact. I am referring, of course, to the fact that the central locus where the events of *Nanon* unfold is a monastery; its brothers are brothers by virtue of their vows, not by birth; they are, as Sand says, "brothers in religion."[22] Indeed, biological brotherhood is linked in this novel with one of the most hateful aspects of prerevolutionary aristocratic family politics, primogeniture, which Nanon describes as a form of soul murder:

> Emilien de Franqueville was born intelligent and resolute. To prevent him from claiming first rank in the family, there was a concerted effort to kill his soul and spirit. His brother was not, it would appear, as gifted as he, but he was the elder, and in this Franqueville family, all the younger brothers had been ordained. It was a law that had always been observed and that was transmitted from father to son. Emilien's father the marquis thought it excellent; it was a measure of order that improved upon the law of the State. (p. 45)

Though the novel bears the name of its plucky heroine, who serves as a bridge between Sand's Fadette and Flaubert's Félicité,[23] if we refocus the novel on its male protagonist, we can better make out the contours of what I take to be the novel's central theme: the constitution of a national identity based on a contractual rather than a blood relationship between individuals. And Emilien's exemplary passage from aristocrat into peasant into Frenchman is informed by, indeed predicated on a profound redefinition of fraternity. From the outset Emilien, the sacrificed younger brother of a great noble family, is referred to by Nanon as the "petit frère" because of his place in the monastery. In time, however, this epithet is layered over with a second meaning: for along with an older brother, Emilien has a younger sister whom he dearly loves, and Nanon comes to occupy the place of the sister, before occupying that of wife. In other words, the ideal wife in the new Republican social order is the sister. Innocent about the ways of love and incapable of imagining that an aristocrat such as Emilien could love a peasant such as herself, Nanon translates her deep devotion to Emilien into the only affective code known to her, the vocabulary of family relationships: "We loved each other as if the same mother had brought us into the world" (p. 91).

Sand's fictionalization of sisterhood in this novel both lends weight to and calls into question Juliet Flower MacCannell's view that it is woman *quoad sororem*—if I may paraphrase Freud—who is the great loser in the postpatriarchal brotherly regime:

> It is far less the father than the brother that modern literature calls to account; less the mother than the sister who must be recognized and given her due as the real rather than the imaginary "other" necessary to found male identity and group life; less the son than the younger brother, the son-not-heir who can appear in a new symbolic.[24]

To the extent that Louise, the beloved little sister, is in fact the bad woman who will eventually have to be left out of the utopian community, *Nanon* stages, albeit in a modern version, the ritual sacrifice of the sister by the brothers. Louise is killed off in the end because she is an impenitent aristocrat but also because, in an interesting update of the figures of negative femininity in Sand's utopian novels of the 1840s, in the new economic order *Nanon* salutes, she represents the new figure of demonized femininity that inherits the negative attributes of the earlier incarnations of the all-too-feminine woman—the coquette, the adulteress, the madwoman in love: the female consumer. Louise's premature death is directly linked to her spendthrift ways: "From then on he [Costejoux, Louise's bourgeois husband] set about becoming rich to satisfy his wife's frivolous tastes and he is now one of the wealthiest men in the land. She died still young and leaving him two charming daughters, one of whom married her cousin, Pierre de Franqueville, my eldest" (pp. 234–35).

Becoming a Frenchman, taking his place "in the sunshine of civil equality," means for Emilien a whole series of ruptures with his aristocratic family: first his cruel father, then his rival brother, and ultimately and most wrenchingly his beloved sister. But as each familial role is vacated, a nonfamily member comes to occupy the empty slot: in the place of the father, there is Emilien's adopted father, the aptly named Père Fructueux who runs the monastery; in the place of his royalist brother, there is Costejoux, his bourgeois and Republican brother-in-law; and in the place of his snobbish and spendthrift sister, his wife, the upwardly mobile and enterprising capitalist Nanon. But that is not all; Emilien, like Sylvinet, joins the Republican army, not to escape an untenable personal conflict but to acquire citizenship in the new French nation. Thus, unlike Sylvinet, he pays the penultimate price: an all-too-symbolic mutilation, the loss of his forearm. Like Jane Eyre, Nanon marries her social superior but only after he has been deprived of a key index of privilege—both phallic and social. The redefinition of the fraternal order takes then the form of a marriage that signifies both the fusion of the classes and the demise of a feudal social order based on caste in favor of a new capitalist social order in which women have begun to obtain a measure of equality through economic independence.

The redefinition of the fraternal contract in Sand necessarily issues on a reconsideration of the genealogical bond; to substitute a purely contractual relationship—such as marriage—for those based on blood ties is to be forced to come to terms with the patriarchal order as it is bound up with notions of hereditary class privilege, in a word, aristocracy. To the extent that Sand never stopped rethinking marriage, it can be said that she never stopped grappling with what is arguably one of the greatest questions of her time: reconciling the social contract theories inherited from the Revolution with notions of heredity that passed disturbed but not destroyed from feudalism to positivism. If as a feminist Sand was encumbered by the unresolved contradictions of Enlightenment social thought, as a descendant of an illustrious family she was equally weighted down by the unresolved contradictions of her personal origins. Espousal of contract theories of social organization did not automatically mean a total renunciation of class privilege. As Michèle Hecquet demonstrates, an early novel such as *Mauprat* (1837) both signals the promising beginning of what Hecquet aptly calls the "era of contracts" and marks a regressive promotion of aristocratic social and aesthetic values.[25] Indeed, what that novel makes clear is that in order for the happy marriage that is, finally for Sand, the most glorious social contract into which women can enter to occur, the daughter must break with the father and the old order he represents.

Transmissions:

Histoire

de ma vie

Full fathom five thy father lies;
Of his bones are coral made;
Those are pearls that were his eyes;
Nothing of him that doth fade,
But doth suffer a sea-change
Into something rich and strange.
                    Shakespeare, *The Tempest*

In materialism we find *mater*. Can we not then see idealism,
which opposes and represses materialism, as a *paterialism?*
                    Jean-Joseph Goux, *Symbolic Economies*

During the cold crisp night of January 18, 1821, George
Sand had, according to her *Histoire de ma vie* (*Story of My
Life*), what may well be a unique experience in the annals of
autobiography: like some sort of female Aeneas, led by her
Virgilian tutor Deschartres, the seventeen-year-old Sand literally descended into the family crypt and emerged, if not
to found an empire, to write the family epic, the story of her

father. The occasion for this bizarre expedition into the shady underworld was the death of Sand's paternal grandmother, who had raised her after her father's premature death in a fall from a horse. In the course of readying the family crypt to receive the grandmother's coffin, Deschartres, who had been Maurice Dupin's tutor, was, according to Sand's account, suddenly overcome with the impulse to lift the lid of the coffin containing his beloved pupil's remains. As Deschartres described the experience to the impressionable young Aurore: "The head had come away by itself. I lifted it up and kissed it. I took such great comfort from that—I, who had not been able to receive a last kiss from him."[1] So comforting did Deschartres find this necrophilic embrace, that he urged Aurore to follow in his footsteps and pay a similar homage to the remains of her dead father:

> You have to go down there, you have to kiss that relic. It will be a lifetime memory. Someday, you will have to write your father's life story, even if it is only for your children, who will not have known him. Show a sign of love and respect now to one whom you scarcely knew yourself and who loved you so much. I tell you, from where he is now he will see you and bless you. (p. 800/1:1107)

The scene is extraordinary, rivaling anything to be found in the wildest of Gothic tales, including Sand's own: the late hour, the cold, the unsealed coffin, the severed skull, the necrophilic kiss, and above all the injunction to write the father's story. Without overstating the case, one might say that this unforgettable episode—however embellished—was one of the animating factors in Sand's decision to write her autobiography, for Sand's *Histoire de ma vie* is first and foremost the biography of her father, the dashing officer in Napoléon's army who died in 1808, when his daughter Aurore was but four years old.

Indeed, from the moment of its publication in 1854, Sand's autobiography was criticized for what was quite obviously its salient compositional eccentricity: the disproportionate place occupied in the story of Sand's life by the story of her father. In the words of Georges Lubin: "the space given to the father was judged to be excessive. It was said that a better title would have been *The Story of My Life Before My Birth*."[2] There is something of *Tristram Shandy* in this curious autobiography where the beginning of the autobiographer's own life story is postponed

FIGURE 6.

Adela Turin, *Aurore*. des femmes. In this cartoon version of the first part of *Histoire de ma vie* the foundational role of the father is made manifest by the graphic layout: placed exactly at the bottom center of the page, the father's skull, held by the daughter, is framed by an arch of bare tree branches. In this prominently positioned neogothic medallion, the paternal skull becomes by virtue of its contiguity with the overarching trees the very root of the family tree.

until about a third of the way into the text. Sand was well aware of the dangers of this deferral. Midway through her father's story, she pauses for a moment to defend her text against the possible impatience of its readers: "If I continue my father's story, perhaps it will be said that I am putting off keeping the promise I made to tell my own story" (p. 271/1:307). To this anticipated criticism she responds by arguing that the signification of an individual is contextual: the meaning of the page of Sand's life becomes intelligible only when reinserted into the text of "the universal book," as well as that of the family history. And, furthermore, she insists, the private history of a family is bound up with the public history of the nation: "Hence, I have to include a period of about a hundred years in order to tell the story of forty years of my own life" (p. 272/1:308).

Viewed, however, in the context of female autobiography as a subgenre with its own rules and distinctive structural features, the disproportionate place occupied by the father's life story ceases to appear as an aberration in need of justification, for, as Mary G. Mason observed several years ago, "the evolution and delineation of an identity by way of alterity" is a constant of female autobiography from the Middle Ages to the present.[3] Yet, if the central position occupied by the paternal figure in Sand's autobiography is broadly consonant with the poetics of female autobiography, we cannot leave the matter at that, because there remains the matter of the identity of the identity-giving Other.

We might, for example, want to ask about Sand's mother and her place in the biographical scheme, in the paternal epic. That very question is addressed by Sand in the introductory section of *Histoire de ma vie*, where she reflects on the distortions perpetrated by her biographers in her lifetime. She notes with some humor their aristocratic prejudices, especially those of the foreign biographers, who insistently emphasized her glorious paternal lineage to the exclusion of her maternal legacy:

> I especially suspect my foreign biographers of an aristocratic bias, for they have all bestowed on me (those who ought to have been better informed) an illustrious origin while ignoring a very visible stain on my blazon.
>
> One is not only the offspring of one's father, one is also a little, I believe, that of one's mother. It seems to me that the latter is even more the case, and that we are attached to the entrails of the one who gave birth to us in the most immediate, powerful, and sacred way. Hence, if

my father was the great-grand-son of Augustus II, King of Poland, and if on that side I find myself the illegitimate, but nevertheless very real, next of kin to Charles X and Louis XVIII, it is no less true that my bloodlines are tied to the people in a way as intimate and direct; and what's more, there is no bastardy on this side. (p. 77/1:15–16)

Not only Sand's snobbish foreign biographers worked to blot out Mama and occult Sand's popular origins; in a revealing passage, Taine, one of Sand's most astute native admirers and a prime theoretician of the determining role of "race" or class in the constitution of the writerly subject, explains why Sand offers a textbook case for the application of Sainte-Beuve's "l'homme et l'oeuvre" method of literary criticism:

> We know in great detail Sand's mother and father and her grandparents up to the fourth generation; we have their letters, we know their intimate lives, one can follow from King Augustus, the maréchal de Saxe, Mme Dupin, Commander Dupin, down to George Sand herself, the *transmission* of an original temperament, of particular traits that exaggerated, attenuated, renewed, or transformed by successive crossbreedings attained their highest development and their most perfect harmony in the final genius that summed them all up.[4]

Transmission, the passage of a genetic stock from one generation to the next, is for Taine, as for so many of Sand's biographers, imagined as a highly selective and even elitist process. Though we possess, as Taine notes, ample details about both of Sand's parents, what is handed down across four generations is viewed as primarily the paternal legacy, with the maternal genetic pool serving simply as a source of renewal through crossbreeding. The primary genetic code transmitted is paternal, that is, noble; the popular, maternal strain is secondary, a graft onto the aristocratic line of the father. Transmission is conjointly patriarchal and aristocratic. This insistent patriarchalization of transmission is perfectly consonant with theories of reproduction going back to Aristotle and has far-reaching consequences for theories of idealism, for as Jean-Joseph Goux reminds us: "While the male is associated with the transmission of a pattern, a model, the female braves the contradiction of a material reproduction and is merged with what is *other* in relation to constant ideal form: that is, with amorphous, transitory, inessential material."[5] Further, as Sand remarks at a later point in the text, genealogies bear

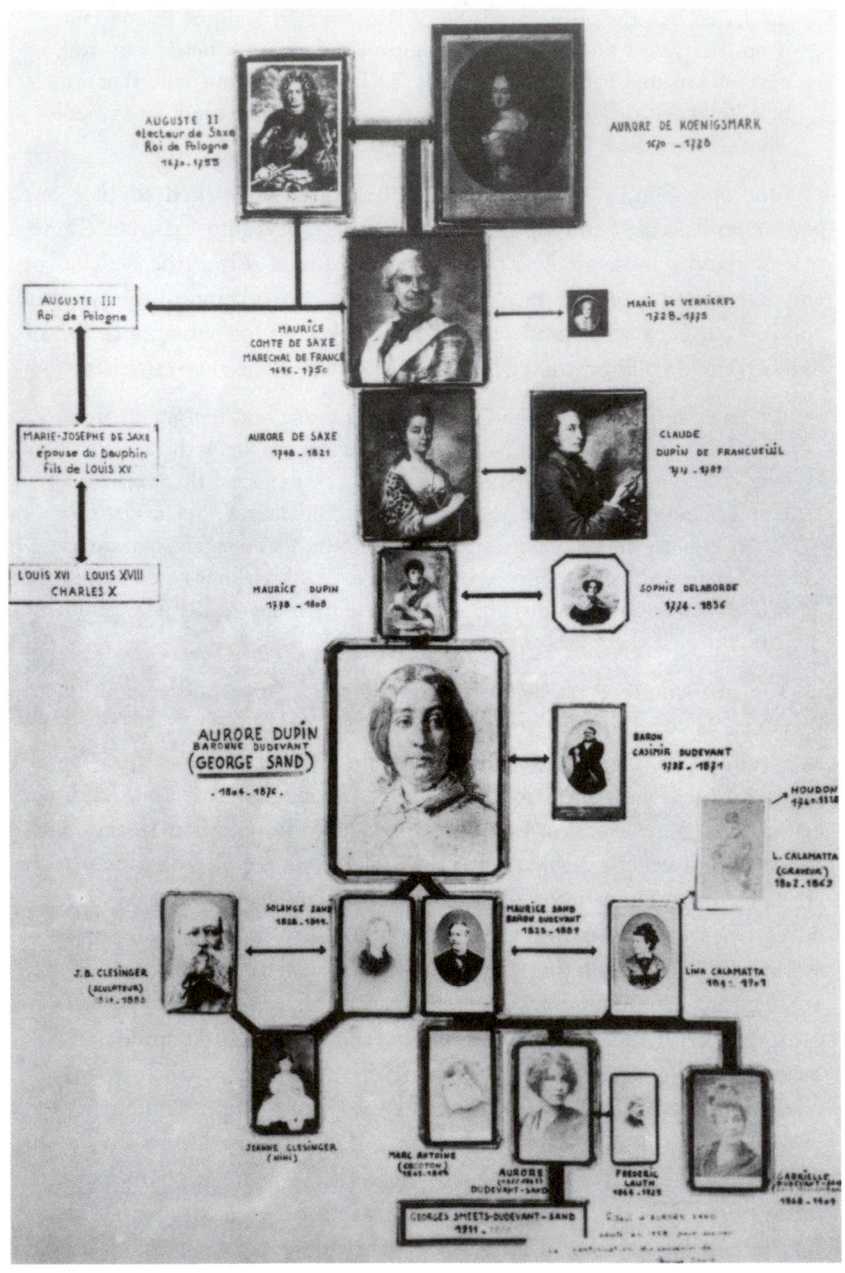

LA FAMILLE DE GEORGE SAND

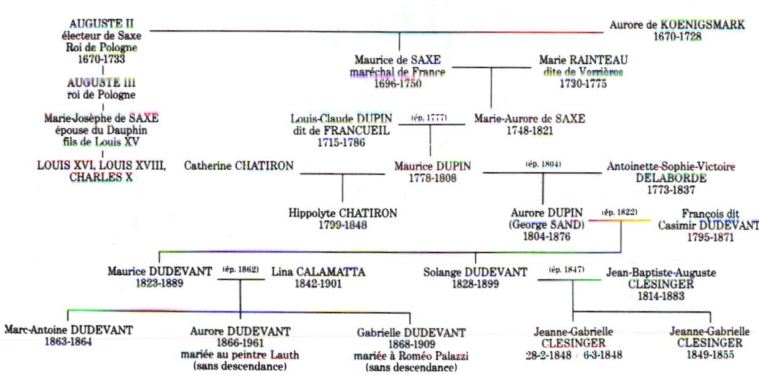

FIGURE 7, 8, 9.

Sand family trees. Musée Gargillesse; Musée Renan-Scheffer; *Oeuvres autobiographiques,* Editions de la Pléiade. The obsession with the laws of heredity that gripped late-nineteenth-century epistemology and haunts fin-de-siècle fiction persists in the most recent presentations of the Sand family tree. As the thoroughly unscientific, homemade family tree on display at Gargilesse—Sand's rustic retreat in the Berry—vividly demonstrates, the legend overwhelmingly favors the paternal branch. Despite its more sober presentation, the family tree furnished by the Renan-Scheffer Museum in Paris perpetuates the emphasis on the paternal line. It is only in the family tree that appears in the Pléiade edition of *Histoire de ma vie* that the proper balance is restored and the maternal lineage adequately accounted for. And yet even this most objective genealogy is selective, excluding illegitimate half-brothers and half-sisters on both paternal and maternal sides.

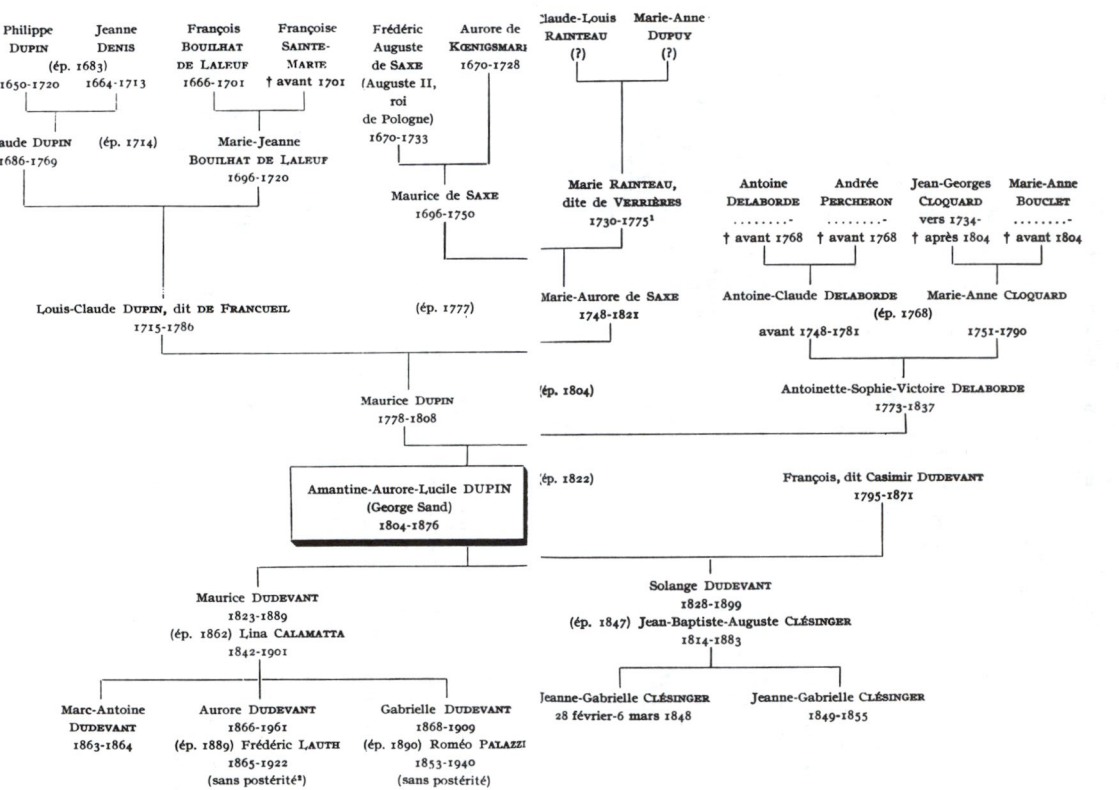

Philippe
DUPIN

(ép. 1683)

1650-1720

Jeanne
DENIS

1664-1713

François
**BOUILHAT
DE LALEUF**
1666-1701

Françoise
**SAINTE-
MARIE**
† avant 1701

Frédéric
Auguste
de **SAXE**
(Auguste II,
roi
de Pologne)
1670-1733

Aurore de
KŒNIGSMARK
1670-1728

Claude-Louis
RAINTEAU
(?)

Marie-Anne
DUPUY
(?)

Claude **DUPIN**
1686-1769

(ép. 1714)

Marie-Jeanne
BOUILHAT DE LALEUF
1696-1720

Maurice de **SAXE**
1696-1750

Marie **RAINTEAU**,
dite de **VERRIÈRES**
1730-1775[1]

Antoine
DELABORDE
. . . .
† avant 1768

Andrée
PERCHERON
. . . .
† avant 1768

Jean-Georges
CLOQUARD
vers 1734-
† après 1804

Marie-Anne
BOUCLET
. . . .
† avant 1804

Louis-Claude **DUPIN**, dit **DE FRANCUEIL**
1715-1786

(ép. 1777)

Marie-Aurore de **SAXE**
1748-1821

Antoine-Claude **DELABORDE**

avant 1748-1781

(ép. 1768)

Marie-Anne **CLOQUARD**
1751-1790

Maurice **DUPIN**
1778-1808

(ép. 1804)

Antoinette-Sophie-Victoire **DELABORDE**
1773-1837

(ép. 1822)

**Amantine-Aurore-Lucile DUPIN
(George Sand)
1804-1876**

François, dit Casimir **DUDEVANT**
1795-1871

Maurice **DUDEVANT**
1823-1889
(ép. 1862) Lina **CALAMATTA**
1842-1901

Solange **DUDEVANT**
1828-1899
(ép. 1847) Jean-Baptiste-Auguste **CLÉSINGER**
1814-1883

Marc-Antoine
DUDEVANT
1863-1864

Aurore **DUDEVANT**
1866-1961
(ép. 1889) Frédéric **LAUTH**
1865-1922
(sans postérité[2])

Gabrielle **DUDEVANT**
1868-1909
(ép. 1890) Roméo **PALAZZI**
1853-1940
(sans postérité)

Jeanne-Gabrielle **CLÉSINGER**
28 février-6 mars 1848

Jeanne-Gabrielle **CLÉSINGER**
1849-1855

1. Ce tableau d'ascendance ne peut faire état du fils que Marie Rainteau eut du duc de Bouillon : Charles-Godefroid-Marie de Beaumont-Bouillon (1750-1823), demi-frère d'Aurore de Saxe et grand-oncle de George Sand.
2. Mme Aurore Lauth-Sand a adopté en 1958 M. Georges-André Smeets (1911-1970).

the mark of class, indeed serve to constitute and perpetuate class differences: "The genealogies of ordinary people cannot compete with those of the rich and powerful. . . . The poor man dies in totality" (p. 114/ 1:71).[6]

Having denounced the biographers' favoring of the more glorious paternal branch of her family tree, Sand proceeds to repeat their matricidal gesture, first by devoting a disproportionate part of her text to her father's story and second by revealing the seamier sides of her mother's life, the blots on the maternal escutcheon. Repeating the gestures of both Sand and her biographers, I, too, will be concerned in what follows with the story of Sand's father, which does not, of course, mean that I, any more than they, deny the importance of the mother.[7] The argument I will make is that Sand's choice to devote such a prominent place to her father's life story rose less from her own aristocratic prejudices than from her espousal of an aesthetics of idealism. Or rather, to reestablish the more plausible order of events, Sand's idealist aesthetics draw their affective impetus from the idealization of her dead father. Regardless of whether Sand espoused idealism because of the injunction to idealize the father or idealized her father because of her espousal of an aesthetics of idealism, what interests me are the overdeterminations of Sand's aesthetic choices, situated, as all such choices are, at the always permeable border between the specificities of a personal myth and the play of larger social formations. Even if, as the ironist might argue, the injunction is nothing but a prosopopoeia fabricated after the fact to legitimate the autobiographical enterprise *en abyme*, and even if, as the ironist might further argue, one should always beware of loose causalities, I will maintain that a crucial link exists between the autobiographer's selective genealogy and her larger aesthetic project.

Sand's self-described aesthetic project was, as we have seen, idealistic. When I speak of Sandian idealism I am not—it should by now be abundantly clear—referring to her espousal of some Gallic version of German romantic aesthetics, rather to her participation in elaborating what Joseph Frank has described as the second of the "two romanticisms" available to European authors who came of age in the 1830s—that is, native French social romanticism.[8] But whereas Frank stresses the continuity between French social romanticism and realism, I have argued throughout what precedes that, for all its embryonic naturalist elements,

French social romanticism—at least as it was exemplified by Sand—relied heavily on techniques of idealization that strained against the particularization we (and she) associate with realism.

Autobiography as a genre constitutes at least in theory[9] a unique exception to Sand's idealist poetics: whereas the fictional enterprise is for her essentially idealistic, the ideal autobiography is necessarily (though reluctantly) realistic. As Sand acutely perceives, in autobiography idealization quickly shades into self-idealization and ultimately autodivinization, that is, a confusion between the idealizing self and the ideal. Just as for Roland Barthes, autobiography for Sand is constantly threatened by the lures of the imaginary.

> The habit of speaking about ourselves seems easily to lead to self-praise, and that, doubtless quite involuntarily, by a law instinctive to the human mind, which cannot keep from embellishing the object of its contemplation. . . . But this self-enthusiasm which inspires such audacious surges toward heaven is not the milieu in which the soul can settle in order to speak of itself to humankind. In that mood, it loses the sense of its own weaknesses. It identifies with the godhead, with the ideal that it embraces. (pp. 71–72/1:6)

But for Sand, unlike for Barthes, the danger of the imaginary is not so much the illusion of plenitude and self-presence that it gives as the threat it poses for the legitimating pedagogical efficacy of the autobiographical text. If the autobiographer takes himself for his ideal, he makes it impossible for his readers to identify with him; he ceases, in other words, to provide a viable specular model. Entranced by his idealized self-image, the autobiographer identifies with God, and that transcendental identification transports him beyond the identificatory reach of the merely mortal potential reader. And identification between autobiographer and reader is the very condition of an autobiography's readability:

> It is surely impossible to believe that the penchant of poets for idealizing their own existences and making of them something abstract and impalpable is a lesson complete in itself. Useful and vivifying it is without doubt, for everyone's spirit is uplifted with those of the inspired dreamers; everyone's sentiments are purified by following them across those rapturous regions, but what is missing in this subtle balm spread by them over our failings is very important—reality.

> Naturally, it takes something for an artist to mirror reality; those who get their pleasure this way are really very generous! As for me, I cannot carry the love of duty that far, and it is not without great effort that I am going to descend into the prose of my subject. (p. 72/1:7)

Sand's very praiseworthy and unimpeachable pedagogical concerns do not, however, constitute the only argument in favor of a resolutely dei-dealized presentation of the autobiographical self. There is another more compelling, more personal, and ultimately more suspect reason for her refusal of idealism in autobiography. From her earliest attempt at writing her memoirs to her mature achievement in this genre, Sand was at great pains to emphasize her own inadequacy as a subject for idealization. In the *Voyage en Auvergne,* she describes herself as follows:

> Looking at myself in the mirror I can say . . . that I never pleased myself much. . . . A woman must love herself a great deal to have an expressive look when she contemplates herself and to find herself pretty. If I saw myself in the eyes of someone who loves me, I would no doubt be more satisfied with my mother's work.[10]

There is at the outset an advertised specular failure that can only be remedied by the gaze of the amorous other; it is only when refracted by another's eyes that the mother's child—it is significant that the deva-lorized subject in need of a narcissistic boost from the outside is merely mothered—acquires value in her own eyes. When in *Histoire de ma vie* Sand seeks to refute the imputation or assumption of the autobiographical character of her feminocentric fictions, she enlists the same self-depre-cating argument. Once again the mirror is hopelessly mimetic:

> I am too romantic ever to have seen the heroine of a novel in my mirror. I never found myself beautiful or pleasing enough, nor consistent enough in the interplay of character and behavior to be of poetic or even general interest. I would have tried to embellish my person and dramatize my life, in vain; I would never have come to the end of it. My own self, coming to haunt me face to face, would have given me the chills.
>   . . . I was cut from too mottled a cloth ever to lend myself to any type of idealization. (p. 922/2:160)

Before we can begin to address the critical question of Sand's adherence to her credo of realism in autobiography in regard to her own self-portrait, we must first ask whether she respected her credo in the section devoted to her father. The answer, according to Georges Lubin, the preeminent Sand scholar of our time and editor of the Pléiade edition of *Histoire de ma vie*, is no. Although the paternal section is made up largely of the correspondence of Maurice and his mother—that is, of authentic documents drawn from the family archives—it would appear that in integrating them into her work, Sand revised them, often quite dramatically:

> Alas! George Sand immediately swerves away from the line of conduct she had set herself, as soon as the principle must be put into practice. Those letters of her father's, those firsthand documents that she has the good fortune to possess in her secretary at Nohant . . . the novelist that she is cannot prevent herself from rewriting them, reworking them, recasting them, blending them to give them a literary form, and yes, from betraying them sometimes, betraying them often. (1:xxiv)

But, I would argue, Sand's rewriting of her father's letters is motivated less by the imperatives of fictionality than those of idealization; it is *Sand the daughter* more than *Sand the novelist* who betrays the paternal originals in translating then into the prose of autobiography. In fact, if one compares Sand's reworking of her father's letters to the originals, one is led to conclude that Sand, in Lubin's words, "veiled the paternal nakedness" (1:xxiv).

Several questions then arise: Why in the process of appropriating her father's correspondence does Sand reenact the paradigmatic veiling gesture of Noah's daughters? How is the daughterly autobiographical enterprise bound up with the idealization of the father? What is the place of the mother in the scenario of idealization? What benefits accrue to the autobiographer from idealizing the parents? What exactly are the mechanisms of idealization?

I

Psychoanalysis, like poetics, is overwhelmingly wedded to the reality principle, which is why, as Freud himself remarked, "Psycho-analysis has been reproached time after time with ignoring the higher, moral, supra-personal side of human nature." It is not until the 1914 "On Narcissism: An Introduction" that the notion of the ideal makes its official entry in Freudian metapsychology side by side with the concept of narcissism and not until the postwar texts, *Group Psychology and the Analysis of the Ego* (1921) and especially *The Ego and the Id* (1923) that the ideal, through its linkage with the superego, is accommodated in Freud's remapping of the topography of the mind. As Paul-Laurent Assoun made clear in a lucid and thorough study of the "genealogy" of the ideal in Freud, the emergence of the ideal in psychoanalysis accompanied a major Freudian reconceptualization of the subject, which involved a radical shift in perspective from an object- to an ego-centered theory of the libido. This shift occurred in stages beginning with the essay on narcissism and culminating in *The Ego and the Id*. "The theory of the ideal plays precisely this role of valuable relay between narcissism and the second topography."[11]

However, one brief early text, the 1908 "Family Romances," deserves mention at the outset because it adumbrates so many of the themes that will concern us in the later texts. Of particular interest in this slight but suggestive text is the way sexual differences insinuate themselves to the detriment of women into the account Freud gives of the play of fantasy in early childhood life. What is at stake in this text, which is closely linked to another text written that same year, "Creative Writers and Day-Dreaming," is the power to reshape reality through that prestigious faculty, the imagination. And the female imagination demonstrates its superiority in Freud only in the sadomasochistic fantasies of the disciplined girl-child of "A Child Is Being Beaten."

Women are, it appears, doubly disadvantaged or displaced in the protofictional family romance. First, in the early asexual stage, boys are more likely to experience the feelings of rage and rivalry that give rise to the fantasizing activity: "Here the influence of sex is already in evidence, for a boy is far more inclined to feel hostile impulses toward his father than toward his mother and has a far more intense desire to get free from *him* than from *her*. In this respect the imagination of girls is apt to show itself much weaker."[12] Second, in the later stage, after the child has learned the facts of life, sexual difference returns in a different guise, in this instance not separating boy from girl but mother from father. Armed with the knowledge that " '*pater semper incertus est*' while the mother is '*certissima*,' " the child must refashion the family romance to coincide with the fact of the mother's stable identity: "The family romance undergoes a curious curtailment: it contents itself with exalting the child's father, but no longer casts any doubt on his maternal origin, which is regarded as something unalterable" (p. 239). The fixity of the mother does not exempt her from the child's—the male child's, one assumes—active fantasy life, but whereas the family romance works to idealize the father, it gives license to lower the mother by imagining that one's hated rivals for her affections, that is, one's siblings, are in fact illegitimate. There are then two quite opposite outcomes of the family romance: in the first instance, it is the *author* of the fiction who imagines himself to be illegitimate; in the second, the author of the fiction displaces the illegitimacy onto his or her *siblings*. In Freud's words: "An interesting variant of the family romance may then appear, in which the hero and author returns to legitimacy himself while his brothers and sisters are eliminated by being bastardized" (p. 240). Sand's family romance interestingly combines elements from these various scenarios: in her autobiography she both idealizes her father and lowers her mother; thus, while claiming to clear her mother's reputation, Sand makes public her elder half-sister's illegitimacy.

What emerges most forcefully from our reading of this early essay is the link Freud establishes between the paternal and idealization.[13] If we go on to consider Freud's subsequent theorizations of the ideal, we find perhaps not surprisingly that they all work to amplify and support the association between the father and the ideal. Nowhere is this clearer than in the all-important third chapter of *The Ego and the Id*, "The Ego and the Super Ego (Ego Ideal)." It is there that Freud spells out in intricate detail—most of which need not be rehearsed here—just how it is that the subject comes under the sway of the ego ideal, which is here synonymous with the superego. The key mechanism in the differentiation of the superego from the ego is identification. Already in the transitional *Group Psychology and the Analysis of the Ego* Freud had argued that the mechanism whereby a number of individuals merge to form a group involves a double process: identification with the other members of the group with whom one shares an ego ideal and the replacement of the ego ideal by the person of the leader. However, in the case of the Catholic church, identification operates both vertically and horizontally—the believer both identifies with Christ and idealizes him. And so it is, according to Freud, with the child, who like the believer both identifies with and idealizes the quasi-divine figure of the father. It is at this junction that this extremely complex chapter takes a turn that is of particular interest to me. Speculating on the "origin of the ideal," Freud writes: "Behind it there lies hidden an individual's first and most important identification, his identification with the father in his own personal prehistory."[14] In a crucial footnote appended to this sentence, Freud adds: "Perhaps it would be safer to say 'with the parents'; for before a child has arrived at definite knowledge of the difference between the sexes, the lack of a penis, it does not distinguish in value between its father and its mother" (p. 31). And then, amazingly: "In order to simplify my presentation I shall discuss only identification with the father" (p. 31). The mere sake of simplicity does not, of course, command Freud's decision to focus on the paternal identification, any more than it does his privileging of the identificatory trajectory of the *male* child. The father is, as we have already seen, *the* parent of idealization, and this, as we shall see in a moment, is not without far-reaching consequences for women in their relationship or rather alleged nonrelationship to the ideal.

In actual fact Freud does not limit himself strictly in the rest of the chapter to paternal identification. Because of the inherent bisexuality of the human subject Freud is quick to recognize that the Oedipus complex rarely presents itself in its paradigmatic, that is, masculine and so-called positive form: "An ambivalent attitude to his father and an object-relation of a solely affectionate kind to his mother make up the content of the simple positive Oedipus complex in a boy" (p. 32). With the dissolution of the Oedipus complex a number of outcomes, four to be exact, are possible: in the case of a positive Oedipus complex, a boy will identify with his father, and a girl with her mother; in the case of a negative or inverted complex, a boy may identify with his mother and a girl with her father. This combinatory of identifications leads Freud to conclude: "*The broad general outcome of the sexual phase dominated by the Oedipus complex may, therefore, be taken to be the forming of a precipitate in the ego, consisting of these two identifications* [the paternal and the maternal] *in some way united with each other. This modification of the ego retains its special position; it confronts the other contents of the ego as an ego ideal or super-ego*" (p. 34).

If the superego or ego ideal is, in Freud's own words, a "precipitate" of *both* the father and the mother identification, why does he explicitly privilege the paternal identification? Why does the maternal identification drop out of consideration? Because the passage from parental identification to the formation of the superego is bound up with repression: "The ego ideal," writes Freud, "had the task of repressing the Oedipus complex; indeed, it is to that revolutionary event that it owes its existence" (p. 34). And in this heroic act of renunciation of gratification, it is from the father's no, Lacan's "non du père," that the child draws his strength. Again I quote Freud:

> Clearly the repression of the Oedipus complex was no easy task. The child's parents, and *especially his father*, were perceived as the obstacle to a realization of his Oedipus wishes; so his infantile ego fortified itself for the carrying out of the repression by erecting this same obstacle within itself. It borrowed strength to do this, so to speak, from the father, and this loan was an extraordinarily momentous act. *The super-ego retains the character of the father.* (p. 34; emphasis added)

For feminists, the problem with this account of the creation of the superego is that, because the daughter's credit is not as good as the son's, it is much harder for her to obtain a loan from the paternal bank. Because, as Freud repeatedly noted, notably in "Femininity" and "Some Psychological Consequences of the Anatomical Distinction between the Sexes," women's lack of a penis deprives them of a key incentive for exiting the Oedipus—that is, the fear of castration—women suffer from a grievous deficiency in the area of the superego, hence a congenital ethical inferiority. Freud's formulation of this situation in "Anatomical Differences" is particularly eloquent, not to mention notorious:

> I cannot escape the notion (though I hesitate to give it expression) that for women the level of what is ethically normal is different from what it is in men. Their super-ego is never so inexorable, so impersonal, so independent of its emotional origins as we require it to be in men.[15]

Lack of a penis translates in the Freudian schema into a lack of idealism; ethics in Freud is phallic. What then are we to make of Sand's idealism or, indeed, of her idealization of her father? I hasten to note that Freud is quick to qualify his misogynistic generalizations by granting his feminist critics "that pure masculinity and femininity remain theoretical constructions of uncertain content" (p. 258). Exceptions to the rule abound. Nevertheless, the question remains: what are the means whereby the daughter can overcome within the Freudian conceptual system her constitutional inferiority in regard to the ideal? Two paths lead to idealization for the daughter. One lies through a persistent identification with the father: "Analysis very often shows that a little girl, after she has had to relinquish her father as a love-object, will bring her masculinity into prominence and identify herself with her father (that is, with the object which has been lost), instead of with her mother. This will clearly depend on whether the masculinity in her disposition—whatever that may consist in—is strong enough."[16] Clearly, Sand's disposition to masculinity was sufficiently strong to support such a persistent identification. Thus, in *Histoire de ma vie*, she writes:

> I continue the history of my father, since he is, no pun intended, the real author of the story of my life. This father whom I hardly knew and who has remained in my memory like a shining apparition—this artistic young man and warrior has remained wholly alive in the flights of my fancy, in the pitfalls of my constitution, in the features of my face. My being is a reflection—weakened, no doubt, but rather complete—of his. . . . My exterior life has differed as much from his as the period in which it developed; but had I been a boy and had I lived twenty-five years earlier, I know and I sense that I would have acted and felt in all things like my father.[17] (p. 169/1:156–57)

Doubly bound to her dead father as reflection and reincarnation, Sand's excessive identification culminates in an imagined rebirth as a boy, a sort of fraternal twin to her father. The fact that Sand's father's death occurred when she was very young is, of course, a crucial factor in the elaboration of this scenario, indeed in the genesis of her idealism; as Lacan observes: "The death of the father, at whatever stage of development it occurs and according to the degree of achievement of the Oedipus tends . . . to exhaust by freezing it the progress of reality."[18] To paraphrase another statement of Lacan's, one might say that *the dead father is the father of idealization.* Sand's autoidealization is inseparable from her idealization of her father: by identifying so strongly with her idealized (dead) father, Sand surreptitiously circumvents the censoring of her own self-love. In the apt words of Hartmann and Loewenstein: "The setting up of the ego ideal can be considered a rescue operation for narcissism."[19]

This seductive formula, which summarizes a widely shared psychoanalytic wisdom, forces us to double back to the genealogy of the ideal in

Freud, as well as to reconsider Sand's repeated protestations of narcissistic deficiency, specular inadequacy. As we noted at the outset, following Assoun, the ideal mediates between the concepts of narcissism and the superego. But what we did not make clear is that in the shift from narcissism to the superego the ideal undergoes a crucial transformation. In fact, two rather different ideals are at work in Freud's metapsychology: *the ideal of narcissism is not the same as that of the superego*. In a distinction Lacan in particular did much to bring out and give meaning to, in the essay on narcissism Freud distinguishes between two facets of the ideal, the *idealich* (ideal ego) and the *ichideal* (ego ideal),[20] and this distinction can in turn be enlisted in an attempt to bring gender to bear on psychoanalytic theorization of the ideal. The *idealich* is the repository of infantile narcissism, of the stage of "early perfection" where, according to Freud, what the child "projects before him as his ideal is the substitute for the lost narcissism of his childhood in which he was his own ideal."[21] This preoedipal ideal is first internal and then projected onto exterior objects, whereas the oedipal *ichideal* is the product of parental identification, the result of the internalization of external models and prohibitions. Pressing this distinction further, I would speculate that the ideal of primary narcissism (the *idealich*) is the unacknowledged maternal counterpart of the paternal ideal of the oedipal superego. As Daniel Lagache writes: "The ideal ego viewed as a narcissistic ideal of omnipotence cannot be reduced to the fusion of ego and id, but includes a primary identification with another being, cathected with omnipotence, that is to say the mother."[22] Thus Sand's idealization of her father masks or provides a cover for the gratification of the less valorized form of idealization from which she explicitly disassociates herself, that of the mother's child. When, as we saw earlier, Sand insisted that she did not idealize herself in her fictions and theorized that she should not idealize herself in her autobiography, what she guarded against was not idealization as such but the idealization that redounds to the mother, the regressive form of idealization that refers back to the archaic fusion of mother and child. Much of Sand's oeuvre can be seen as driven by a constant struggle to overcome the pull of the discredited maternal idealization, in favor of the more prestigious paternal.

Before returning to the strict letter of Freudian theories on women and the ideal I want to open the discussion by considering the psychoanalytic theories of a thinker whose case bears fruitful comparison with Sand's, that of Lou Andréas-Salomé, whose extraordinary life, loves, and friendships have fascinated biographers to the same extent as Sand's have. What makes the detour via Salomé so compelling is that on the one hand Salomé was, according to the illuminating account of her "(life)styles" provided by Biddy Martin, a serial idealizer of the men in her life, an optimist given to what Salomé nicely called *Schönfarberei* ("excessive optimism" in Martin's translation),[23] and on the other an important psychoanalytic theoretician of the ideal, arguing contra Freud that in this area, which is to say the area of ethics, daughters, far from being disadvantaged are in fact advantaged "in relation to the father as ideal" (p. 198). However farfetched such a statement might be, I would go so far as to say that had Sand been born at a different time and had she gone to Vienna and met Freud, given what I believe to be her pre-Freudian intuitions of the workings of the unconscious (see chapter 4), she might have produced a theory of women and the ideal something like Salomé's.

Basing herself on her earlier theorizations of narcissism, in her brief but important essay "The Consequences of the Fact that It Was Not a Woman Who Killed the Father" (1928),

> Salomé subtly insists on the often forgotten distinction in Freud's own 1914 narcissism essay between ego ideal and superego, or conscience; Salomé makes conscience the fate of the male and the unpunitive ego ideal the daughter's difference. Woman is less likely to confuse desire with ethics [as do men, who typically love anaclitically according to Freud] and, hence, has greater sobriety in relation to the law. The daughter, Salomé writes, resolves her own tendency to idealize the father through a series of ever more subtle, more refined sublimations without having to murder the father or repress her narcissistic sense of connectedness; therefore, desire and self-assertion coexist more peacefully in her. (p. 220)

Whereas in men ethics are inseparable from the primal murder of the father and always bound up with repressed aggressivity, in women, for whom there is no such founding rupture, ethics is on a continuum with the idealization of the father. Far from being an impediment to female ethics, the idealization of the father is its very bedrock. If daughters are at a disadvantage in relation to the superego, they are privileged in relation to the ego ideal; and if ethics are more firmly grounded in the ego ideal than in the superego, then female ethics are both different in kind from and preferable to male ethics.

Like all the psychoanalytic thinkers who theorized the ideal after Freud, Salomé appropriated and amplified distinctions Freud made between agencies of the ideal (ego ideal/superego, *ichideal/idealich*) to her own ends. And her ends, unlike others', are feminist in that they involve the promotion of an alternative but ultimately more stable access of women to the realm of the law—or rather a more harmonious access to a different law. Yet however brilliant and relevant Salomé's correction of Freud's misogynistic theorization of the formation of ethics, it is only partially satisfying, in that it leaves undisturbed, indeed reinforces the Freudian equation of the ideal and the paternal. It is woman qua father's daughter who in Salomé's theory becomes the agent of the ideal; the mother remains as absent from the scene of the formation of the ethical in Salomé as she is in Freud, serving as nothing more than the invisible ground against which the daughter deploys her idealization of the father.

After this detour, which will have served to indicate just how difficult it is even for so independent a daughter to go beyond Freud and the tradition he represents, let us now return to Freud's texts and explore the other, less secure, but more curious path by which Freud claims women can attain to the ideal enforced by the superego, one that originates in the transmission of a phylogenetic heritage rather than identification. Behind the law-giving father of the individual subject, there lies the originary father of the symbolic, the dead father of the primal horde. And although men, as descendants of the primal horde of brothers, are favored in the anthropological as well as the metapsychological version of the creation of the superego, women, too, can share in the legacy of morality and religion, albeit secondarily: "The male sex seems to have taken the lead in all these moral acquisitions; and they seem to have then been transmitted to women by cross-inheritance."[24]

Transmission returns here, but what is being transmitted has changed: in the Freudian schema what the daughter inherits from the father and only from him are not class privileges as in Taine et al. but the capacity for repression, morality, idealism, in a word: civilization. Troubling questions immediately arise, notably: why invoke Freud at all given the vulgar misogyny of his theory of the ideal, which seems to exist less to explain women's alleged ethical inferiority than to naturalize it? For two reasons: first, because Freud's metapsychological speculations constitute to my knowledge the most sustained reflection on the psychic mechanisms of idealization, as well as one of the most complete accounts of a pervasive and powerful cultural myth of women's alleged ethical inferiority, and, second, because Sand's case both spectacularly confirms and confounds Freudian theories of the formation of the ideal. Let me develop each of these points in turn.

"Ethics," as Denise Riley recently wrote, "has a history,"[25] and what she calls the "implausibility" of women as ethical subjects must be understood as a relatively recent phenomenon whose root cause was identified by Ian Watt when he wrote: "It is very evident that the eighteenth century witnessed a tremendous narrowing of the ethical scale, a redefinition of virtue in primarily sexual terms."[26] The restriction of the ethical to the sexual conjoined with the increasing conflation of the sexual and the feminine, which was on the rise throughout the eighteenth century, resulted in the nineteenth century in the disenfranchisement of women as ethical actors that began (at least) with Hegel and culminated in Freud.[27] Freud's account of women's ethical lack must be viewed as the ultimate product of two centuries of uncoupling of femininity and morality. Indeed one might speak here of a Rousseauist-Freudian continuum, for as Carol Pateman has demonstrated on more than one occasion Freud provided the explanatory system for Rousseau's misogynistic barring of women from civil society:

> No explanation was available of why women are less able than men to sublimate their passions, or how the "special stamp to the character of females as social beings" comes about until Freud formulated his psychoanalytic theory. Rousseau can tell us that men and women differ in this respect—and he prescribes an education for girls that will reinforce their disorderly natures and indifference to justice. . . . Freud argues that the explanation for women's lack of, or deficiency in, a sense of justice is the differential passage of the two sexes through the Oedipus complex and a consequent difference in the developments of their super-ego.[28]

As Pateman also argues, a bizarre feature of the Rousseauist tradition is that in it "women are seen as guardians of order and morality as well as inherently subversive" (p. 25). We are confronted here with yet another turn of the classical paradoxes of the patriarchal order: exiled from the lofty sphere of the ethical, woman is nevertheless condemned to represent and reproduce the ideal. I come now to my second point.

The fit between the particularities of George Sand's case and Freud's theories is, as I and other critics have repeatedly noted, uncannily close; it is nevertheless not airtight. I want now to sketch out what I see as Sand's third and in Freudian terms deviant path to the ideal, a path that calls into question the supposedly essential relationship between the paternal and the ideal and the exclusion of women from the highest spheres of the ethical it serves to legitimate. For if Sand deidealizes her own biological mother, making her an unfit parent of idealization, this deidealization does not apply to all maternal, all female imagoes in her life.

Thus, in the convent where she is sent to be educated, Sand finds what she had so sorely lacked in her childhood, *an ideal or idealizable mother, a fit mother for her idealism*. Speaking of Mother Marie Alicia, the mother she adopts, Sand explains:

> I needed a wise mother. . . .
>
> I needed someone to cherish and place in my thoughts above all other beings; to imagine perfection, tranquility, power, and fairness through that being; to venerate an object superior to me, and to give heartfelt, assiduous worship to something like God. . . . This something took on the features of Marie-Alicia. She was my ideal, my holy love, my chosen mother. (p. 679/1:924, 925)

If we have learned anything from Lacan, it is that biological paternity does not prevail in the realm of the symbolic. Sand's autobiography suggests that a similar but much, much more difficult debiologization is called for in regard to the maternal instance: *the mother of the ideal need not, indeed most likely can never be the biological mother*. Because of the intractability of the mother-child link—"*mater semper certissima est*" (or in Sand's own words: "We are attached to the entrails of the one who gave birth to us")—the birth mother is not, as we saw earlier, readily available for idealization and becomes instead a target for lowering. What Sand's autobiography demonstrates is that this fact of life need not affect the mother as a sponsor of idealism: the mother of the ideal is the adoptive mother.[29]

II

Feminist criticism and theory have been to a remarkable and entirely understandable degree obsessed with the mother: her relationship to her children, but especially her daughter, her relationship to the text, her erotic body, and her reproductive rights. Yet despite feminism's founding insistence on separating the socially constructed from the biologically determined, despite recent advances in reproductive technologies that have dramatically reconfigured traditional notions of maternity and paternity, the figure of the mother has remained largely impervious to the trend toward deessentialization: embodied maternity continues to be conterminous with the maternal. Though twice a biological mother herself, for Sand, the best mother is rarely the birth mother but instead the adoptive mother in a variety of guises: from the idealized nuns she loved in her adolescence to the maternal lover that she became in her maturity. Certainly the most explicit and also the best-known fictional thematization of Sand's idealization of the adoptive mother is *François le champi* (*The Country Waif*), where under the cover of a foster relationship, the son is enabled to marry the (adoptive) mother without guilt or retribution.

I want to suggest that *François le champi*, like *Histoire de ma vie*, is only the most spectacular instance of the slow, indeed lifelong elaboration of Sand's most enduringly successful fictional creation, one that goes beyond the persona created through the parental identifications of her autobiography and that cannot be located in any particular text. I am speaking of her truly astonishing transformation of herself from an object of scandal into the supreme figure of propriety, the good mother par excellence, the popular public persona and cultural artifact that came to be known as the "Bonne Dame de Nohant."

Although it is impossible to date this transformation with any precision, based on contemporary evidence it seems to have been completed in the mid-1850s, which is to say that it coincides with the publication of Sand's autobiography (1854–55). Thus, in his *George Sand*, published in 1854 in the popular "Les Contemporains" series, Eugène de Mirecourt describes the "patriarchal" life Sand leads at Nohant in the following quasi-religious terms:

She greets affectionately the village folk who surround her, receives them at her table, listens to them, encourages them, comforts them in their sorrows, their illnesses, and gives them remedies for themselves and their children. They look to her as to a saviour always certain of being succored.

An old woman covered with a sort of leprosy came one day to ask for her aid.

—Look, my good lady, she said, pulling at her rags, you don't disgust me: see what a state I am in.

Madame Sand had a room in her chateau opened, led the poor woman there, dressed her sores herself, and took care of her until she was completely cured.

Such a deed needs no comment; it is a page out of the Gospel.[30]

Interestingly, this literal canonization of Sand—the image of Sand in her chateau tending the leper's sores plays on two registers, the religious, obviously, but also the patriotic, recalling as it does the founding French myth of patriarchal goodness, Saint-Louis's hands-on cure of the scrofulous on the day of his coronation—goes hand in hand with the rejection of her utopian politics, for Mirecourt is careful to offset the hagiographic celebration of Sand's noblesse oblige with a critical repudiation of Sand's revolutionary belief in progress.

When I first began to work on Sand, I felt an almost missionary zeal about rescuing her from the grip of the army of adoring biographers who had despite their devotion kept the Sand legend alive by participating in the erasure of her achievements as a writer. Now, as I near the end of my book, I have come to recognize that ultimately any good reader of Sand's fiction must confront and come to terms with the Sand of Masterpiece Theater, Nohant, and competing films about the Sand-Chopin affair. In the time—admittedly lengthy—it has taken me to bring this book to its conclusion, two new films loosely based on different moments in that episode in Sand's love life, James Lapine's *Impromptu* and Andrzej Zulawski's *La Note bleue*, have appeared to mixed reviews, and no fewer than four highly romanticized biographical studies have been published in France, some to much fanfare: Huguette Bouchardeau's *George Sand: La Lune et les sabots* (1990), Jean Chalon's *Chère George Sand* (1991), Jacques-Louis Donchin's *George Sand, l'amoureuse* (1992), and the latest entry into a field that shows no signs of being saturated, Yves Monin's *George Sand: Troubadour de l'éternel vérité* (1992). Nor is the ongoing commodification of the Sand legend restricted to the more conventional mass cultural modes of biographies, made-for-TV bio serials, films, or the upscale Sand china plate settings edited several years ago by Christofle (the botanical motif of the original Nohant china competing head on with the stunning yellow and blue geometrics

FIGURE 10.

Edward Frascino, "George Sand Has Some People in for Drinks." *The New Yorker.* For the sophisticated American reader, cartoon representation (or being named in the annual Yule poem) in *The New Yorker* represents the ne plus ultra of cultural iconicity. Both Chopin and Sand's stellar guests at Nohant (e.g., Delacroix, Lizst, Balzac) are diminished here by their Americanization, not to say suburbanization: Frederic becomes Freddy, George is stuffed into what looks to be a costume, the guests hold what appear to be martini glasses in their hands, transforming the entire event into a very anachronistic cocktail party.

FIGURE II.

Notorious Woman. BBC. The Sand-Chopin affair is a central component of the Sand legend, and visual representations of the couple in close proximity to a piano are a topos of the Sand filmography. In 1974, at the height of the feminist movement, the BBC produced a serialized biopic on Sand's life *Notorious Woman,* which was aired soon after on America's equivalent to the BBC, the Public Broadcasting System. In this version of the piano scene, Sand (Rosemary Harris), is in the dominant position, her attitude protective. The emphasis is on her silent strength rather than his tormented artistry. Chopin is played by George Chakiris (of *West Side Story* fame!). One can measure what a long way we have come by comparing this scene to the one in *Impromptu* where Sand lies literally at Chopin's feet, under the piano, enraptured by his genius.

Monet designed for Giverny); it has now been extended to geographical mapping, as the sleepy Vallée Noire Sand did so much to promote, not to say invent, is in the process of being packaged as a "parc romantique" for cultural tourists.

Rather than deploring this popularization of the Sand legend—as almost all serious Sand scholars are wont to do—it is my sense that our increasingly nuanced sense of the cultural field in which a writer deploys her activities has made it possible, if not imperative, to devise a reading strategy that will further our understanding of how the author of *Lélia* became the "Bonne Dame de Nohant," of how Sand's family romance became both the wellspring of her quickly forgotten fiction and the source of her lasting enshrinement as a cultural icon.

For me that reading strategy has consisted in the retrieval and rethinking of the category of idealist fiction whose canceling out by realism coincided with the decanonization of its most significant French practitioner, George Sand. Charting the rise and the fall of the idealist novel, which parallels Sand's literary fortunes, has led me almost inevitably to reconsider the relationship between the author's life and her fictions and to conclude at least tentatively that for Sand idealism came in time to be more than an aesthetics, more than a politics—it became a way of life, indeed of afterlife. And yet the posthumous Sand legend has fastened less on the self-fashioned image of the benevolent chatelaine and doting grandmother—Sand is always represented as a young woman or, more popularly, as a young dandy—than on the scandalous lover of a sickly genius. Replacing Sand in the canon must then be a two-pronged effort, involving on the one hand the exhumation and revalorization of her idealist counterdiscourse and, on the other, the deidealization of the legendary subject of autobiography and biography, for whether portrayed as "la Bonne Dame de Nohant" congenial to Third Republic morality or the cigarette-smoking, cross-dressed liberated woman for our times, as a cultural icon Sand is idealized. Given Sand's particular profile, it is not enough as in the case of other marginally canonical figures simply to craft a revisionist poetics of reading in order to endow her writings with legitimacy. To make sense of the fused texts of her fiction and her life, what is demanded is a joining of the proven insights of poetics with those promised by cultural studies.

Living

On:

Flaubert's

Idealism

Idéal: Tout à fait inutile.
Flaubert, *Dictionnaire des idées reçues*

At George Sand's funeral on June 10, 1876, Gustave Flaubert, whom Sand addressed fondly in their remarkable thirteen-year correspondence as her "vieux troubadour" (old troubadour) wept "like a calf."[1] His deep grief over the loss of his beloved "chère maître" (dear master) was made all the more poignant by its timing, in the midst of his work on a tale Flaubert claimed to have written expressly for Sand, just as some years earlier he had undertaken *L'Education sentimentale* for Sainte-Beuve: "How I miss her! How I need her! I began *A Simple Heart* exclusively for her, solely to please her. She died when I was in the middle of my work. So it is with all our dreams."[2] During the dark year 1875–76, when Flaubert struggled against the depression brought on by his diminished financial and literary prospects, Sand had given him a crucial piece of advice: "Write something more down to earth that everybody can enjoy."[3] That something was to be *Un Coeur simple*.

Much of the critical debate over this most enduringly popular of all Flaubert's writings has focused on the problematic status of irony in a tale that constantly strains toward pathos. In keeping with its intended receiver, Flaubert defended his text against the ironical reading: "This is not at all ironical as you may suppose," he writes to Mme des Genettes, "but on the contrary very serious and very sad. I want to move tender hearts to pity and tears, for I am tender-hearted myself."[4] Nevertheless, despite Flaubert, the ironical reading has, with some rare exceptions, prevailed, simultaneously obscuring the tale's pathos and Flaubert's debt to Sand. In what follows I want to consider what it might mean to read *Un Coeur simple* bearing in mind its structure of address. My concern in twofold: On the one hand, to show how reading Flaubert *with* Sand might inflect our interpretation of this "overread" (N. Miller) text. On the other, to show how at the very moment when Sand's idealism was about to be expunged from literary history, some vestige of it, some trace of it survived to become enshrined in the canon, but encrypted in the writing of a French male writer, whose own idealism has never received its due. To read Flaubert *with* Sand is to be led inevitably to reconsider Flaubertian idealism. In thinking about the posterity of Sandian idealism, which at the end of the nineteenth century and the beginning of the twentieth appears to be exclusively male, we will need to be exceedingly attentive to the tension between various strains of idealism, to the ways in which in the works of writers such as Flaubert and Proust Sand's antirealist, feminist, utopian, and narcissistic idealism comes into contact with, nourishes, and is eventually supplanted by other forms of idealism and notably an aesthetic idealism in which she does not share.

I

What would it mean to read *Un Coeur simple* in the light of Flaubert's debt to Sand? What is a structure of address, and how does it differ from what was once called the study of influence? Influence comports, as we know, a complex choreography of power; to be influenced is in a traditional male rendition of literary history to be placed in a submissive position in relation to a dominant, more potent literary partner.[5] To speak of coming *under* someone's influence is more than a figure of speech, as influence always implies a master and a disciple, a predecessor and a follower, a top and a bottom, an activity and a passivity. It is this sadomasochistic scenario that most expert readers of *Un Coeur simple* vigorously reject, not so much because it implies a hierarchy but because the hierarchy it implies—Sand *over* Flaubert—appears unnatural, wildly out of line with the received system of values of the French canon.[6] The three pages the author of the preface to a recent edition of the Flaubert-Sand correspondence devotes to this vexed question exemplify the lengths to which critics will go to contest the notion that Sand might have in any manner "influenced" the author of *Un Coeur simple*. At first the prefacer seems evenhanded in his argument against influence, refuting with equal assurance any suspicion that Sand was influenced by Flaubert (that she renounced her idealism in favor of a Flaubertian realism) and, conversely, Flaubert by Sand:

> Fundamentally, her position will not change from 1866 to 1876. She will never adopt either the techniques, or the style, or the aesthetic and social ideas of Flaubert. . . .
>
> The same is true for Flaubert. The vigorous protestations he addressed to his friend in 1876 are identical to those of 10 years previous—down to the terms enlisted.[7]

The neat symmetry of the mutual noninfluence of Sand and Flaubert is, however, but a smoke screen for what is in fact the main thrust of the discussion: Sand's supposed influence on the writing of *Un Coeur simple*: "It has often been suggested, texts in hand, that the sweet and tender figure of Félicité (in *Un coeur simple*) was conceived under the influence of George Sand" (p. 11). These suggestions are, Jacobs then sets about demonstrating, both misinformed and mystified. Misinformed, because they do not take into account Flaubert's biographical circumstances at the time he undertook to write *Un Coeur simple*, circumstances that have a great deal more to do with the tale's genesis than any part Sand might have played in the project, despite what Flaubert says in his celebrated letter to Sand of May 29, 1876: "You will see from my *Story of a Simple Heart* (*in which you will recognize your own direct influence*) that I am not so stubborn as you believe. I think you will like the moral tendency, or rather the underlying humanity, of this little work."[8] According to Jacobs, this *"texte à l'appui"* is in fact an afterthought; the Sandian influence acknowledged by Flaubert is a post facto fabrication designed to please his dear friend: "And it is only belatedly, after having a firm outline and having written the first part of his text, that he realizes the pleasure reading his tender story will provide his 'chère maître' " (p. 12). And this brings us to Jacobs's second point: the proponents of a Sandian influence are also mystified, because they do not factor in Flaubert's penchant for self-aggrandizement. When Flaubert in the equally celebrated letter of August 29, 1877, (cited above) addressed to Maurice Sand after his mother's death claims to have written *Un Coeur simple* exclusively for Sand, one must recognize a characteristic instance of Flaubert's tendency to flatter or impress his interlocutors:

> Did he not also say that *L'Education sentimentale* had been written "for" Sainte-Beuve? Flaubert's sincerity, especially when he wants to "impress" or please his correspondent, is a complex problem, and his naive mania of always amplifying, always exaggerating, is well known. . . . The passage in question, which was obviously written to underscore in the eyes of the son the depth of his friendship for the mother, is according to us one of the most typical specimens of this mania. It would be dangerous to take it literally. (p. 12)

The conclusion is thus inevitable: "It seems unquestionable to us that Flaubert, had he never known George Sand, would have written his short story anyhow and the 'moral tendency' and 'human side' of the work would not have been any different" (p. 12). QED. In the context of another reading of *Un Coeur simple*, about which I shall have more to say below, Raymonde Debray-Genette ironically defends the same conclusion. Taking issue with those who see in *Un Coeur simple* a variant of the servant novel, Debray-Genette writes: "Such was never Flaubert's intention, even if he claimed to 'be down to earth' and to show *his good George Sand*, who had died too soon to read it, that he could write with a heart that was pure, if not simple."[9]

What these strenuous denials of Sand's influence on Flaubert point to is not just the threat such an influence poses to entrenched hierarchies of value; they also emphasize the necessity to rethink issues of influence, and not merely in terms of opposing a nonconflictual relationship between women writers to the titanic oedipal struggles between men, as was the case at an earlier stage of feminist criticism.[10] What I am calling for here is a more nuanced, more painstaking, and surely messier mapping of the complex field of intersubjectivity that would begin to account for the subtle, intricate exchanges that take place in a long-term and largely epistolary relationship such as Sand and Flaubert's. Such a mapping would of necessity entail a special sensitivity to and a suspicion of the linguistic medium of these exchanges, bearing in mind Flaubert's own awareness of the ways in which language functions as a means of both distorting (through metaphor) and facilitating (through clichés) communication.[11] Between two subjects engaged in the heightened form of communication that is love and/or friendship—and as we shall see Sand and Flaubert's relationship hovered on that obscure border—language is always opaque, a means of self-idealization, a locus of misfires and misunderstandings. Of Léon's and Emma's first meeting in Rouen, Flaubert writes: "This was how they would have wished to be, each setting up an ideal to which they were now trying to adapt their past life. Besides, speech is like a rolling machine that always stretches the sentiment it expresses."[12]

II

As a necessary preliminary to reading Flaubert *with* Sand, we need to consider their full correspondence (and not just the circumstances of Flaubert's biography) as the context of the writing of *Un Coeur simple*, the text that may or may not have been written *for* Sand, in all the multiple meanings that one may attach to this preposition—*for* but also *in lieu of*.[13] And we need at the same time to recognize that this correspondence is an artificial construct when isolated as a circumscribed text from the still wider context of both authors' general correspondences. Ideally, any reading of the Sand-Flaubert correspondence would have to situate it in relation to the multiple correspondences each had with other correspondents.[14] Since such a vast undertaking clearly exceeds the scope of this chapter, I shall frame my reading of the Sand-Flaubert letters by looking at Flaubert's correspondence with another older woman, the provincial *femme de lettres*, Mlle Leroyer de Chantepie, whom Flaubert never saw but with whom he carried on an extraordinary epistolary exchange that ended only with his death. Mlle de Chantepie's misprision on receiving her very first letter from Flaubert—an answer to a fan letter she had written him regarding the then-serialized *Madame Bovary*—is of particular interest to me: "At first I thought your letter came from George Sand, because your way of writing certain letters is deceptively similar; the author of *Lélia* has sometimes done me the honor of writing me."[15]

Well before the beginning of the Sand-Flaubert relationship, that famously puzzling connection was prefigured by Mlle de Chantepie's mistaking the one's handwriting for the other's. A voracious and well-informed reader of contemporary literature and philosophy, Mlle de Chantepie never stops talking to Flaubert about Sand and linking through her admiration the authors of her two favorite books, as though in her mind there existed a sort of affinity, a secret kinship between the two that is made manifest by an uncanny graphological resemblance. What is more, nothing in Mlle de Chantepie's letters suggests that this connection was in any way daring, bizarre; clearly, for her there was no incompatibility in her double identification: she felt herself to be a kindred spirit of Flaubert's on the one hand and a sort of sisterly double of Sand's on the other.

The Chantepie-Flaubert correspondence gives the lie to a hardy myth that the Sand-Flaubert relationship was somehow unnatural or at any rate would have been perceived as such in the context of the nineteenth-century literary scene. To take account of the insight Mlle de Chantepie offers us into this extraordinary relationship, we will have to be acutely sensitive to the subtle ways in which Sand's and Flaubert's characters, desires, fantasies interlock.

Unquestionably, as many have noted, Sand and Flaubert form the oddest of literary couples: on the one hand a writer celebrated for her prolixity, on the other hand a legendary perfectionist; on the one hand the good lady of Nohant, author of classics of children's literature, on the other hand the hermit of Croisset, the precursor of modernism and postmodernism. The oppositions between Sand and Flaubert are not merely anecdotal, superimposed on the correspondence; to read their correspondence is to become aware that it rests precisely and very explicitly on a series of homologous oppositions, which can be arrayed as follows:

he is alone/she is surrounded by her loved ones
he lives for literature only/she lives only for others
he hates nature/she loves nature
he neglects his body/she lives a healthy life
he hates the bourgeoisie/she loves humanity
he has money problems/she is comfortable

The entire series of oppositions could be reduced to that of two places, two metonyms: Croisset versus Nohant, the hermitage versus the community. Or, if we press the reduction a little further, the fundamental opposition at work here is that between pathology and health, and that opposition is aligned with and secured by the opposition between celibacy and family. A debate that in the latter half of the nineteenth century divided the bourgeoisie against itself lies at the heart of this correspondence: that between celibacy—especially male—and familialism. Against Sand, especially the grandmotherly Sand of the later years—after the great cut-off constituted by the events of 1870–71—Flaubert, the unhappy uncle, represents the dysphoric discourse of the bachelor.

And yet, as their correspondence demonstrates, their differences—and they are not exhausted by the differences in their familial circumstances— enabled and enlivened their dialogue, rather than impeding it. On more than one occasion Sand articulated the benefits to be derived from friends, and especially from writers, whose aesthetics and writing practices are radically opposed. Implicit in these statements is *a theory of the formation of the writerly ego* that accords a special privilege to the complementary processes of expulsion and absorption, differentiation and identification, and that theory singularly complicates our understanding of the Sand-Flaubert relationship. Thus in an early letter Sand writes Flaubert:

> Bring the copy. Put in it all the criticisms which occur to you. That will be very good for me. People ought to do that for each other as Balzac and I used to do. That doesn't make one person alter the other; quite the contrary, for in general, one gets more determined in one's *moi*, one completes it, explains it better, entirely develops it, and that is why friendship is good, even in literature, where the first condition of any worth is to be one's self.[16]

We are here very far from the common notions of influence, where the effect of one writer on another is viewed as overwhelming, invasive, humiliating, where the possible interaction between two creative subjects is reduced to unilateral and univocal power plays. What Sand is suggesting is the very opposite of the anxiety of influence—that is, *a positive and beneficial reinforcement of each author's singularity in the encounter and negotiation between contending equals*. In contrast with a parental Freudian model of literary influence, what we have here is a model of brotherly or sisterly literary exchange. But more is at stake than a reciprocal egotistical enhancement of each individual author; the authorly ego is formed not only by distinguishing self from nonself, from Other, but at the same time by a process of taking into itself aspects of the Other with which one identifies, in which one is lacking:

> We are, I think, the two most different workers that exist; but since we like each other that way, it is all right. The reason each of us thinks of the other at the same hour, is because each of us has a need of his opposite; we complete ourselves, in identifying ourselves at times with what is not ourselves.[17]

There are then two complementary mechanisms at work in this relationship between opposites: on the one hand a reinforcement of each partner's singularity, on the other an absorption of the other's alterity.[18] Though both modalities of intersubjectivity coexist at all times, identification might be said to be the ground of differentiation.

The relationship between Sand and Flaubert was not simply that of two writers but that of two subjects—two differently gendered subjects at that—and those two factors must be brought into play in order to make sense of that relationship. Indeed, beyond or beneath the theorization of the relationship between two antithetical writerly sensibilities, there is another theory—and it is always Sand who does the theorizing here—which is quite simply a theory of friendship or, to be more precise, of friendship in maturity. And this theory repeats while at the same time subtly displacing the terms of the first. What distinguishes mature from youthful friendship is the absolute respect for the other's alterity that is the mark of wisdom. Outgrown is the aggressivity of the formative mirror stage, transcended are the struggles for prestige and power of the master/slave dialectic, abandoned is the quest for perfect reciprocity. In order to express this new concept of friendship Sand spins out a lovely neoclassical allegory that emphasizes the analogy between friendship and aesthetic appreciation; in both instances what is prized is disinterestedness, and this disinterestedness goes hand in hand with a decathecting of the ego, a sort of hemorrhaging of the self:

> One gets, being old . . . a new idea of everything and of affection above all.
>
> In the age of power and of personality, one tests one's friends as one tests the earth, from the point of view of reciprocity. One feels oneself solid, one wants to find that which bears one or leads one, solid. But, when one feels the intensity of the *moi* fleeing, one loves persons and things for what they are in themselves, for what they represent in the eyes of one's soul, and not at all for what they add further to one's destiny. It is like the picture or the statue which one would like to own, when one dreams at the same time of a beautiful house of one's own in which to put it.
>
> But one has passed through green Bohemia without gathering anything there; one has remained poor, sentimental and troubadourish. One knows very well that it will always be the same, and that one will die without a hearth or a home. Then one thinks of the statue, of the picture which one would not know what to do with and which one would not know where to place with due honor, if one owned it. One is content to know that they are in some temple not profaned by cold analysis, a little far from the eye, and one loves them so much the more. One says: I will go again to the country where they are. I shall see again and I shall love always that which has made me love and understand them. The contact of my personality will not have changed them, it will not be myself that I shall love in them.
>
> And it is thus, truly, that the ideal which one does not dream of grasping, fixes itself in one because it remains *itself*. That is all the secret of the beautiful, of the only truth, of love, of friendship, of art, of enthusiasm, and of faith.[19]

Whereas in the theory of writerly intersubjectivity there is room for two egos of equal power, and thus the possibility of the introjection of the attractive traits of the other, in the theory of mature friendship, there is a conjoined renunciation of specularity and egocentrism. To detach oneself from the other, to give up on possessing him or her necessarily entails a loss of narcissism. No longer taking oneself for a god, one no longer tries to shut up the Other in a private temple where, under the cover of idealizing the Other, the real religion one practices is the cult of the self.

We come here then to what we may term *the end of idealism* or at any rate the vanishing point of idealization, and this may be the moment to sum up what we may term *the four modalities of idealization in Sand,* which do seem to correspond at least loosely to developmental stages. They are:

Maternal Idealism. This is by far the most prevalent and most negatively valorized form of idealism, the one connoted as regressive, even pathological. What I am calling "maternal idealism" is the fusional model of idealism that manifests itself most acutely in the sphere of eroticism: the maternal idealist idealizes the love object and longs to merge with it. This idealist (incestuous) desire for union is maternal in that it is motivated by the desire to recover the original mother-child bond (or rather a fantasy of that bond), to be once again one with a completely receptive and nurturing specular other. Maternal idealism is the idealism of the imaginary, of primary narcissism, and, if satisfied—which (should I say happily?) it almost never is or for very long—it can be lethal. The idealism identified with the mother is the discredited idealism inherent in the literature of romance.

Fraternal Idealism. This is the most optimistic, most luminous, but also most vulnerable form of idealism, the one that is often described as naive. In this instance the idealist attempts to organize society along the lines of an idealized fraternal relationship, one fantasied as impervious to the drives of possessive individualism. Fraternal idealism is in its most euphoric and inspiring form an ideal of community that transcends the bounds of the personal, the subjective; it is the idealism inherent in early forms of communism and running through much nineteenth-century French utopian social thought. At best fraternal idealism is the most political, the most revolutionary form of idealism; at worst it is the most phallocentric. If maternal idealism is deadly because it entails a loss of self, fraternal idealism is doomed because it hampers individuation and denies sexual difference and the conflict of desires.

Paternal Idealism. This is, not surprisingly, the most prestigious and the most enabling form of idealism, the one identified with the highest forms of human achievement. Unlike maternal idealism, which is coextensive with the imaginary, paternal idealism deploys itself, indeed merges seamlessly with the realm of the symbolic; it is paternal in that it is informed by theories of paternity that insistently link the paternal with the ideal (*eidos*, the superego). The paternal idealist seeks not to lose himself in the idealized Other but rather to introject his (or her) qualities. Paternal idealism gratifies narcissism but does so in a way that enhances the narcissist instead of diminishing him. Pushed to the extreme the paternal idealist does not seek to fuse with the Other (let alone share with him, as in the case of fraternal idealism) but to become in turn an ideal for others. Paternal idealism is the idealism of those that set themselves up as models for others (autobiographers), of writers who also view themselves as leaders (poet-magi, writers *engagés*).

Amical Idealism. Perhaps because it is not modeled on a familial relationship (however, as in the case of the ideal father, disembodied), this form of idealism is, when achieved, the supreme form. But its manifestations are exceedingly rare and precarious, because they are always in danger of collapsing back into the familial. In the amical mode of idealism, one neither fuses with, nor shares with, nor emulates, nor seeks to change the Other, but asymptotically approaches what may well be the end point of idealism: a renunciation of the exaltation of the self and an aesthetic delight in the other's alterity. In the amical mode one continues nonetheless to idealize both self and Other, but in this instance the Other becomes the prized means for enhancing one's individuality within an economy of caring and complicity. In amical idealism we are confronted with the irreducible measure of idealism—idealization of the self and the Other—that pervades all forms of subjectivity and intersubjectivity. Idealism in this mode is revealed to be an integral aspect of symbolization; to be in language is to be in idealism.

Obviously the four types of idealism I have just teased out of my reading of Sand are themselves idealized, and they are gender neutral. And yet at every stage, including the final one, gender inflects intersubjectivity. This brings us to the extremely delicate issue of the play of sexual difference in the Sand-Flaubert correspondence.

What can be asserted at the outset is that this correspondence tends to situate itself beyond sexual difference; the differentiation between ego and Other is not in this particular instance gendered or, to be more precise, gendered in any stable way. It is around issues of gender that the oppositional structure appears most reductive, least adequate. Because of her age—"I am old," writes Sand to Flaubert in the inaugural letter of their correspondence (January 28, 1863)[20]—Sand immediately locates her discourse in a state of post-femininity. For Sand, femininity is bound up with nubility and not with the possession of specific sexual organs.

To paraphrase Simone de Beauvoir's celebrated formula, for Sand, as for many of her contemporaries, not only is one not born a woman but one does not remain one: "Now that I am no longer a woman, if God were just I would become a man. I would have physical strength and I would say: let's go on a trip to Carthage or elsewhere. But we are heading toward infancy, which has neither sex nor energy."[21]

Flaubert shares this notion of gender as age-specific. When Mlle de Chantepie tells him her age—she is fifty-seven years old when she first writes him—he answers with obvious relief: "Let me first thank you for having told me your age. That puts me more at ease. We will chat together like two men."[22] But, one might well object, neither of these statements really signals a transcending of sexual difference; rather, they both constitute a reaffirmation of male superiority, not to say of woman's inexistence: gender is not so much transcended as negated. This interpretation seems to be confirmed by this surprising declaration by Sand:

> And still further, there is this for those strong in anatomy: *there is only one sex*. A man and a woman are so entirely the same thing, that one hardly understands the mass of distinctions and of subtle reasons with which society is nourished concerning this subject. I have observed the infancy and the development of my son and my daughter. My son was myself, therefore much more woman, than my daughter, who was an imperfect man.[23]

If one unpacks this passage, one finds in it a curious combination of the radical and the conventional. Unlike late-twentieth-century sexual rebels who "bend" gender by refusing not so much anatomical destiny as binary models of thinking, who promote multiple differences, Sand couples the bold rejection of the anatomical ground of gender difference with the tame assertion of a single, undifferentiated sex, although just exactly what sex she does not really say. It would appear that the single sex she has in mind is on the order of the androgyne. Single sex does not mean equality of the sexes: according to Sand, the masculine daughter loses out on both counts, whereas the son adds the prestige of the maternal heritage to the privileges of masculinity. What is more, Sand's sexism is also a heterosexism: when she speaks of her son's femininity and her daughter's failed masculinity, she is closer to the "trapped soul paradigm" of late-nineteenth-century discourse on homosexuality than to a contem-

FIGURE 12.

Photograph of George Sand, Paul Nadar. Bibliothèque Nationale. In the abundant Sand iconography, which includes many well-known photographs by Félix Nadar, this image by his son Paul of the aging Sand stands out. Whereas the only prop to be found in Félix Nadar's widely reproduced frontal portraits is an enigmatic regal wig, Paul Nadar has posed his famous subject standing full length against the conventional artificial, idealized landscape of the early photographer's studio, Whereas Félix's full-face, close-up portraits of Sand are outstanding examples of vivid, psychologically complex realist portraiture, Paul's remote, abstracted view makes manifest the deadliness that lurks in idealist representation.

porary understanding of the inadequacies of a theory of sexual identity rooted in a heterosexual norm.[24]

If, as Martine Reid argues, misogyny (as well as heterosexism) underlies Sand and Flaubert's complicity, one must not therefore conclude that sexual difference is absent from either their relationship or their correspondence. For if Sand is a transsexual, Flaubert, for his part, describes himself as a hysteric and thus a hermaphrodite: "I believe that men are hysterics, just like women, and I am one. . . . I am of both sexes."[25] If according to both Sand and Flaubert age deprives women of their femininity, according to Flaubert it enhances men's: "I was drier, harsher, twenty years ago than I am today. I've been feminized and softened by wear and tear—which harden other people."[26]

But there is more: the Sand-Flaubert relationship resembles neither the asexual relationship Flaubert had with Mlle de Chantepie nor especially that of Sand with her old friend Rollinat: "Rollinat, my double in this life, the veritable friend whose feeling for the differences between the sexes had never hurt our pure affection."[27]

Sand's "perfect" friendship with Rollinat became in time for her the very paradigm of the nonsexual male-female relationship and provides an excellent foil for her friendship with Flaubert. The important pages Sand devotes to Rollinat in *Histoire de ma vie* are the occasion for her to make explicit her ideas on the possibility of intersexual platonic friendships and, by the same gesture, to take issue with the misogyny that underlies women's exclusion from the Western literature of friendship. For, as she discovers early on from her reading of Montaigne, who both exalts his friendship with La Boétie and declares women congenitally unfit for friendship, there is a crucial link between the incapacity for amical idealism and the "moral inferiority" attributed to women "in every reading of philosophical teachings, even in religious books."[28] Indeed, as Sand understands Montaigne to be saying, the capacity for amical idealism is the royal road to philosophy. To be barred from one is to be barred from the other; to claim equal rights to the highest form of intersubjectivity is to claim equal access to the highest form of intellectual activity. And in order to gain access to these supreme forms of idealism—friendship (with a man) and philosophy—Sand is, typically, willing to concede that there exists an essential difference between men and women, a certain essentialism being for her the gauge of recognition as an ethical and intellectual subject:

> That woman may differ from man, that the heart and mind answer to a sex, I do not doubt. . . . But must this difference, essential for the harmony of things and the noblest enticements of love, constitute a moral inferiority? . . . I did not see why Philosophy was too great a lady to grant us equality in her esteem, just as God grants us equality in His promises of heaven. (pp. 899–900/2:127)

Sand's aspiration to be part of the society of brothers—which is to say, a philosophical fraternity—culminates in her double fantasy both of playing La Boétie to Montaigne's Montaigne and of reenacting with Rollinat that legendary virile friendship: "Thus, I was going along nourishing a dream of male virtue to which women could aspire . . . and I wondered why Montaigne would not have liked and respected me as much as a brother, as much as La Boétie" (p. 899/2:127–28). "Rollinat never preached to me except by example. . . . With him and for him I formed a code of true and sound friendship, a friendship not unlike Montaigne's conception, wholly by choice, wholly selective and perfect" (p. 901/2:129).

But Flaubert was not Rollinat, the perfect friend of a lifetime.[29] However problematic Sand and Flaubert's attempt to locate their relationship beyond gender, there is no doubt that sexual difference is constantly at work in their relationship. If their correspondence constitutes an exemplary attempt at carving out an intersubjective arena where sexual identity is shifting, mobile, severed from anatomy, unhampered by social norms, it is also true that sexuality is not absent from this relationship where friendship becomes indistinguishable from love, if that opposition means anything at all. Castration, it might be said, is the hidden pivot on which this correspondence turns. This is particularly true in the case of Flaubert's address to Sand. There is an extraordinary instability in his gendering of his correspondent; in fact, she unites all the attributes he finds attractive—she is both man and woman, friend and mother. Hence his feelings for her are unique, unclassifiable: "What constellation were you born under, to be endowed with so many qualities, so diverse and so rare? I don't know what to call the feeling I have for you; it's a very *particular* kind of affection, such as I have never felt for anyone until now."[30] "I dislike eating alone. I have to associate someone or the idea of someone with the things that give me pleasure. But that someone is rare. I, too, ask myself why I love you. Is it because you are a great man or a 'charming human being'? I have no idea. What is certain is that for you I have a *particular* feeling, one I cannot define" (2:101/p. 122).

There is a real lovers' discourse in this correspondence, and it is coiled up in the sharpest exchanges between the two troubadours. Thus, speaking to Flaubert of the "Response to a Friend" provoked by their political disagreements during the Commune, Sand explains the distinction she makes between their private disagreement and the anonymous debate she makes public: "Our real discussions ought to remain between ourselves, like caresses between lovers, and even sweeter, since friendship also has its mysteries without the storms of personality."[31] To which Flaubert responds: "Besides, you can always say everything to me, to me! everything! Your blows will be caresses to me" (p. 228/353). The difference between love and friendship has then nothing to do with the presence or absence of physical contact, with penetration—blows and caresses are exchanged between friends just as they are between lovers— the difference lies rather in the space occupied by what Sand calls so euphemistically "the storms of personality."[32] One may say that there are caresses and blows between friends, but no friction.

Ultimately—for, of course, it is in the nature of a friendship, especially a loving friendship, to evolve over time and in the nature of all human relationships, even those situated in an experimental space, to resolve themselves into familiar, not to say familial patterns—Sand came to occupy consciously and explicitly the place of the mother in Flaubert's affective economy, and this virtually from the moment when to console her "dear heart" on the loss of his mother, Sand writes him: "In short, my poor child, I can only open a maternal heart to you which will replace nothing, but which is suffering with yours."[33] And in the following months Flaubert writes her: "More than ever, I should like to have you now in my poor Croisset, to have you sleep near me, in my mother's room" (p. 253/388; translation modified). Or on another occasion: " 'My poor old mother' loved you very much. It would be sweet to have you here in her house, when she has been gone only such a short time" (p. 252/385). The substitution of Sand for Mme Flaubert rests both on a temporal proximity and a spatial contiguity, on a resemblance and an election. In the end Sand had become a second mother to Flaubert, as evidenced by his famous letter to Maurice after Sand's funeral: "It seemed to me that I was burying my mother the second time" (p. 372/534).

That the Sand-Flaubert relationship ultimately resolved itself into a mother-son relationship is, of course, not news; what is perhaps less often noted is that this oedipal scenario is complicated by the fact that Sand already had a son, and one close in age to Flaubert. The Flaubert-Sand relationship is then doubled and made more problematic by the Flaubert-Maurice relationship within which Maurice becomes another opposite against whom Flaubert measures himself and whom he envies, first because Sand is his mother and second because Maurice has a family. In some sense it might be said that Flaubert displaces his envy of Sand onto her son: "How I envy your son. What a nice, regular, healthy life he has";[34] "Maurice seems to me to be the type of human happiness. What does he lack? Certainly, he is no more envied by anyone than by me."[35] "Maurice is right. He has arranged his life well. If only I had done the same."[36]

It is then against this complex set of relations—here only sketched—that we must read the aesthetic debate that runs throughout the correspondence and that reaches a crescendo in its final phase. We must first note that in keeping with Sand's need for an Other against which to define and reinforce her singularity, Flaubert came to occupy the place and function of Balzac. Just as in her beginnings as a writer she had defined herself through a series of binary oppositions with Balzac, so in her final years she reaffirmed her singularity vis-à-vis Flaubert. The Flaubert-Sand rehearsal of the realism/idealism debate is but a repeat of the earlier dialogue. Yet there is another level of resonance and repetition, because at the same time that the Flaubert-Sand debate echoes that between Sand and Balzac it also recalls Flaubert's dialogue with Louise Colet, which is also informed by a gendered axis of competing aesthetics.

Sand's debate with Flaubert even echoes, at a distance of nearly half a century, the very terms of her debate with Balzac, the friend and model of her youth. Flaubert writes to Sand: "You, always, in whatever you do, begin with a great leap toward heaven, and then you return to earth. You start from the *a priori*, from theory, from the ideal. . . . I, poor wretch, remain glued to the earth, as though the soles of my shoes were made of lead: everything moves me, everything lacerates and ravages me, and I make every effort to soar."[37] Flaubert's apparent and "feminine" humility contrast sharply with Balzac's condescending and phallocentric assertions (see chapter 1), but the terms of the opposition remain the same. Flaubert's "inferiority" is coded as a failure of aerodynamics, an inability to take off, that contrasts with Sand's instantly airborne elevation above the piercing circumstances of the real.

But the heart of their difference turns on the issue of morality and its place in literature; it is on that issue Sand and Flaubert disagreed most interestingly during the final years of their correspondence, and *Un Coeur simple* is in my view the scriptural trace of that critical exchange.

The shared conviction of Flaubert and his fellow realists was, as the young Henry James sarcastically observed, "that art and morality are two perfectly different things, and that the former has no more to do with the latter than it has to do with astronomy or embryology."[38] For Sand—and this perhaps explains why in the nineteenth century her literary fortunes exceeded Flaubert's among both Russian- and English-speaking readers—art and morality were, on the contrary, intimately linked. Hence Sand totally rejected Flaubert's vaunted doctrine of impartiality, his belief, as he famously expressed it to her, that "the Artist must appear in his work no more than God in nature."[39] According to Sand, the writer, far from being absent from his work like a *deus absconditus*, must intervene, judge his characters, and above all provide his readers with a moral compass. To "make a mystery of the moral and beneficent meaning of his book" (2:229/p. 518), as Flaubert did in *L'Education sentimentale*, is to court the reader's indifference, even rejection. But what Flaubert termed the "essential difference" between himself and Sand lies elsewhere, for in the final analysis what Sand objected to in Flaubert's writing was less its failure to take a moral stance than its refusal to provide moral examples: "Don't hold true virtue to be a cliché in literature. Give it its representatives; portray the honest and the strong, along with the maniacs and dolts you so love to ridicule" (2:230/p. 519). Unambiguously virtuous characters are indeed in short supply in Flaubert's fictional universe, peopled as it is with a depressing conglomeration of deluded, self-centered, or cynical characters entirely lacking in any redeeming virtue. One can count on one hand the representatives of goodness in Flaubert's fiction: Catherine Leroux, the exploited domestic servant who is awarded a medal at the agricultural fair in *Madame Bovary*; Dussardier, the altruistic worker who dies on the barricades in *L'Education senti-mentale*; and, of course, Félicité. In each instance, goodness is alloyed with stupidity or, at the very least, with naiveté. The situation could not be more different in Sand's novels. The long list of her virtuous characters includes such noble figures as Edmée Mauprat, Fadette, the meunier d'Angibault and the marquis de Villemer. What is more, in Sand's fiction, virtue is always rewarded, unequivocally endorsed by the author. Ultimately, the essential difference between Sand and Flaubert involves ethics and its place in fiction, and it is this difference that, as we have seen, divides Sand from both Flaubert and Balzac—in short, from the major representatives of realism in France.

Altruism, in particular, is, as we have seen, a central component of Sand's Eros. And altruism is, of course, the virtue symbolized by the long-suffering Félicité, who, in Flaubert's words, "loves one after the other a man, her mistress's children, a nephew of hers, an old man whom she nurses, and her parrot."[40] Hers is, like the ignorant Indiana's, the "intellect of the heart." Félicité's serial love objects, unlike those of Flaubert's other protagonists, are none of them narcissistic. Love under the regime of idealism is anaclitic. Whatever else one can say about Félicité's heterogeneous choices, they all testify to her unique capacity to love the Other. After all, what is the parrot if not the absolute Other, first an animal, then inert matter, and finally a transcendental signifier? For all the text's duplicities, for all its manipulations of irony, there is little doubt that in *Un Coeur simple* Flaubert does give virtue its due, does reconcile the poetics of realism with the aesthetics of idealism.

Though idealism as it was theorized and practiced by Sand is not sentimentalism, neither can the two representational modes always be held firmly apart. Thus, to read Flaubert with Sand is to begin by giving full play to what is perhaps *Un Coeur simple*'s most discomfiting aspect, its pathos, often trivialized as its sentimentality, an affective mode almost always connoted as weak, hence feminine, in the context of Western European literature. The author of *Un Coeur simple* was, as Culler has shown, the most critical, the least romantic of sentimentalists, carefully "sloughing off the purely sentimental by subjecting it to a cold and detached treatment."[41] Yet, at least in this tale, he set out to appeal to the sentiments of his reader. When Flaubert writes "I want to move tender hearts to pity and tears, for I am tender-hearted myself,"[42] we must risk taking him at his word. Finally, to read Flaubert with Sand is to recognize—as does Culler—that *Un Coeur simple* is a unique work in the Flaubertian canon and that part of its difference, its uniqueness is, as I have argued, due to its intended reader. It is because Flaubert wrote *Un Coeur simple* for Sand that in it *he* runs the risk of pathos and sentimentality; the intended reader determines how we must read the text, not the other way around.

III

My starting point for this Sandian, which is to say feminist, reading of *Un Coeur simple* is the most subtle and exhaustive recent reading of the tale, Ross Chambers's "An Invitation to Love: Simplicity of Heart and Textual Duplicity in 'Un Coeur simple.' " Breaking with a long tradition of readers who insist that the text must be read *either* as an ironic mockery of its simpleminded protagonist *or*, far less frequently, as a moving "hagiography"[43] of its saintly heroine, Chambers asserts in exemplary poststructuralist fashion that what is called for is what I have called above a "double reading," a reading that takes into account the text's "duplicity": its simultaneous assertion and negation of the value of Félicité's simplicity. Rather than seeking to establish a hierarchy between the ironic and the empathic readings of Félicité's simplicity, the reader must respond to the text's exigency of "a negative and a positive valorization of the character."[44] The reader must give up the search for an authoritative authorial voice that would decide what is left undecidable in the text: "The meaning of the text does not depend here on the *presence* of a narrator, but rather it emerges from the *absence* of any instance that might be appealed to in support of one or other of the two opposed meanings, between which the text does not 'hesitate,' for it simply assumes them, simultaneously and undramatically" (p. 136–37). In short, the reader of this duplicitous text must assume the position of the fetishist whose perversion has come in the wake of deconstruction to serve as the paradigm of undecidable readings. Or to put matters another way, if the canny reader of *Un Coeur simple* must, according to Chambers, adopt the very fetishistic stance that defines Flaubertian irony, it is because, as I have argued elsewhere, Flaubert's irony and Flaubert's fetishism are two aspects of the same phenomenon. The oscillations of the fetishist between denial and recognition of woman's castration are in Flaubert figured by the uncertainties of the ironist.[45]

What complicates this fetishistic approach—which represents a significant breakthrough in the critical thinking on this tale—is that in effect it redoubles the fetishism already thematized in the text itself, for, writes Chambers, what binds Félicité to her mistress and the "bourgeoises" of Pont-l'Evêque is their common fetishism, here defined as a materialist "cult of objects."[46] I am now coming to the point of my disagreement with Chambers's reading. According to Chambers, the positive reading, which is also the conventionally pathetic and identificatory reading of Félicité's simplicity called for by Flaubert in his letter to Mme des Genettes, rests on the assumption of a radical difference between Félicité and the selfish, cruel, and exploitative milieu that she inhabits. What this reading fails to take note of, argues Chambers, is the breakdown of difference between Félicité and her bourgeois others. It is not so much that I disagree with Chambers's assertion of the underlying commonality of masters and servants in a society in the throes of commodification— the point is well taken and illuminating—but that I believe that it works to deny the complex interplay of gender and class that remains one of the largely unexplored dimensions of *Un Coeur simple*.

What I am suggesting is not that we read *Un Coeur simple* as simply another servant novel, a popular subgenre in nineteenth-century French fiction, nor even that we read it as a feminocentric text, in keeping with the protocols of recent feminist criticism. Raymonde Debray-Genette has presented convincing arguments against both approaches, arguing in the first instance that the very title Flaubert chose for his tale signals his distance from the conventions of the genre. Had he wanted to insert his tale into the paradigm of fictions both of and for the lower classes he would have entitled it either *Félicité*, on the model of Lamartine's *Geneviève*, or *Félicité Barette*, on the model of the Goncourts' *Germinie Lacerteux*. Debray-Genette does, however, recognize that "he cannot help but sketch here and there the servant novel."[47] (I will want to return to this point in a moment.) As to the centering of the text and a possible reading of it on the female protagonist(s), Debray-Genette deflects this anticipated feminist reading by arguing that "rich and poor all the women share the same fate" (p. 166), joined in their common exploitation by inadequate men. Hence, instead of focusing on Flaubert's ill-treatment of women, critics (feminist critics, that is) would do well to attend to Flaubert's ill-treatment of his male characters:

> If a very feminist thesis on Flaubert's treatment of women in his novels has been published [e.g., Lucette Czyba], I am surprised that no research has been devoted to his pessimism in regards to men. . . . For all practical purposes, in the manuscripts of "Un Coeur simple," Flaubert sketches out the trial of the "males." (p. 167)

What is striking in both Chambers's and Debray-Genette's otherwise remarkable analyses is their eagerness to head off any interpretive strategy that might remove the text from the purview of their essentially formalistic approaches, and what threatens the formalist readings of the text—and just as *Saint Julien* has become the fetish text of Flaubert's psychocritics, *Un Coeur simple* has been annexed by the formalists[48]—is, of course, any attempt to read it as a realist text from a sociocritical perspective. In some sense, both Chambers's and Debray-Genette's readings, as different as they are in their details, both work to foreclose any threat to the integrity of the text represented by the allegedly extraliterary forces of class and sexual difference. In denying these differences and, with them, ideology, these readings in effect do nothing but play into the hands of Flaubert, whose nineteenth-century bourgeois and male (and some would add colonialist) political unconscious could not accommodate differences. The very leveling of the differences between individuals that Flaubert and others among his contemporaries deplored as a dismaying effect of modernity and democraticization inhabits his fiction. It is by now a truism of Flaubert criticism that, as René Girard pointed out some years ago, "as Flaubert's novelistic genius ripens his oppositions become more futile; the identity of contraries is drawn more clearly."[49]

Given the well-documented tendency of all differences in Flaubert to collapse into identity and interchangeability, it is not difficult to make the case that this tale sustains neither class nor sexual difference, indeed that both forms of differentiation are sketched in only to be erased by the general drift of the tale toward conflation, culminating in the spectacular equation of the stuffed parrot and the Holy Spirit, the inanimate and the transcendental. We know, for example, from Flaubert's marginal comments in the drafts of *Un Coeur simple*, that as he struggled to provide Félicité with a biography he was acutely aware of the dangers of a breakdown of difference between servant and mistress: "Avoid having the formation of her origins resemble those of Mme Aubain."[50] The great "scène du baiser" where the grieving Félicité and Mme Aubain fall into each other's arms in an equalizing embrace becomes then the central scene for a reading of *Un Coeur simple* that would evacuate class difference and with it the question of sexual difference, for the two are here absolutely inseparable. This scene, it will be recalled, affectingly enacts Flaubert's characteristically bourgeois fantasy of class reconciliation as fraternal or sororal embrace, even as it suggests by its reliance on the vocabulary of contractual domesticity that class differences are an irreducible given of modern language and society: "The two women looked at each other and their eyes filled with tears. Then the *mistress* opened her arms, the *maid* threw herself into them, and they clasped each other in warm embrace, satisfying their grief in a kiss which made them equal."[51]

Despite the complicity of Flaubert and some of his finest critics in warding off the ideological, the mutually dependent axes of gender and class cannot be eliminated so easily from the reading of *Un Coeur simple*, for to elide the fact that the tale centers on the relationship between a mistress and her servant is to risk missing some of the reasons for the immense power and popularity of this tale. But can these factors be taken into account without falling into reductive and, worse, predictable sociocritical or feminist models of intelligibility? Is there a way, for example, in which viewing this text as a "servant novel" might disclose aspects of the text that have remained in the shadow, obscured by the blinding light of the tale's formal perfection? What of the "servant novel"?

The salient fact of this fictional subgenre is not, as Debray-Genette would have us believe, its emphasis on class struggle and the exploitation of the servant. It is rather, as the example of *Germinie Lacerteux* most famously illustrates, the effect of class struggle on the representation of women. As Hélène Cixous so aptly phrased it some years ago, in nineteenth-century fiction, "the maid is the mistress's repressed."[52] Sand's *Indiana* is only one of many novels of the period informed by this alignment of class difference with a difference between women. When in the second half of the nineteenth century class difference is brought massively to bear on the representation of women, the result is, as in *Germinie Lacerteux*, a veritable renaturalization of the split between the Virgin and the Whore. Thus in *Germinie Lacerteux* the mistress is an old maid and the servant, a nymphomaniac.

The female servant functions in these novels as the people do more generally in naturalist fiction—in full ascendancy in the 1870s—as the absolute and abject Other, the Other's Other. Viewed in this perspective, we can better appreciate the way in which in his tale Flaubert breaks with the clichés of the genre, not to mention with his own fantasmatic investment in the class-inflected Virgin-Mother/Whore split (as in *L'Education sentimentale*), by making of his servant, his woman of the people, a Virgin. Critics have long known that *Un Coeur simple* is the execution or partial execution—*Madame Bovary* being the other half—of one of a series of interrelated projects Flaubert conceived of in Constantinople in 1850, but they have yet to grapple with the servant Félicité's atypical virginity:

> As for my subjects, I have three; perhaps they are all the same, a thought that galls me considerably. *One: Une Nuit de Don Juan* . . . *Two: Anubis* . . . *Three*: my Flemish novel about the young girl who dies a virgin and mystic after living with her father and mother in a small provincial town, at the end of a garden full of cabbages and fruit trees, beside a stream the size of the Robec.[53]

IV

What then is a Virgin? Why was Flaubert obsessed with the figure of the virgin? What is the significance of Félicité's virginity and, indeed, of the insistence on virginity in the tale (for it is important to note that, though unmarried, Félicité is not portrayed through the grotesque codes of spinsterhood so dear to Balzac, rather through a lyrical anaphorization of virginity throughout the text)? Aside from Félicité's hysterical identification with the virginal Virginie at the moment of her first communion, when Virginie takes her place among the "flock of maidens,"[54] there is another less prominent, but ultimately more suggestive allusion to the centrality of virginity in this text. It occurs in the passage in section one containing the inventory of the contents of Mme Aubain's *salle*. I have in mind a detail that, situated in close proximity to Roland Barthes's barometer, might initially appear to participate in that detail's superfluity, to serve no other function than producing yet another reality effect, but which takes on in this context a meaning beyond the simple work of making real. The object I am referring to is, as Flaubert describes it, "a clock designed to look like a temple of Vesta" (p. 17/44).[55]

In a brilliant article on the goddess Hestia/Vesta, Jean-Joseph Goux has explored the significance of the cult of this "virgin goddess *par excellence*."[56] Goux's point of departure is the observation that alone of her kind, Vesta cannot be represented: unlike temples dedicated to other ancient gods and goddesses, the temple dedicated to Vesta is unadorned, remarkably free of all icons of the goddess. According to Goux, the taboo on the representation of Vesta/Hestia is intimately bound up with her virginity: "Vesta's virginity and her unrepresentability are both protected at once. . . . The inviolable virginity and the strict unrepresentability are identical, as if there were a complicity, on some opposing plane, between 'rape' by manly sexual desire and visualization" (p. 94). What the distinctiveness of the cult of Vesta attests to is the "strikingly coherent solidarity between virginity and nonrepresentation" (p. 95). Further, if Vesta occupies a unique and central place in the pantheon of the ancient world it is because "the absolute virgin, innocent of any sexual relation, is the highest manifestation of the sacred, the essence of what is sacred" (p. 95). Of Félicité, a modern Vesta, Flaubert writes: "Like everyone else, she had had her love-story" (p. 19/45). But, as we know, despite Théodore's repeated assaults on her virtue, despite his attempted rape, she remains inviolate. The disjunction "comme une autre" is misleading, since, as we have seen, Félicité is an exception to the sexual syntax of female servitude.

My point here is not to argue the hagiography thesis—though it gains immensely from this rapprochement—the title of Félicité's story is not after all "The Legend of Saint Félicité." But Goux's illuminating study of the cult of Vesta suggests another possible approach to the text, for Vesta is also Hestia, the goddess of the hearth, and as such attests to the central role played by the feminine in founding any collectivity. "Hestia permits us to think of centrality in terms other than the term 'phallus.' It appears that the center, in a universe which knows and invokes Hestia, is not phallocentric" (p. 100).

Centered on a virginal female protagonist, *Un Coeur simple* does indeed represent a universe that is not phallocentric. If sexual difference tends to collapse in this tale, it is because in it the phallic standard against which difference is measured in phallocentric societies is strangely absent or hopelessly trivialized.[57] And what of representation? If we were simply to apply Goux's theories of iconoclasm to *Un Coeur simple*, we would expect the centrality of virginity in the text to be accompanied by a taboo on representations of the Virgin and indeed a ban on all imagery. Clearly this is not the case, as religious and secular imagery are repeatedly mentioned in the tale, albeit in the rudimentary guise of the "estampes" illustrating the children's geography book and the naive popular imagery of the "images d'Epinal." But when we stop to think of what is at issue in *Un Coeur simple*, is it not precisely the unrepresentability of the divine, in this instance the Holy Ghost rather than the Virgin? Might Flaubert's parrot not be viewed as signifying the grotesqueness of all representations of that which precisely cannot be represented? In the temple of Vesta, all divine imagery is stricken with inanity: there is nothing intrinsically more absurd or comical about representing the Holy Ghost under the guise of a parrot than under any other ornithological guise, for what is at issue is finally the representation of the unrepresentable itself.

Read for the feminine and taking both gender and class into account, *Un Coeur simple* reveals itself as a critique of both phallocentrism and the iconocentrism that accompanies it. Indeed one might go further and say that what is at issue here is the relationship between representation and the ideal. As Derrida points out in his immensely helpful and pertinent article entitled, with the emphasis on the indefinite article, "Une Idée de Flaubert: La Lettre de Platon," throughout most of Flaubert's writings, the idea (and, with it, idealism) is or appears to be enmeshed in the form/content dialectic, bound up with the mimetic theories of representation that undergird the "Platonico-Hegelian continuum."[58] But another idealism is at work or working itself through Flaubert's writings, and this "certain idealism," or "idea of the idea" owes more to Spinoza, for whom his admiration was immoderate, "hyperbolic" (p. 310), than to either Plato or Hegel, both of whom he greatly admired. Spinoza's idea, according to Derrida, "neither is nor gives rise to any representation, mimetic or not, to any idea of the idea, and that Spinoza rightly opposes to the tradition, notably the Cartesian idea, as the act or the affirmation to the reproductive copy, indeed to its model'' (p. 323–24).[59] Having proffered this risky hypothesis, which no citation from Flaubert allows him to back-up, Derrida risks yet another audacious hypothesis in response to the seemingly strange, almost aggramatical question "Who is Flaubert's idea?" "One hears someone whisper: Flaubert's idea is Loulou, between Caroline and Louise, and it's first Caroline the dead sister, the impossible" (p. 323). Just as some years ago Culler punned that Flaubertian realism is a vealism, might one not conclude that Flaubert's idealism is a loulouism?[60]

This chapter has followed a strange course that has taken us from Flaubert's veal-like tears to vealism, from Sand's idealism to Flaubert's very different loulouism, so different indeed that one may wonder at my insistence on reading Sand with Flaubert. If the question of Sand's "influence" on Flaubert remains troubling, it is I think because it is not well posed. What is at issue in their relationship is not, as we have seen, influence, but something I will call *effect*. Whereas influence denotes the reproduction, the miming of the model, effect denotes a very different process, which Sand, once again, aptly and memorably tropes. Writing to Flaubert about the response his letters to her regarding the Commune provoked her to write, Sand says: "Your letters fall on me like a rain that refreshes me and develops at once all that is germinating in the soil."[61] In conclusion, I would hazard the hypothesis that *Un Coeur simple* is the flowering of a seed that the magnificent letters Sand wrote to Flaubert in the months preceding her death, and which constitute her literary testament, brought to life, and it is perhaps this unnatural fertilization that constitutes the veritable scandal of the Sand-Flaubert relationship.

AFTERWORD

Arguments against including new works in the canon almost always involve or invoke some notion of value; the exclusion of a work from the canon is justified by its alleged lack of value, chiefly aesthetic. However, the argument based on value is not foolproof, as so much recent work questioning the eternal, transhistoric, transcultural value of value judgments has shown. There is then a second line of defense of the canon quo, and that is the argument according to pleasure: if a work cannot be kept out on the grounds of its aesthetic inferiority, then its hedonic inadequacies are brought into play. It is not always so easy to distinguish one line of argument from the other, since those who find Sand's *Lélia*—and it is always *Lélia* that is cited in this context—unreadable always imply that if it (she) were any good, it would also be a good read. Needless to say, this standard is double, since no one, at least since its publication, has ever extrapolated from *Salammbô*'s relative unreadability its lack of worth, let alone Flaubert's unworthiness of being included in the canon. The canon is full of works (by men) that one would not necessarily take to a desert island, or at least an island in the Caribbean, unless one were planning to spend one's life there and wanted to improve one's mind.

And yet the question of pleasure is not so easily dismissed. Nor is the problem merely one of boredom: the least pleasurable text by Sand that I read in the course of working on her was not so much boring as it was almost literally nauseating. So powerful was the sickened feeling inspired in me by reading one of her lesser late fictions, *Le Beau Laurence* (1869), which I had picked up somewhat at random, that weeks of a precious leave went by before I could overcome my aversion and go back to reading her again. I can think of no other work I have read in my life as a reader of fiction that provoked in me such a physical sense of repulsion, based not on its content but on its very form—or, rather, formlessness. There was something acutely unpleasurable to me about this text that had little to do with boredom—by no stretch of the imagination can this text be described as difficult—and a great deal to do with what I perceived as its profound and unredeemed structural incoherence. To analyze my somatic reader response, I would have to elaborate some sort of theory of the truly awful in fiction, perhaps organize a colloquium or MLA session—the thought did cross my mind—on "The Esthetics of the Terrible: The Worst Novel I ever Read." Failures including aesthetic ones can, as we know, be instructive. But that is not my concern here, except to the extent that I want to complicate the notions of pleasure and unpleasure, to broaden them to include more violent, less polite forms of rejection than boredom or, conversely, less sexy, more intellectual forms of adoption than pleasure, not to mention jouissance.

The argument that I have made against excluding Sand from the canon is based on a demonstration of the gendering of the aesthetic categories used to keep her out; the arguments for including her are less easily described, less neatly circumscribed, but as the reader of this book has surely noticed they do not involve pleasure. At best my attitude toward much of the material discussed in these pages can be described as ambivalent: if idealism as a politics and an ethics inspires me and fulfills some unmet need for transcendence, and if idealization as a psychic process is a constitutive though troublesome component of my subjectivity, idealism as an aesthetics is for me an acquired taste.

This is not to say that I find reading Sand unpleasurable—I have very much enjoyed reading some of her works, especially the feminist and "Balzacian" (e.g., *Indiana*, *Valentine*, *Isidora*)—but that, perhaps less so than is the case with other Sandistes, my interest in her is not grounded in a powerfully positive affective response to her writing, with the possible exception of her more autobiographical (least idealistic) texts, such as *Histoire de ma vie* and the *Correspondance*. This critical distance from Sand's world may explain in part my not having chosen to write on *Consuelo*, which is curiously both the Sandistes and the non-Sandistes' (not to say antifeminists') favorite novel by Sand. For the first (generally women), it brings together so many of the Sandian themes they hold dear (the woman artist–messiah, music, Venice, grottoes, initiation, the search for the mother); for the second (generally men), it is simply the only major novel by Sand they know, because it was championed by an earlier generation of male romanticist Sand scholars, notably Léon Cellier.

The issue of the pleasure/nonpleasure of the idealist text is thus bound up with another issue: the pleasure and nonpleasure of French high romantic texts. Teaching Sand in two seminars, one undergraduate in English in the early eighties, one graduate in French in the late eighties, as well as in other courses both graduate and undergraduate throughout the eighties and into the nineties, has convinced me that the difficulty American students experience reading her, to the extent that they do experience difficulty, has much, perhaps everything, to do with her romanticism and nothing at all to do with her gender or her lack of canonic status. What makes *Lélia* so very problematic, so disengaging for many of its readers—and not just for my students—is not only that it is short on plot and long on soul searching but that it is steeped in romantic weltschmerz. And whereas the French canon has, as Margaret Waller has shown, enshrined male *mal de siècle*, it has been unable to come to terms with its single female instantiation, which, alas, owes more to Senancour's (even less readable, less canonic) *Obermann* than it does to Chateaubriand's foundational and mercifully short *René*.

The point about *Lélia*, as I have tried to convince my students, is not that it is in fact a good read but that, as Lévi-Strauss says somewhere about myth, it is "good to think." My claim for Sand's oeuvre—and I think this is in the final analysis the only argument that counts for endowing an author with canonic stature—is that it is a worthy conceptual object, that it is not so much readable or rereadable as it is theorizable. In this sense the idealist text could be seen as paradigmatic of the activity of literary criticism and theory, for what I have enjoyed most of all in all my years of working on this project—and they have been many—is *the idea of the ideal*. There is real pleasure in *thinking about the ideal*, but it is cognitive, rather than affective. That the most significant and self-conscious modern European idealist writer happens to be a woman and the major French woman writer of the nineteenth century to boot has enhanced the pleasure immeasurably—indeed, these facts enabled, led to that pleasure, since my intention at the very outset was to "work on" Sand, the preeminent woman writer in my "period." But what matters most to me in the end is that a theory of idealism in writing is an idea whose time has come.

NOTES

Introduction: The Importance of Being George

1. Sand's notorious fictionalization of her stormy affair with Alfred de Musset is the paradigmatic French revenge novel. Later Louise Colet settled her scores with Flaubert and others by writing *Lui*.

2. The expression *around* 1985 more or less deliberately echoes the title of Jane Gallop's *Around* 1981. Like me, in her introduction Gallop notes that in the (too long) time it took her to produce her book, three what she calls "theoretical formations" succeeded each other. This anxiety-producing sense of being caught up in a too rapidly shifting critical scene may well be the postmodernist feminist critical predicament and raises serious questions about the influence of the marketplace on the production of knowledge. Are we really in a period of amazing progress that condemns even today's most radical breakthrough texts to being tomorrow's remaindered specials? Or are these dizzying shifts merely an illusion fostered by the marketing of feminist and gender studies?

3. Roustan. To be more accurate, this book was first spotted by my stepson, Goulven Keineg, who was working the aisle ahead of me. Knowing my interests, he handed the book over to me. According to the title page, the book, which is one of a four-volume series by the same author, is intended for young men and women beginning their post-baccalauréat degrees.

4. N. Miller, "Changing the Subject: Authorship, Writing, and the Reader," in *Subject to Change*, pp. 102–21.

5. At the beginning of "Opponents, Audiences, Constituencies, and Community,"

Edward Said calls the audience for "specialized, advanced (i.e., New New) criticism . . . the real or mythical three thousand" (p. 4).

6. Nesbit, "What Was an Author," p. 240.

7. N. Miller, "Introduction: Writing Feminist Criticism," in *Subject to Change*, p. 14.

8. As J. Miller scrupulously demonstrates, there are important philosophical differences separating the critics of the Geneva school (Marcel Raymond, Albert Béguin, Georges Poulet, Jean Rousset, Jean-Pierre Richard, and Jean Starobinski), but all "replace a concern for the objective structure of individual works with a concern for the subjective structure of the mind revealed by the whole body of an author's writing" ("The Geneva School," p. 307).

9. Foucault, "What is an Author?," p. 151.

10. In her *Essai sur le drame fantastique: Goethe-Byron-Mickiewicz,* which appears in *Souvenirs,* pp. 3–98, Sand makes a point of explicitly contesting Germany's philosophic hegemony, writing "May God keep me from granting to Germany that philosophical superiority to which the least of our advances in the realm of politics gives the lie, for I do not understand a wisdom that doesn't make wise, a strength that doesn't make strong, a liberty that doesn't make free" (p. 4).

11. See Sand's very long disquisition on Schiller's *The Robbers* and its grotesque French adaptation *Robert, chef des brigands* (*Robert, Head of the Bandits*), in which her father played the chief role, in *Histoire de ma vie* (*Story of My Life,* pp. 172–80/*Oeuvres autobiographiques,* 1:161–73). In her *Essai sur le drame fantastique,* Sand readily recognizes that she has closer personal affinities with Schiller than with Goethe—"the nature of his genius responds more directly to the aspirations of my soul" (*Souvenirs,* p. 34)—but she refuses to oppose them, preferring instead to place Byron over and against Goethe (see below).

For a rather different approach to the question of the Schillerian tradition of idealist aesthetics, see Sychrava, *Schiller to Derrida.* Barely touching on Schiller's political idealism, Sychrava focuses on the persistence of the naive/sentimental opposition, first proposed by Schiller in his 1795–96 essay "On the naive and sentimental," in literature from romanticism to poststructuralism. The polemical thrust of Sychrava's book is to undo this post-Kantian (idealist, subjectivist) opposition that always works to ensure the superiority of whatever is aligned with the sentimental and to discredit whatever is designated as naive. Since the naive tends to be equated with the mimetic and the particularistic, Sychrava takes as her exemplary candidate for redemption, a sort of anti-Wordsworth (the fetish poet of recent sentimentalist critics), the nineteenth-century descriptive peasant-poet John Clare.

12. One need hardly rehearse the misogynistic underpinnings of what Derrida terms the "Platonico-Hegelian continuum" ("Une Idée de Flaubert," p. 323). We shall return to Flaubert's participation in this metaphysics of gender in chapter 6. One citation from Hegel should suffice at this point to bear out my argument: "Women may have happy ideas, taste and elegance but they cannot attain to the ideal" (*Philosophy of Right,* p. 263).

13. On Derrida and (linguistic) idealism, see Bennington and Derrida, *Jacques Derrida*, esp. pp. 26–126.

14. Derrida, "Deconstruction in America," pp. 4, 6.

15. M. Butler, "Feminist Criticism." On this unfriendly review of *Reading in Detail*, see my "Rereading in Detail."

16. All page references are to *Souvenirs*.

17. This unquestioned alignment of feminism and materialism may now be ripe for reassessment, as J. Butler argues in her provocative essay, "Bodies that Matter" (forthcoming in *Engaging with Irigaray*).

18. But also as an aesthetics, since in nineteenth-century aesthetic debates realism and materialism are often equated. See *French Realism*, where Weinberg summarizes the position of the critical enemies of nascent realism as follows: "*Réalisme, matérialisme*: the words are synonymous. The new school is an *école matérialiste*; it answers to the 'tendance toute *matérialiste* de notre époque' " (p. 133).

19. Leroux, *Oeuvres*, p. 149. The translations are mine.

20. Sand, *Story of My Life*, p. 923/*Oeuvres autobiographiques*, 2:162.

21. See, for example, *Histoire de la littérature*, where Lalou classifies Villiers under the rubric "l'idéalisme" and speaks of his "idéalisme militant" (p. 80). Throughout her extensive introduction to the long-awaited paperback edition of *L'Eve future*, Nadine Satiat speaks of Villiers's idealism (see especially pp. 22–25 on Villiers and Hegel). Just as Villiers's *Axel* fascinated an earlier generation of modernist critics, *L'Eve future* has acquired something of cult status among the current postmodernist generation; see Michelson, "On the Eve of the Future," and Gasché, "The Stelliferous Fold," among others.

22. See Schor, "Female Fetishism."

1. Idealism in the Novel: Recanonizing Sand

1. Leslie Fiedler as quoted by Meese, "Sexual Politics," p. 86.

2. Though "upgrading" the status of a woman author already marginally in the canon does entail rethinking the grounds of canonicity, at the same time it raises the specter of the token woman and the negative consequences such tokenism inevitably entails. Even as Sand occupies a marginal position in the canon, her presence there serves to obscure the achievement of other contemporary women writers, to provide an alibi for not reaching beyond the canon to pull in other known nineteenth-century French women writers. There seems to be a law—the very law of tokenism—that makes it impossible for two women (or black, or Albanian) writers to share the spotlight; one's rise to prominence entails the other's fall into obscurity. Describing the phenomenon of mutual exclusivity that characterized the relationship between Flora Tristan and George Sand, Stéphane Michaud notes: "the two women cannot coexist, one must erase the other" ("En miroir," p. 199). Recanonizing Sand must not foreclose work on other nineteenth-century women writers but rather pave the way to rewriting the entire literary

history of nineteenth-century France. However much Sand may have been "male-identified" in her intellectual tastes and friendships, her work exists in a context that includes Flora Tristan, the Saint-Simonian women, Louise Colet, and Daniel Stern (among others), figures with whom she was in constant if not always harmonious dialogue.

Whatever our differences, neither Robinson nor I take the more radical, indeed the extreme, position that questions the need for a canon altogether, arguing against both canons and (re)canonization. However much I may agree in theory with the anticanon position, I do not think that the question of the canon, at least the literary canon, is open, that one is free to vote for it or against it. At best one can question its constitution, show up its exclusions, argue for its expansion, in short shake up and relativize it, but the time constraints that operate outside but especially inside the classroom are such that a certain process of selection is inevitable: one cannot read/teach the entire library, and as soon as one begins to make choices or substitutions, there is canonization.

3. Showalter, introduction to *The New Feminist Criticism*, p. 11.

4. And it is as an author of rustic fiction that she survives in those ultimate repositories of the French canon, the *"manuels"* (e.g., the Lagarde et Michard series) destined for high-school students preparing for the baccalauréat examination. In a recent survey of women as they are represented in textbooks, the author of the section on literature notes of Sand: "Her oeuvre is generally reduced to her rustic novels, whereas her production is very diversified" (Crabbé et al., *Les Femmes dans les livres scolaires*, p. 57). According to the authors of this volume, women writers are subject to two strategies of exclusion: "Occultation and reduction characterize the treatment of women's writing" (p. 57). As one of the two "monuments" of nineteenth-century French literature—the other being, of course, Germaine de Staël—Sand's contribution cannot be elided, hence the "reduction" of her immense oeuvre to her country fiction.

5. FAGUET, *Dix-Neuvième Siècle*, pp. 395, 398.

6. Pellissier, *Le Mouvement littéraire*, pp. 243–44.

7. Cellier, *La Porporina*, p. 1.

8. Van Tieghem, *Histoire de la littérature française*, p. 468.

9. See chapter 6 of Dickenson, *George Sand*, for a nice survey of Sand's international reputation.

10. Rocheblave, introduction to *George Sand*, n.p.

11. Pellissier, *Le Mouvement littéraire*, p. 243.

12. Woolf, *Three Guineas*, p. 188 n. 49. To complicate this already confusing picture of the vicissitudes of Sand's literary fortunes, one might note that, according to Ellen Moers, the revival of interest in Sand's work "started quietly in France in the 1930s" ("Fraternal George Sand," p. 222). Thus, around the same time when Woolf was speaking of Sand as "half-forgotten," "two eminent Frenchmen, Edouard Dolléans and Alain," were in the process of rereading and recovering her. But it is the biography of Sand, *Lélia: The Life of George Sand*, by André Maurois, a student of Alain's, "that gave the Sand revival wide and international currency" (p. 222).

13. Panofsky, *Idea*, pp. 105–10. In his book *Ethical Idealism*, Rescher has this to say about the history of the substantive form of the ideal:

1. Idealism in the Novel: Recanonizing Sand

The employment of *ideal* as a noun is relatively recent. Lessing informs us that it was first so used by the Italian Jesuit Francesco Lana (d. 1687). The adjective *ideal* is older; we find it (as *idealis*) in use by Albert the Great (d. 1390), and by later scholastics. It is clearly related to one sense of the word *idea*—namely, its Platonic sense as an idealized exemplar (*paradeigmon*, that is, *idea prima = exemplar primum seu archetypon*). (p. 114)

He goes on to say that "the modern conception of an 'ideal' was disseminated through the philosophy of Kant" (p. 114). For more on the history of the ideal, see Michel, *Le Beau Idéal*.

14. Panofsky, *Idea*, p. 126.

15. Lewes, *The Principles of Success*, p. 83. Lewes is in many ways a crucial figure in this realm of aesthetics. A significant interpreter and disseminator of Hegel's idealist philosophy, an insightful supporter of women novelists (Charlotte Brontë, Sand, and, of course, Eliot), Lewes emerges as one of the prime theoreticians of realism/idealism in Victorian criticism. In fact, for Lewes, who espoused what one commentator has called a "modified Realism," idealism and realism were not incompatible, not true opposites; for him, writes Alice Kaminsky, "idealism is simply a special kind of realism" (*George Henry Lewes*, p. 45). Thus Lewes writes: "Realism is . . . the basis of all Art, and its antithesis is not idealism but Falsism." Despite Lewes's modification of terminology and his promotion of realism in all its forms, including idealism, which is here clearly subsumed to realism, we are dealing once again with a fundamentally oppositional structure. The false realism/idealism opposition has merely been displaced by the more accurate paradigm realism/falsism.

For Lewes on Sand, see "Balzac and George Sand" and "George Sand's Recent Novels."

16. Idealism is, of course, not realism's only meaning-giving Other. For example, as Laurie Langbauer reminds us in her recent *Women and Romance*, the realist novel defines itself explicitly as against romance, and however much the meaning of both terms may shift, romance is "yoked" to woman, and thus the realist novel's superiority to its allegedly feminine origin is firmly secured. And this "scapegoating" of the feminized, maternalized romance is at work both in men's and women's fiction.

The imperative to contextualize realism more adequately works both ways, of course: just as nineteenth-century realism depends on earlier, chiefly neoclassical idealism to make it meaningful, nineteenth-century idealism, as we shall see, is molded and given significance by the rise of an increasingly hegemonic realism. Each term must be read in terms of its historic counterpart.

17. Published in 1937, Bernard Weinberg's invaluable *French Realism* remains the best account we have of the basic tenets of realism in painting and literature and the fierce idealist opposition it encountered in the middle third of the nineteenth century. See in particular chapter 4, "Criticism of Realistic Painting (1840–1860)," and chapter 5, "Theory and Opposition (1840–1870)." The order in which Weinberg proceeds— first painting, then literature—and the distinctions he draws between the issues and debates in the two fields are highly enlightening; the objection to the realists' "disdain

for the ideal" (p. 130) is, however, according to Weinberg's survey of the journalism of the period, the most common complaint of the critics of both media. Though, as Weinberg interestingly observes, "For most critics, realism was antiromantic, rather than anticlassical" (p. 130), he seems to suggest that the opposition to realism was more classical than it was romantic. The "quest for the beautiful and the ideal" was, however, "considered to be the essential aim of [both] those schools" (p. 130). These remarks have a direct bearing on the case of Sand: by displacing the emphasis away from her romanticism onto her idealism, one not only avoids having to decide the question of the degree of her romanticism, one also sees clearly how and to what extent allegiance to an idealist credo defined her dissent from the rising school of realism and aligned her at least initially with a contested romantico-classical aesthetics.

18. Pellissier, *Le Mouvement littéraire*, p. 233. Cf. C. Robinson, *French Literature*, whose survey of nineteenth-century French literature is informed by the opposition between "idealists" and "pragmatists," an eternal opposition given renewed impetus in the nineteenth century, "not only because of the crisis of values caused by the social cataclysm of the end of the previous century, but also because continued progress in the sciences undermined belief in accepted notions of reality itself" (p. 8). Robinson further complicates his model by distinguishing two types of idealism: "Most thinkers were profoundly dissatisfied with the world as it was. The question was: could the moral improvement of man be derived from his material progress or should he look to values outside material existence?" (p. 103). Curiously, Robinson's generalization of the category of idealism to include most major developments in nineteenth-century French literature does not lead to a reevaluation of Sand's fiction. Of the writer who was arguably the preeminent idealist of her time, he writes: "Even a thinker so congenitally feeble as poor George Sand could see," that during the July monarchy

> problems of social inequality were substantially moral problems too. It is the very core of her revolt against society in those novels compounded from a jumble of absurd utopian and spiritualist theories, e.g. *Consuelo*; it underlies such ludicrous idealizations of the peasantry as *Petite Fadette* or *François le Champi*. Even in her early novels, with their grotesquely melodramatic stylisations of adultery at its most clichéed, *Indiana* or *Jacques* . . . , the moral corrosion effected by the social structure is constantly felt as a primary cause of individual inadequacy. (pp. 105–6)

19. More accurately, Sand and idealism are forever linked in the half-life of the literary manuals, where the pace of change is inscribed in the longest of *durées*; like a fossil preserved in amber, the Sandian idealist novel remains embalmed in the unscientific sample of manuals and introductions to French literature I have consulted.

Although she is by far the most famous representative of idealism in nineteenth-century French literature, Sand is not, as I have already noted, the only one. The case of Lamartine would bear close investigation in this context, particularly the tendency of his contemporaries to discredit his writings and politics by insisting on his/their femininity. Flaubert's contributions to this tradition are relatively well known; less known is the following telling *boutade*, according to which Lamartine is, "the female genius, or

222

else he would have been called Lemartin" (Orcel and Boddaert, *Ces imbéciles croyants de liberté*, p. 83).

Dating the disappearance of idealism as an aesthetic category in twentieth-century writings on the nineteenth-century novel would be an instructive exercise: it is no accident that in this chapter I cite only two modern critics, Bernard Weinberg and Harry Levin, for whom idealism remains alive as a notion. This suggests that the erasure of idealism is a fairly recent phenomenon that has accompanied the rise of Theory, which has perhaps now reached its end point.

20. Taine, *Derniers essais*, pp. 130–31. Cf. Henry James, who in his essay on George Sand included in *French Poets and Novelists* and explicitly indebted to Taine's, also linked Sand's falling out of fashion with the dissemination of realism: "During the last half of her career, her books went out of fashion among the new literary generation. 'Realism' had been invented, or rather propagated; and in the light of 'Madame Bovary' her own facile fictions began to be regarded as the work of a sort of superior Mrs. Radcliffe" (p. 168).

21. Hémon, *Cours de littérature*, p. 43. Cf. Rocheblave, who explicitly links Sand's literary fortunes to a long-deferred return to the ideal: "Until the public, finally disillusioned by a sad realism, returns completely to idealist literature" (introduction to *George Sand*, n.p). James, in his aforementioned piece, is far less sanguine about the prospects for a return to Sandian idealism, imagining instead that in a future "world . . . given over to a 'realism' that we have not as yet begun faintly to foreshadow, George Sand's novels will have, for the children of the twenty-first century, something of the same charm which Spenser's 'Fairy Queen' has for those of the nineteenth" (*French Poets and Novelists*, pp. 180–81). While it may be argued, as Katherine Hume does in *Fantasy and Mimesis*, that realism was a short-lived movement and that postmodernism marks a return of the fantasy repressed by realism, the return of fantasy is not the same as the return of idealism, though there is a definite connection between the two.

22. Brunetière, *La Renaissance de l'idéalisme*, pp. 18–20. In the course of his talk, Brunetière alluded to the historical context in ominous terms, describing the current hour as "somber . . . dark and confused" (p. 21), and his "Avant-propos" suggests that this darkness may have had something to do with the Dreyfus affair, since Brunetière defends himself there against an attack sparked by his talk in Drumont's paper, *La Libre Parole*. For more on Brunetière's involvement in the Dreyfus affair, see his *Discours de Combat*.

23. Beauvoir, *The Second Sex*, p. 688.

24. Radway, *Reading the Romance*, p. 99. See also Fowler, *The Alienated Reader*.

25. Radway, *Reading the Romance*, p. 98.

26. For my purposes, Langbauer does not sufficiently distinguish Eliot's rejection of romance from her rejection of idealism and idealization. And this points to what may be Langbauer's own blind spot: her tendency to follow the general Marxist rhetoric of devalorizing idealization, speaking for example in her chapter on Dickens of his "humanist idealization" of life (*Women and Romance*, p. 139). To a limited but significant extent, the ideal becomes her scapegoated category, which only demonstrates that no system, however self-aware and self-reflective, escapes the ritual of the *pharmakos*.

27. Thomson, *George Sand and the Victorians*, p. 183, emphasis added.

28. Levin, *The Gates of Horn*, p. 66.

29. Eliot, *Adam Bede*, pp. 221, 222, 223.

30. Eliot, *Essays of George Eliot*, p. 270.

31. Eliot, *Adam Bede*, pp. 224–25.

32. At the conclusion of his interesting reading of chapter 17 of *Adam Bede*, J. Miller also makes the point that the difference Eliot promotes between "irrealism" and "realism" tends finally to collapse. See *The Ethics of Reading*, especially pp. 66–70 and 78–80.

In *The Industrial Reformation of English Fiction*, Catherine Gallagher begins her chapter on Eliot's representational realism with a charming anecdote that purports to feature a debate between a female idealist and a female realist but in fact recounts a conversation between George Eliot and Harriet Martineau, two female realists with different conceptions of realism:

> In a London art gallery in 1861, two middle-aged women stand before a painting of a stork killing a toad. The painting provokes a short argument. The older woman dislikes it intensely, calling it coarse and amoral; the younger woman admires it, explaining somewhat condescendingly, that the purpose of art is the careful delineation of the actual. Good art, she insists, must show the world as it is. The older woman then pointedly asks whether it would be good art to delineate carefully men on a raft eating a comrade. According to the older woman's later report, the question silences her companion. (p. 219)

On Eliot's struggles to reconcile realism and idealism, see U. C. Knoepflmacher, *George Eliot's Early Novels*.

33. Barthes, *S/Z*, p. 59. Cf. Pellissier who writes: "Now because of the way we are constituted, the exaggeration of evil finds our credulity much more accommodating than that of good. Thus the word *realism*, diverted from its true meaning, is applied to works of raving idealization, so long as they idealize man in his perversity and his stupidity" (*Le Mouvement littéraire*, p. 249).

34. That Taine and Proudhon represent the major theories of art in the latter half of the nineteenth century and that their theories are both bound up with the idealism rejected by the realist-naturalists is confirmed by Zola's critical responses to both in *Mes haines*: "Proudhon et Courbet" (pp. 41–54) and "M. H. Taine, artiste" (pp. 63–83). See Ehrard, "L'Esthétique de Zola," pp. 133–50, esp. 135–37. "The words *idealist* (used 6 times), *idealism* (1 time), *idealize* (3 times), *idealization* (1 time), *ideally* (1 time), very rare, always have a pejorative value, a negative meaning" (p. 136). In keeping with his own aesthetic positions, Zola rejects both hyperbolizing (Taine's "essential characteristic") and meliorative (Proudhon's socialist realism) idealism(s): "No more than the formal ideal, the moral ideal is not for Zola the principle of the plastic arts" (p. 136). For more on Zola and idealism, see note 53.

For an interdisciplinary but unusually precise definition of idealism, see Brunetière, *La Renaissance de l'idéalisme*, pp. 18–20.

35. See the cover of the original edition of Nochlin, *Realism*, which features a portrait of Proudhon, a blown-up detail of the painting "Pierre-Joseph Proudhon and His Family."

36. Proudhon, *Du principe de l'art*, p. 29.

37. See Panofsky, *Idea*, for the incidence of the subject/object distinction in the idea/mimesis debate. It is not until the Renaissance, with its invention of perspective, that this alignment occurs (pp. 50–51).

38. Proudhon, *Les Femmelins*, p. 27. This little volume is a facsimile reprint of the edition of Proudhon's work put out in 1912 by the Maurassian Cercle Proudhon, and, according to the author of the preface, the target of the Action Française circle is Rousseau, the first of a line of "femmelins," the origin of society's corruption, the rise of pornography, and the dissolution of the family: "He is the first of these *womanlets* of the intellect in whom, the idea being troubled, passion or affect overcome reason and who, despite eminent and even virile qualities, cause literature and society to go into decline" (p. 30).

39. For a useful rehearsal of this sorry tradition, see Naginski, *George Sand*, pp. 221–23. Naginski sees the "derogatory myth of Sand's writing" as three-pronged: "The first is its very liquidity, metonymized by milk or murky water. The second is the dubious nature of the liquid, seen as the very anti-thesis of pure spring water. . . . The third is the uncontrollable nature of the writing which emerges without shape or style," (p. 223).

40. An egregious recent example of this particular smear tactic by two contemporary publicists should make clear that the rhetorical devices of misogyny are transhistoric. In their book, *Ces imbéciles croyants de liberté*, Orcel and Boddaert—who insistently refer to Sand as "la Dupin"—establish a link between her sexual promiscuity and her logorrhea that serves to underwrite the link between her writing and her lowest bodily functions: "Is not this collectionitis the flip side of the scriptural logorrhea of she who was to die some forty years later of an intestinal occlusion?" (p. 82).

41. See Gilman, "Black Bodies, White Bodies."

42. Sand, it should be noted, held Proudhon's political theory in grudging respect. But as she writes to Mazzini (November 22, 1848) with reference to Leroux: "Proudhon is much more powerful than he in absolute and personal theories. But he's the spirit of Satan, and woe unto us if we thus kick the ideal out! Leroux has too much of the ideal, but I cannot deal with Proudhon any longer because he does not have any at all" (*Correspondance*, 8:175). For Sand on Proudhon, see also *Correspondance*, 8:594–95, 9:38–39, 11:184–85.

43. Taine, *Derniers essais*, p. 132.

44. Taine, *Philosophie*, 1:33.

45. Cf. Levin, who writes: "If we rated authors by their humanitarian sympathies, rather than by their comprehension of human beings, we should rate George Sand and Victor Hugo above the authors on our list" (*The Gates of Horn*, p. 82).

46. It is only at the very end of his chapter on the ideal that Proudhon introduces a moral concern by defining art as *"an idealist representation of nature and ourselves, with a view to the physical and moral perfecting of our species"* (*Du principe de l'art*, p. 43). Morality intervenes as an aspect of the work of art's intended *effect* on the human race and not as an aspect of the work itself.

47. Sand, *Story of My Life*. p. 923/*Oeuvres autobiographiques*, 2:161–62). Cf. the

recasting of this dialogue in the "Notice" of *Le Compagnon* (1869), pp. 1–2. Sand's account of her conversation with Balzac should be read alongside Balzac's account to Mme Hanska of his conversations with Sand, because such a juxtaposition complicates what appears to be a simple assertion of sexual identity in this passage. What emerges from Balzac's letter is that he, like so many of his contemporaries, did not view Sand as a woman or at least, as André Maurois suggests, wanted to convince Mme Hanska of that fact:

> She is masculine, she is an artist, she is great-hearted, generous, devoted and temperamentally chaste. She has all the finer characteristics of a man; *ergo* she is not a woman. . . . What it all comes to is that she is a man: all the more so since she wants to be one. She has given up playing the woman, and is *not* a woman. (cited in Maurois, *Lélia*, p. 254)

See also Balzac's *Béatrix*, for his fictional portrayal of Sand as Camille Maupin.

Pellissier provides yet another interesting gloss when he observes that as idealists neither Sand nor Balzac mime reality: "Even in the novel, realism can never be the faithful reproduction of reality, because art necessarily involves two processes, abstraction and idealization, the first eliminating unimportant traits, the second more forcefully emphasizing those that the artist has selected. . . . For all that he abstracts and idealizes, Balzac does not cease to be a realist" (*Le Mouvement littéraire*, p. 248).

48. This is the thrust of a refreshingly polemical work by Raymond Tallis, *In Defence of Realism*, that provides one of the first sustained responses to the Althusserian critique of "classical" realism as exemplified by Catherine Belsey in her book *Critical Practice*. For a fairly recent assessment of the status of reflection theory, see the special issue of *Critical Inquiry* entitled *The Sociology of Literature*, edited by Ferguson et al.

49. The same objection could be made to Tallis, who totally fails to take gender into account in his "defense of realism," disposing of the entire problem in a preliminary note explaining his use of the masculine pronoun throughout: "I should prefer that my feminist credentials were judged by my ideas rather than by a nervous linguistic tic. If those who defend realistic fiction have natural allies, they are to be found among the ranks of feminists" (*In Defence of Realism*, n.p). Yes, but . . .

50. For two rather different, indeed conflicting, approaches to the question of women and the sentimental, see Poovey, "Mary Wollstonecraft," and Tompkins, *Sensational Designs*. In the late-eighteenth-century British context studied by Poovey, Mary Wollstonecraft discovers in the process of writing *Maria* that her "political insights" into the rights of women are "dangerously at odds" (p. 112) with the sentimental structure, whereas in the mid-nineteenth-century American context studied by Tompkins, the sentimental structure offers Harriet Beecher Stowe a powerful vehicle for promoting the rights both of slaves and women. For the one, the sentimental novel is a mixed generic blessing for women since it is rooted in a bourgeois ideology of individualism that is inimical to women and to the expression of their sexuality; for the other, it is a privileged genre that allows women writers to propose alternatives to a materialistic patriarchal society.

1. Idealism in the Novel: Recanonizing Sand

Beyond a common emphasis on domesticity, however, Poovey and Tompkins's notions of sentimentalism in fiction share little, and though the institution of marriage is certainly central to Sand's political and fictional project (see below, esp. chapter 3), domesticity can hardly be said to be the distinguishing feature of idealist fiction. I can only gesture here at a future rearticulation of the commonalities and differences among the three closely allied feminine or feminized genres: romance and the sentimental and idealist novels. Because as a feminist reader of Rousseau Sand shared with Wollstonecraft the same contradictory enlightenment legacy and as a literary critic wrote on Stowe—the two writers are often compared—she should occupy a crucial position in this yet-to-be-written reconsideration of gender and genre as it shifts across historical time and national spaces. What appears clear even at this preliminary stage is that the split within sentimentalism diagnosed above lies at the heart of Sandian idealism, which shares with late-eighteenth-century sentimentalism a preoccupation with the wrongs of romanticized Eros and with mid-nineteenth-century sentimentalism a concern with utopian refashionings of the social order.

51. I am alluding here to Brooks, *Reading for the Plot,* a major critical work on narrative that, as Brooks's feminist critics have been quick to point out, does not include any work by a woman novelist, hence my critique of the universalist claims of the chief theoreticians of plot from Aristotle to twentieth-century narratologists.

52. See Tallis, "Anti-Realism in Practice," in *In Defence of Realism*, pp. 93–119, which concludes that antirealism, except in very short takes, is a figment of the theoretician's imagination: "Anti-realism or consistent anti-realism does not exist because it could not exist. The truly anti-realistic novel would be unintelligible and therefore unrecognizable as a novel" (p. 118).

53. Laclos, *Oeuvres complètes*, p. 688.

54. Zola, *Oeuvres complètes*, p. 772. The very fact that in *L'Oeuvre* the writer character is called Sandoz indicates that Zola's relationship to Sand was more complex and ambivalent than one might at first surmise and confirms the intimate relationship of idealism and naturalism, for Sandoz combines both Sand and a partial anagram of Zola. My thanks to Philippe Hamon for reminding me of this connection.

55. For more on the detail-woman association, see my *Reading in Detail*. Interestingly, in Eliot, according to J. Miller, the gendering of the realism/idealism paradigm is reversed: "The impulse toward falsehood is given an implicit male gender, the gender of the narrator himself [in a peculiar strategic gesture, Miller insists on referring to Eliot throughout as "he"], whereas the faithful representing of commonplace things is therefore implicitly female" (*The Ethics of Reading*, p. 68). If Miller is right, we can perhaps identify Eliot's writing as inaugurating the transvaluation of the traditionally negative association of femininity and detailism pursued by modern feminist critics who have often (re)claimed the realistic representation of (female) experience as the hallmark of women's writing.

56. James, *French Poets and Novelists*, p. 155. Aptly characterizing James as the "sort of friend who puts enemies out of work" (*George Sand*, p. 126), Dickenson views him as one of, if not the chief, architects of Sand's decanonization, at least in Britain and

the United States. For more on her estimation of James's nefarious role, see pp. 166 and 168–72.

57. James, *French Poets and Novelists*, p. 185.

58. See, for example, Flaubert who writes: "What I fault women for above all . . . is their need to poeticize; they don't see either the true when it presents itself, or beauty where it is found" (cited in Carlut, *La Correspondance de Flaubert*, p. 43). This is an especially vicious modulation of the cliché because it links women's inability to look truth in the face with their incapacity to see beauty; feminine poeticization, which is meant to embellish, perversely blinds to the beautiful, because, in keeping with Flaubert's Platonic logic (which Sand, that other great Platonist, also subscribes to), truth and beauty are one.

59. That this should be so is hardly surprising given the sexism of the major avantgarde movements and their chief exponents. Critiques of representationalism are, as the history of twentieth-century avant-garde movements eloquently demonstrates, not necessarily allied with critiques of phallocentrism. The case of Alain Robbe-Grillet, who never stops setting up Balzac as a straw man for promoting the new novel and never stops reinventing misogyny, is to my mind exemplary but not unique. On sexism and the avant-garde, see Suleiman, *Subversive Intent*, esp. pp. 11–32 and 51–71.

60. I am thinking here of the work of what might be thought of as the English or Cambridge school of critics (Tanner, Heath, McCabe, Prendergast) who, working in the wake of Barthes, are engaged in rethinking realism. Significantly, however scathing their critique of realism, it has remained completely divorced from a critique of the canon. The work of Prendergast is in this respect symptomatic: while recognizing fleetingly that the laws of verisimilitude repress "feminine desire" with a particular vengeance, Prendergast's corpus is resolutely male. The surprising annexation of Nerval's *Sylvie* as a standard work in the library of realism only serves to point up the critic's blind spot; indeed, one almost suspects that *Sylvie* was appropriated in lieu of a text by a woman. (See Tanner, *Adultery in the Novel*; Prendergast, *The Order of Mimesis*; Heath, "Realism, Modernism, and 'Language-Consciousness.'") There are, however, encouraging signs of movement in this area. In a forthcoming book focusing on the early 1830s, that is the "origins" of French realism, Sandy Petrey devotes a provocative chapter to *Indiana*, in which he demonstrates the neat fit between realism as a form of social contract and constructionist theories of gender.

This is perhaps (also) the place to make explicit what is implicit throughout this chapter: to say that Balzac is the paradigmatic realist (or Sand, the paradigmatic idealist) is not to endorse the reductionism of the canon. Balzac's representational versatility, his own practice of (Sandian) idealism are not the issue here. What is at issue is that the same criteria of canonicity (derived from and confirmed by Balzac's realist fiction) that serve to decanonize Sand serve to decanonize Balzac's (and other writers') nonrealist fiction.

61. James, *French Poets and Novelists*, p. 181.

62. Taine, *Derniers essais*, p. 132.

63. Cf. what Michèle Hecquet calls *"euphemisation"* ("Contrats et symboles," p. 38).

1. Idealism in the Novel: Recanonizing Sand

Sandian idealism is both literally and figuratively euphemistic in that it involves a blurring of contours as well a preference for "general terms rather than the vocabulary of concrete practices, toned-down terms rather than violent ones."

64. Sand, "*L'Education sentimentale*," p. 421. For more on Sand and realism, see also Champfleury and Sand, *Du réalisme*.

65. Auerbach, *Mimesis*, p. 445. See also Swales, "The Problem of Nineteenth-Century German Realism," pp. 68–84. Sand's well-known debt to Goethe—*Jacques*, for example, rewrites the *Elective Affinities*—but also her condemnation of Goethe's lack of social conscience (see her "Essai sur le drame fantastique" in *Souvenirs*, pp. 3–98) appear here in a new light, because, according to Auerbach, Goethe's aesthetic choices, particularly his aristocratic rejection of realism, decisively inflected the history of German literature. It is because Goethe is the central canonic figure of German literature and because Goethe eschewed bourgeois realism that realism failed to take hold in Germany.

66. Sand, *Story of My Life*, p. 921 / *Oeuvres autobiographiques*, 2:159.

67. Sand, *La Marquise*, in *Nouvelles*, p. 45.

68. Chambers, *L'Ange et l'automate*.

69. Sand, *La Marquise*, in *Nouvelles*, p. 60.

70. Sand, *Story of My Life*, p. 931 / *Oeuvres autobiographiques*, 2:173.

71. The translation is mine, from a letter by Latouche cited by Georges Lubin in Sand, *Correspondance* 2:88 n. 1 (cited by Didier in her preface to *Indiana*).

72. My reading of the opening pages of *Indiana* differs from that of Naginski, for whom Sand's privileged intertext is Chateaubriand's *René* (*George Sand*, p. 57). As I read it, the opening scene, and especially the description of the curious *ménage à trois* grouped around the hearth with its static tableau and painterly chiaroscuro effect, is a clear pastiche of Balzac's neo-Dutch realist mode.

73. George Sand, cited in Didier's "Notes et variantes" in *Indiana*, p. 380 n. 13.

74. Salomon, *George Sand*, p. 29. The issue of Sand's representation of her male protagonists is a persistent preoccupation in Sand criticism, dating at least as far back as the reception of *Indiana*. While Sainte-Beuve in his article on *Indiana* did not take Sand's portrayal of Raymon to signify the author's allegiance to realism, he did take it to betray her sex, writing that Raymon is "exposed in all his miserable selfishness in a way no man, not even a Raymon, would ever have been able to see or dared to say" (*Les Grands Ecrivains français*, p. 45). Proudhon speaks of Sand's "androphobia" (*Les Femmelins*, p. 89). Sandy Petrey argues in "George and Georgina Sand" that Sand's demonstration in *Indiana* of the constructedness of gender is an instance of her realism. Indeed, according to Petrey, there is no room for the ideal in the realist framework in place in *Indiana*, because the ideal itself is shown there to be dependent on collective ratification rather than a timeless absolute or essence:

> The entire binary structure of the opposition between Real and Ideal . . . is radically incompatible with the historicized vision of existence that unites *Indiana* with the work of Stendhal and Balzac. Within that vision, the reality that counts is a social construct instead of an objective given, the ideal a social validation instead of a subjective dream.

Because in Petrey's terms realism and with it "realist gender"—i.e., Raymon's—depend entirely on the consensus of a given society, "where there is no *monde* there is no realism"; thus in *Indiana* idealism with its inevitably "essentialist ideology" is to be found only in the valley of Bernica.

75. Sand, *Indiana*, p. 46/89. This reference is to the English and French editions, respectively.

2. Idealism and Its Discontents

1. Sand, *Lélia*, p. 113/176. Here and in all other double references to *Lélia* in the text and notes, the first is to the English translation and the second to the French edition published in 1985.

2. Sand, *Story of My Life*, p. 946/*Oeuvres autobiographiques*, 2:196–97.

3. *Lélia*, p. 350.

4. For two helpful attempts to track the sequence of nonevents in *Lélia*, see Naginski, *George Sand*, pp. 105–37, and Waller, *The Male Malady*.

5. Quoted in *Lélia*, pp. 592–93.

6. Cf. this excerpt from a review of *André* and *Leone Leoni* by Adolphe Groult, cited by Iknayan in *The Idea of the Novel in France*:

> Generally the action gets off to a good start, the exposition is natural, but no sooner have the actors been named and produced, than the poet, carried away by her own movement, transports heavenward the drama begun on earth; her figures become larger, elevated, idealized; but at the same time, and by a necessary consequence, they leave earth and lose their footing, and the scene, which had opened in the Beauce or the Berry, on such day of such year, ends up in time and space. (p. 121)

7. Todorov, *Theories of the Symbol*, p. 199.

8. Didier, introduction to Sand, *Lélia*, 1:31.

9. In all fairness to Didier, it should be pointed out that she is no more interested in the psychological realism of Lélia's confession than she is in the allegorical dimensions of the text, hence her intriguing decision to reprint the more overtly feminist 1839 version of the novel. And yet in the final paragraph of her introductory essay, she writes: "Granted it is not easy to write the novel of a mystic; and it is perhaps there that resides the lack of understanding with which the *Lélia* of 1839 was met. And yet one might well wonder whether in the final analysis, the character is not more real and more present in 1839 than in 1833" (p. 46).

10. Sand, "Préface de 1939," in *Lélia*, p. 350.

11. Sand, *Story of My Life*, p. 922/*Oeuvres autobiographiques*, 2:161.

12. Quoted in *Lélia*, p. xxxix. See Naginski, "*Lélia*: The Novel of the Invisible," in *George Sand*, pp. 105–37.

13. On ethical idealism, see Rescher, *Ethical Idealism*, which although written in a mode I find completely alien, does contain some useful insights.

2. Idealism and Its Discontents

14. de Man, "Allegory (*Julie*)," p. 206.

15. Bossis, "L'Homme-dieu," p. 186. Bossis's exact words are: "Sand's heroes suffer from the malady of ideality."

16. See Chasseguet-Smirgel, *The Ego Ideal*, esp. pp. 10–25; see also her *Ethique et esthétique de la perversion*. If one can fault Bossis with missing what is perhaps most applicable to Sand of Chasseguet-Smirgel's theories—that is, as we shall see below (chapter 5), her insistence on the narcissistic aspects of "la maladie d'idéalité"—then one can surely fault Chasseguet-Smirgel's failure to take any account of Lacan's parallel and contemporary theorization of the same pathology.

17. An early version of this analysis was originally presented at a session of the Thirteenth Annual Conference on Nineteenth-Century French Studies held at Northwestern University in Fall 1987. During the discussion period, my copanelist, Leslie Rabine, asked me a simple question pinpointing an amazing and embarrassing omission in the final section of my paper: "What about Pulchérie?" In other words, repeating Sand's gesture, I, too, had become fascinated by the main protagonist, to the exclusion and erasure of her sister, the only other major female character in the book.

18. Beauvoir, *The Second Sex*, p. 202.

19. Warner, *Monuments and Maidens*, p. 199.

20. For more on the crucial distinction between women's writing and feminist writing, see N. Miller, *Subject to Change*, esp. pp. 5 and 8–10.

21. Pointon, *Naked Authority*, p. 64. The relationship of gender and allegory is also discussed at length in the final chapter of the book, "Guess Who's Coming to Lunch? Allegory and the Body in Manet's *Le Déjeuner sur l'herbe*." Based on Pointon's readings of these two canonic nineteenth-century French visual texts, it would appear that female allegory—and allegory is here always coded as female versus male realism—cannot hold, that the representation of the naked or seminaked female body on which allegory relies so heavily introduces an unruly and ultimately destabilizing element into the space of representation, one that ends up problematizing allegory itself. Unfortunately, since her concern is exclusively the male canon, Pointon does not address the issue of female uses of allegory.

Remaining within the domain of painting—though not at first the domain of gender— one might note that another major icon of nineteenth-century French painting poses by its very enigmatic subtitle the problem of the relationship of allegory and its incompatibility not with idealism but rather with realism. I refer, of course, to Courbet's *Atelier du peintre: Allégorie réelle*. As Champfleury, Courbet's ardent promoter, wrote: "An allegory cannot be real any more than a reality can be allegorical" (*Du réalisme*, p. 73). Champfleury solved or eluded the problem posed by the oxymoronic subtitle by separating out those figures he deemed allegorical (figures on the left) from those he qualified as real (central and right-hand figures). The notion that the central female figure might embody the dilemma of fusing allegory and realism is totally absent from Champfleury's reading.

This is as good a place as any to note that in his aesthetic writings Delacroix firmly aligns himself with the idealists, rehearsing all the standard idealist arguments against realism, which he equates with detailism. See Delacroix, "Réalisme en idéalisme," in *Oeuvres littéraires*, pp. 57–68.

22. Sand, *Correspondance*, 8:391–92.

23. See *Correspondance*, 8:400–408.

24. Having opted for a discussion of the works over the life, or having at least temporarily bracketed the life, Dickenson, for example, founds her analysis of Sand's (faulty) feminism on a distinction between the fiction and the essays: "In the essays, this dogma of 'separate but equal' often degenerates into 'certainly separate, and not so equal as all that.' In the novels, paradoxically, women are often presented as different and *superior*" (*George Sand*, p. 47). In some sense, my move here is the opposite, perhaps because it is not motivated by a search for a better feminism, especially of the eighties' variety that Dickenson identifies with Carol Gilligan's ethics of caring.

25. Sand, *Lettres à Marcie*, p. 165.

26. Sand, *Indiana* (1978), n.p.; "Préface de l'édition de 1842," *Indiana* (1984), pp. 46–47.

27. Rabine, "George Sand," p. 2.

28. Sivert, "*Lélia* and Feminism," p. 47.

29. See J. Butler, *Gender Trouble*. At the very moment when I began writing this text, I noted in the program of the 1990 MLA that a session was to be devoted precisely to this question. The session was entitled "Toward a Definition of Sand's Feminism," and the titles of the talks to be given under this rubric were: (1) "*Consuelo*: The Fiction of Feminism," Pierrette Daly; (2) "The Limits of Sand's Feminism: Marriage in the Novels of Her Maturity (1857–76)," Lucy M. Schwarz; (3) "Un idéal mythique de la femme," Simone Vierne; and (4) "Textual Feminism in George Sand's Early Fiction," Françoise Massarider-Kenney. One might conclude on the basis of these titles that the reading of Sand's fictional feminism remains the dominant trend in Sand studies.

30. Maurois, *Lélia*, p. 324.

31. O'Brien, "George Sand and Feminism," p. 89. O'Brien's conclusion is the following: "For women of the nineteenth century there was no dilemma as to whether or not Sand was working for the cause of women" (p. 88). We judge her feminism according to anachronistic criteria at the risk of dehistoricizing it: "To select several tenets of feminism held in our day by some feminists and say that all who do not hold these views are inimical to the cause is ahistorical" (p. 89). O'Brien's cautionary note is welcome, although, as I will attempt to show, some of the problems posed by Sand's feminism have a very contemporary dimension.

32. Chonez, "George Sand et le féminisme," pp. 77 and 79. What follows is worth quoting but needs no comment:

> In any case today she would be a woman who votes and wears pants. . . . Some analysis would have freed her of her frigidity or naturally freed in her the expression of physical love, but a mother adoring her brood, a cautious woman in the face of violence, a good traditional housewife, she would almost surely be totally opposed to the MLF [Mouvement de Libération des Femmes]. (p. 79)

33. Vareille, *Socialité, sexualité*, p. 397. Of all the discussions of Sand's feminism, I

find this to be the most thoughtful and the most enlightening; my only reservation is that Vareille seems unfamiliar with contemporary feminist theorists.

34. Dickenson, *George Sand*, p. 73.

35. Macherey, "Un Roman panthéiste," p. 41.

36. Sand, *Correspondance*, 3:713.

37. The interdiction that affects this relationship in Sand has less to do with some intellectual deficiency in women—an argument Sand always ridicules—than with the danger that certain *bad* philosophies, such as that of the Saint-Simonians, present for female virtue. Thus in a letter to François Rollinat dated October 16, 1835, Sand writes: "It is not easy for a woman to be both a philosopher and chaste at the same time" (Sand, *Correspondance*, 3:58).

That this issue was timely in the very intellectual circles in which Sand operated is indicated by an article by Lerminier, "Des Femmes philosophes," which appeared in the *Revue des Deux Mondes*. What is most interesting about this article (a review of two anonymously published works of religious philosophy by women) is that it demonstrates that the familiar essentialist line of argument—women do not have the inborn qualities necessary for pursuing speculative inquiry—is in fact subordinated to another—female intellectual activity is not good for the complexion and thus makes women less attractive to men. In other words, the essentialist argument is undone, shown up for what it is by the recognition that women can engage in higher mental activity and what prevents them from doing so is male anxiety: "Is it in the depths of a library, in a solitary study, her complexion pale from her nightly labors that we like to imagine a woman? No, that is not her place, that is not her life, and nature calls her elsewhere" (p. 678).

38. Sand, *Lettres à Marcie*, p. 229.

39. Scott, "The Sears Case," p. 174. Cf. Sand's analogous comments in her article on socialism:

> You attempt in vain to confuse the meaning of the word equality with identity. No, men are not identical with each other. The diversity of their forms, their instincts, their faculties, their appearances, their influence is infinite. There is no parity between one man and another. But these infinite diversities consecrate equality instead of destroying it. ("Socialisme," in *Questions*, pp. 258–59)

40. Sand, *Lettres à Marcie*, p. 229.

41. Scott, "The Sears Case," pp. 174–75.

42. On this topic, see Perrot, *Histoire de la vie privée*. It would appear, according to the women historians of private life, that whereas the Revolution initially marked a rupture with the splitting off of public/private, masculine/feminine, that was set into place throughout the eighteenth century—the public invading everything as the private became suspect—in the long run it was merely written into law and customs:

> The eighteenth century had refined the distinction between the public and the private. . . . The French Revolution operates in this evolution a dramatic and contradictory rupture, whose short-term effects must, moreover, be distinguished. In the immediate, "private" or "particular interests" are suspected to be a shadow

favorable to plots and treachery. . . . In the longer term, the Revolution accentuates
the definition of the public and private sphere, valorizes the family, differentiates
sexual roles by opposing political men and domestic women. (Perrot, "Avant et
ailleurs," *Histoire de la vie privée,* p. 17)

43. My emphasis here on the centrality of Sand's endorsement of the separation of
spheres should not be taken to signify that there were not other reasons for her opposition
to women in public life, notably one: the troubling issue of power. For as Heilbrun
forcefully reminds us, until very recently there was a veritable taboo on women's admitting
to a desire for power. In the nineteenth century, the "prohibition" on women wanting
to exercise power is the unspoken, unspeakable ground on which women's complicity
in their confinement to the domestic sphere rests. See Heilbrun, *Writing a Woman's Life,*
esp. the introduction.

44. Perrot, *Histoire de la vie privée,* p. 10.

45. Vareille, *Socialité, sexualité,* pp. 410–11.

46. This sweeping generalization needs to be checked against the evidence provided
by the history of French feminism, notably against the case of Saint-Simonian feminism.
Following Weil, I think the appropriate question here is: Is the feminism of the Saint-
Simonian women (as distinct from the men) in fact utopian? In a paper entitled
"Feminocentric Utopias and the Paris of the Saint-Simoniennes," Weil comments apropos
of Claire Démar's manifesto ("Appel d'une femme"): "Démar's vision is non-utopian
in the sense that it depends on no image and no plot of reunification" (np).

47. This expression was used by Hélène Cixous in the course of a debate that followed
the talk given by Francine Demichel at the conference on "Lecture de la différence
sexuelle," at the Collège International de Philosophie, October 18–20, 1990. For an
American listener or eavesdropper (myself), the violence of the debate that followed the
talk of a jurist who argued for the entrance of women into the "system" (by presenting
themselves for the entrance exams to the "grandes écoles," notably the ENA—Ecole
Nationale de l'Administration) was both very striking and significant, for it showed how
much the tendency to valorize the private feminine sphere remains alive in France, whereas
in the United States, however strong the separatist trends within the women's movement,
one knows that refusing to enter the system amounts to playing into the hands of the
most conservative, the most misogynist right wing. This does not, of course, mean that
the recuperation of the women's movement is not a permanent danger and that one
must not at all times play the double game of integration and of the preservation of the
revolutionary values of feminism.

The horror that the word *feminism* inspires in France and the utopianism that
accompanies its diversion are illustrated by the answer Perrot gave in an interview
published in a special issue of the *Nouvel Observateur* entitled "La Guerre sans dentelles,"
when the *Nouvel Observateur* asks her point-blank the question "Are you a feminist?":

The struggle for equality between men and women is not over. On the visible
horizon of history, one sees only a male domination. Male society is not always
a success. In the future, I hope that one will arrive at something else and, from

this point of view, I am a feminist. That does not mean that one should impose on women masculine values. What one must aim for is an equality that preserves the difference of identities. But as soon as women assert their difference, men tend to confine them in inferiority. ("Un Entretien," p. 170)

48. On the question of the difficult inheritance of the French Revolution for French feminism, see Fouque, "Women in Movements." See also chapters 3 and 4 of the present volume.

3. The Politics of Idealism

1. Brecht, "Against Georg Lukács," p. 69.
2. Jameson, "Reflections in Conclusion," p. 200.
3. Ibid., pp. 200–201.
4. Jauss, "The Idealist Embarrassment," pp. 191–92.
5. Surprisingly little in Marx's own aesthetic writings relates to this question and what there is does not intersect with the few mentions of George Sand. When Marx does comment on the ideal in literature, his remarks are consistently and not surprisingly negative: he scorns the idealism in his own early efforts at writing poetry, steadfastly rejects the idyllic aspects of nineteenth-century German literature, demystifies the romantic idealism of Lamartine, and in perhaps his most significant statement on the subject opposes Shakespearian realism to Schillerian idealism, when it is not Rembrandt to Raphael. On Marx's aesthetics, see Prawer, *Karl Marx and World Literature*.

To the extent that Marx does mention Sand, that mention is favorable. He chooses to end his attack on Proudhon in *The Holy Family* with a ringing quotation from one of Sand's most-forgotten texts, *Jean Ziska*. In Sand's *Correspondance* is a copy of a letter from Arnold Ruge asking to meet with Sand, then at the height of her political idealist phase, to discuss "the democratic interests of France and Germany, whose intimate union should serve as the base for a publication . . . we have just founded in Paris" (March 11, 1844, *Correspondance*, 6:476–77). The "we" refers, of course, to Ruge and Marx. The journal (*Deutsch-französische Jahrbücher*) was short-lived, and it appears that the projected meeting between Sand and Marx never took place. One can only dream about what they would have said to each other.

Though the question of whether Marx was actually introduced to Sand in 1844 remains unanswerable, her correspondence does contain one angry letter to Marx as editor regarding an inflammatory canard he had published in the *Neue Rheinische Zeitung* regarding her role in Bakunin's exile from France. Marx complied with her request and published her letter in a following issue of his newspaper (July 20, 1848, *Correspondance*, 8:546–48).
6. Coward and Ellis, *Language and Materialism*, p. 2.
7. In her book *Critical Practice*, Belsey traces the concomitance of idealism and empiricism back to New Criticism and its avatars.
8. On conventionalism as a new, degraded form of empiricism and hence of idealism,

see Lazarus, "Doubting the New World Order," esp. pp. 115–28. The slippery slope whereby the attack on empiricism as an idealism leads right back to the very idealism that is being denounced goes as follows: "Postmodernism prematurely extirpates *realism* in the course of its campaign against *empiricism*, resorting to an epistemological conventionalism that shades almost inevitably into idealism, pragmatism, and 'judgmental relativism' " (p. 115).

9. See Lazarus's illuminating and passionate case for realism, "Doubting the New World Order." Lazarus's concern is, of course, with postmodern social theory and Marxist epistemology, not literary criticism, but when he insists on the existence of objects "independently of their discursive inscription" (p. 118) and retraces the linguistic turn in recent structuralist/poststructuralist thought, it is not hard to see how these debates impinge upon theories of literary realism and the self-righteous critique of "naive" referentiality. In fact, no incompatibility exists between reconsidering idealism in the novel and grounding new epistemological claims for realism because, as I noted in chapter 1, the idealism/realism paradigm in aesthetics only makes sense if one assumes an exterior reality available for but also independent of representation.

10. Eagleton, *Criticism and Ideology*, pp. 125–26.

11. This formula has a certain inevitability—one finds it, for example, in Williams, *The Country and the City*—since, and this point is, of course, of critical importance in any serious discussion of the place of idealism in Marxist aesthetics, socialist realism was virtually by definition at the same time a socialist idealism, a programmatic fusion of realist representation and revolutionary romanticism. This observation is not destined to improve Sand's standing in a Lukácsian perspective, since Lukács had, as is well known, little use for the heroic worker types of socialist realism; rather, it is meant to emphasize how thin is the line between realism and idealism within the context of Marxist aesthetics when the link between idealism and idealization is fully grasped.

12. It should come as no surprise that Brunetière, one of the architects of the canon of French literature, dismisses Sand's social thought in the following patronizing terms: "Rather than having tried to set the classes against each other, we must thank her for having 'married' them. . . . It's childish as a solution to the social question; but at least it's not done reluctantly—and it's so feminine" ("La Transformation du lyrisme," p. 319).

13. It is of more than passing interest for the sake of my general argument that when in *Isidora* (1845) Sand does return to "the woman question": (1) She takes the opportunity to enunciate her critique of Rousseau, having her heroine Julie/Isidora say, "The sublime Rousseau did not understand women. . . . In spite of his goodwill and good intentions, he could not conceive of them as anything but second-class social beings. To them he left traditional religion, from which he liberated men. He did not anticipate their need for the same faith and the same morals as their fathers, husbands, and sons, nor that they would feel degraded by having a different temple and a different doctrine. He created nursemaids, thinking he had made mothers. He mistook the maternal breast for the generative soul. Last century's most spiritual philosopher was a materialist in regards to the question of woman" (*Isidora*, p. 68). (2) She does not, as she does in her

feminist fiction of the thirties, separate issues of class from those of gender (Sourian, preface to Sand, *Isidora*, pp. 21–23, 27). (3) She adopts, as in *Lettres à Marcie*, a generically mixed form that combines diary, social treatise, omniscient narration, and letters.

14. Sand, *Le Péché de Monsieur Antoine*, p. 154.

15. A. Michel in her article "Structures romanesques" was the first to detect an ambiguity in what she calls Sand's "marriage novels," and she ascribes this ambiguity to a contradiction in Sand's feminism, "which maintains together two equally powerful tendencies, one which makes marriage odious and another which makes of it a state of perfection" (p. 37). Because she takes as her paradigmatic antirealist novel, *Consuelo* (cf. Naginski, *George Sand*), Michel casts her analysis in terms rather different from mine: for her, the crucial opposition is that between desacralized and resacralized marriages. But, despite our different emphases, we concur in seeing the promarriage novels as embodying a faith in the necessary fusion of love and marriage. The marriage that is exalted is not a *mariage de raison* but a love union sanctified in the case of the socialist idealist novels by higher social imperatives that are also ethical.

16. Sand, *The Journeyman Joiner*, p. 383/379. This and all subsequent double references to *The Journeyman Joiner* in the text and notes are to the English and 1988 French editions, respectively.

17. If one wanted to pursue this line of thinking further, one would have to consider what Johnson calls "the unavowed sadism of idealization" as it is manifested in Petrarchan love poetry; see her "Gender and Poetry," p. 181 n. 27. Johnson is referring here to Vickers's reading of Petrarch in "Diana Described."

18. Not only the main protagonists are idealized here. As Lucette Czyba has shown in a very pertinent article, "La Femme et le prolétaire," one of the most heavily idealized figures in the novel is la Savinienne, who represents "la femme du peuple." As we shall see later, Sand's representation of working women breaks with two separate but equally negative stereotypes: that produced by a reactionary conservative tradition of depicting the "laboring classes" as "dangerous" and, more troubling for feminists, the tendency in nineteenth-century women's fiction to portray the working-class woman as an exemplar of a "degraded female subjectivity."

For more on Sand and the representation of the people, see her letter to Louise Colet of February 1843, where she takes Colet to task for representing the people as abject without any compensatory analysis of the causes of the people's misery (*Correspondance* 6:51–53).

19. Sand, *Le Compagnon* (1988), p. 31.

20. See Robin, *Le Réalisme socialiste*, pp. 244–329, esp. pp. 271–329. She herself draws on Mathewson, *The Positive Hero*. As one critic remarks, "The problem of the positive hero is obvious; how to give him life" (Rodney Livingstone in Scriven and Tate, *European Socialist Realism*, p. 18). It is, of course, consistent with Lukács's well-known preference for bourgeois realism that he is particularly critical of the positive hero figure in the works of socialist realists.

21. Sand, *Le Compagnon* (1988), p. 31.

3. The Politics of Idealism

22. On this point I disagree with Czyba. According to Czyba, "her [Sand's] generous utopia does not separate the rehabilitation and emancipation of the worker from that of women" ("La Femme et le prolétaire," p. 21). And yet, as she herself acknowledges, this linkage of socialism and feminism does not preclude, indeed entails, the reinscription of a hierarchy within the "ideal couple," wherein the heroine becomes the apostle of her messianic companion. More disturbing still, for reasons that will become apparent, the precondition for Yseult's promotion to the dignity of protagonist is, as Czyba rightly observes, her decorporealization. And even though both members of the transgressive couple are similarly made to submit to this loss of embodiment, the imperative unquestionably weighs more heavily on the female protagonist.

The crucial point to be made here is that in the world of Eros, idealization always entails disembodiment. As Green writes, "Idealization rests on two closely related notions: overestimation and disembodiment" ("L'Idéal," p. 31). See also the very pertinent analysis by Chasseguet-Smirgel of the metaphysical nature of courtly love, the supreme form of idealizing Eros, *The Ego Ideal*, pp. 57–60.

23. Didier, preface to Sand, *Le Meunier*, p. 11.

24. For more on Sand and Scott, see her important letter of about July 13, 1846, to Anténor Joly in Sand, *Correspondance*, 7:55–56, as well as p. 73.

25. Emmanuel Leroy-Ladurie on plebeian romance literature, as cited in Fowler, *The Alienated Reader*, p. 14.

26. It is no accident that in his very pertinent study *Literarisch-politische Avantgarde in Frankreich*, Biermann also chooses to focus on the same three novels by Sand.

27. My criteria for defining my corpus are shared with Biermann but not with the author of a major study of Sand's political idealism, Hecquet. In her *thèse d'état*, *Contrats et symboles: Essai sur l'idéalisme de George Sand* (1990), Hecquet limits her corpus to five novels: *Le Compagnon du tour de France*, *Horace*, *Jeanne*, *Le Meunier d'Angibault*, and *Le Péché de Monsieur Antoine*. Two comments are in order here: (1) Like me and like Biermann, Hecquet explicitly excludes *Consuelo* from her corpus, confirming my sense that *Consuelo* does not belong in a study of Sand's socialist fiction. (2) If I have not included *Horace* (1841), Sand's depiction of cross-class relationships in a Parisian student milieu, it is because it lacks another key feature of her socialist fiction as I read it: the provincial setting. It is as though there were a necessary (though not sufficient) link between Sand's regionalism and her socialist fiction.

For a summary of Hecquet's thesis, see "Contrats et symboles" in *George Sand: Une Oeuvre multiforme*. Though we share a common conviction that Sand's idealism is ripe for reconsideration and though we concur on several points (see chapter 1), for Hecquet, Sand's idealism is purely political and studied only as it is manifested in the five novels listed above.

28. Sand, *Le Meunier d'Angibault*, p. 37. This and all successive citations are to the edition listed under Sand in the references.

29. I am indebted in what follows to Shoshana Felman's reading of *Novembre* in "Modernité du lieu commun."

30. Sand, *Indiana*, pp. 272–73/291. This and all subsequent references to *Indiana* in the notes and the text are to the English and French editions, respectively.

3. The Politics of Idealism

31. Schor, "Female Fetishism."

32. I refer here to Gallop's reading of Lacan's "Le Stade du miroir" (The mirror stage) in "Where to Begin," in *Reading Lacan*, pp. 74–92.

33. See Vareille, *Socialité, sexualité*, pp. 57–70, esp. p. 63. Though scrupulously fair and judicious in her reading, Vareille nevertheless downplays the elements that make this first Sandian utopia so problematic. It is, of course, essential to her argument in favor of the utopian closure of the novel that Bernica be the site of a coming-to-sexuality for Indiana.

34. Earlier in the novel, Sand quite explicitly links the absence of children with an absence of sexual fulfillment when she says of Colonel Delmare: "Too enfeebled by age and hardships to aspire to become a father, he had remained an old bachelor in his home, and had taken a wife as he would have taken a housekeeper" (p. 251/271).

35. Sand, *Correspondance* 7:56.

36. Cited in Caors, addenda to Sand, *Le Meunier* (1990), p. 298.

37. Caors, preface to Sand, *Le Meunier* (1990), p. 5.

38. Didier, preface to Sand, *Le Meunier* (1985), p. 17.

39. The issues raised by *Le Meunier* are indeed traditional questions debated in France from romanticism up until the present regarding the proper relationship between utilitarian, engaged writing and *l'art pour l'art*. Throughout the mid-nineteenth century, Sand's writings were at the heart of this debate, which was carried out mainly in the newspapers of the time. On the critical response to the humanitarian novel, see Iknayan's invaluable *The Idea of the Novel in France*, especially pp. 94–95.

40. Sand, "Quelques mots sur chacun de mes romans," in *Souvenirs*, p. 99.

41. Perdiguier, "Lettres," p. 441.

42. As quoted in Larnac, *George Sand révolutionnaire*, p. 63.

43. Lerminier, "Poètes et romanciers," p. 97. For more on the generally hostile contemporary reception of Sand's social novels (including the pastoral trilogy), see Mayr, *Studien*.

44. Writing of *Consuelo*, Hubert Juin attributes Sand's decanonization to her utopian politics: "In *Consuelo*, George Sand, between the 'lightning bolt of July' and the wet firecracker of 1848, made herself the impious priestess of 'remythifying' liberty. She had convinced herself that *hope* should speak. This is perhaps why she is so despised today!" (*Lectures du dix-neuvième siècle*, p. 198).

45. Chow, "The Politics and Pedagogy," p. 29.

46. Sand, *Correspondance* 6:616.

47. Given my inability to provide a reference for this quotation, I propose a new term to cover this sort of scholarly failure: loc. lost.

48. Caors, preface to Sand, *Le Meunier*, p. 296.

49. Sand, *Correspondance*, 6:623.

50. Biermann, *Literarisch-politische Avantgarde*, p. 100.

51. Kaplan, *Sea Changes*, p. 168. I shall be drawing heavily in what follows from Kaplan's illuminating essay "Pandora's Box," pp. 147–76.

52. Kaplan, "Like a Housemaid's Fancies," p. 62.

53. See Orr, *Headless History*, pp. 17–18 n. 25.

54. This citation from Rousseau's essay *Politics and the Arts* gives the title to Carol Pateman's useful reflections on the misogyny of most contract theories and the problems this misogyny poses for theorizing woman's participation in democratic societies.

55. Kaplan, *Sea Changes*, p. 161.

56. Barthes, *S/Z*.

57. Letter from H. de Latouche to George Sand, reprinted in the "Annexe" to Sand, *Le Péché de Monsieur Antoine*, p. 386. This and all subsequent references to *Le Péché* are to the edition listed in the bibliography.

58. Bloch, *The Utopian Function*, pp. 245–64 and 265–77, respectively.

59. Faced with the challenge of coming up with a title that was not simply the name of a character, Sand experienced unusual difficulties. The rejected possibilities also included, among others, *"Le Vieux et le neuf," "L'Amour et l'argent,"* and even *"Hier et aujourd'hui."* See Sand, *Correspondance*, vol. 7., esp. pp. 51–53.

60. Bloch, *The Utopian Function*, p. 262.

61. I borrow this Ricoeurian notion from Jameson's luminous chapter on Ernst Bloch in *Marxism and Form*, p. 119.

62. Suvin, *Metamorphoses of Science Fiction*, p. 37.

63. Bloch, *The Utopian Function*, p. 130.

64. Jauss, "The Perfect as the Fascinosum," p. 14. See also his "On the Origins of the Differentiation," which directly precedes that essay.

65. Suvin's complete definition of utopia, arrived at after a coruscating survey of previous definitions is:

> Utopia is the verbal construction of a particular quasi-human community where sociopolitical institutions, norms, and individual relationships are organized according to a *more perfect* principle than in the author's community, this construction being based on estrangement arising out of an alternative historical hypothesis. (*Metamorphoses of Science Fiction*, p. 49; emphasis added)

Cf. Jauss's reminder that Rousseau was in some sense the first modernist in that in his second *Discourse*, he was the first to call for the substitution of the notion of *perfectibility* for that of *perfection*, which had been "usurped by art":

> Measured in terms of the human capacity for self-perfection (whether for better or worse, since Rousseau's neologism has no teleological intent), perfection must lose its ontological primacy, and must finally be given up once its illusory nature has been perceived: "Ne cherchez point la chimère de la perfection, mais le mieux possible selon la nature de l'homme et la constitution de la société." ("The Perfect as the Fascinosum," p. 24)

66. Rancière, *Aux bords du politique*, pp. 81–84, esp. p. 81.

67. Leroux, *De l'egalité*, p. 174. Cf. Derrida, *Séminaire* 1990–91, where Derrida probes the consumption/excretion cycle. As he remarks: "What one eats is always the Other, a member of the community" (November 11, 1990). In the light of his remarks, one might well ask: *Who* is being eaten at this great fraternal banquet? Who is being sacrificed?

3. The Politics of Idealism

That utopia in Sand always entails "an obligatory passage through loss, sacrifice, or separation" (p. 37) is a point also made by Hecquet in "Contrats et symboles: Essai sur l'idéalisme de George Sand," where she notes that for this very reason Sand's utopias are not regressive. Hecquet, however, does not take note of the gender of the sacrificial victim.

68. Schor, "The Portrait of a Gentleman."

69. Freadman, "Of Cats, and Compagnons," p. 129.

70. In the course of an interview with Pierre Nora, first published in *Le Débat*, Fouque, the chief theoretician of the "Psych et Po" movement of French feminism, develops at some length her analysis of the incompatibility of the women's movement and the society of brothers. For her, it is not patriarchy but rather what she calls *filiarchy* ("le filiarcat") that constitutes the root of women's problems in modern societies: "Nothing excludes girls more than brotherhoods do" and "The coming together of sons and brothers after the regicide to establish democracy radically and a priori excludes women" ("Women in Movements," p. 19). Filiarchy is inherent in Christianity, but the society of brothers is a modern, even a contemporary phenomenon—at one point, Fouque describes the era of fraternity in France as an effect of the events of May 1968. Given the grounding exclusion of women from the democratic order set into place by the "coming together of sons and brothers after the regicide," there is no other solution from Fouque's separatist perspective than rewriting the Republican motto and system to include a fourth term to take us beyond fraternity: "There are two sexes. It is a reality that the history of human rights, if it wants to remain worthy of its ideals, should make its fourth principle, after liberty, equality, and fraternity. The Women's Movement has brought with it, from the beginning, this fourth revolution that I used to call the revolution of the symbolic" (p. 22).

The notion that we live under the regime of the band of brothers, in the era of a dominant narcissistic homosocial order, is, of course, not new in terms of feminist cultural analysis. The difficulty with this model is that of periodization; the danger is always of slipping into a dehistoricized notion of a timeless parricide by a mythical horde of brother-sons. The problem of historicization is further complicated by debates over the role of the French Revolution as absolute initiator or mere accelerator of transformations already under way. To reduce an immensely complex tangle of issues to a simple question: Was the fraternal compact a cause or an effect of the Revolution?

71. For a more strictly American formulation of the same dilemma, see Cornell, "The Doubly-Prized World." Cornell's attempt is to think through a position beyond the essentialism debates that would mediate between Catherine MacKinnon's hard-nosed endorsement of absolute equality and Carol Gilligan's valorization of a higher female ethics. "Feminism calls us to the dream of a utopia of sensuous ease in which the reality of the castrated subject appears as a nightmare from which we are trying to awaken" (p. 699).

4. *The Fraternal Pact:* La Petite Fadette *and* Nanon

1. Moers, "Fraternal George Sand," p. 225; emphasis added.

2. Pateman, *The Disorder of Women*, p. 40. In this extremely pertinent chapter, Pateman fails to take note of important differences between French and English, which may give a linguistic ground to the vaunted differences between English and French feminisms: whereas in English, it is possible to distinguish brotherhood from fraternity, in French, *fraternité* is the only word that adequately conveys both these meanings. There is, of course, the word *confrérie*, but it signifies a (religious) brotherhood or sisterhood, a confraternity.

3. Derrida, "The Politics of Friendship," p. 642.

4. Sand, *Correspondance*, 8:430–31.

5. As Lubin comments, "This letter informs us that G.S. was on the Arch of Triumph with the provisional government," in Sand, *Correspondance*, 8:430 n. 1.

6. On the relationship between the social and the sexual contract, see, in addition to Pateman, Armstrong, *Desire and Domestic Fiction*, pp. 30–42. For more feminist analyses of the disastrous consequences for women of the replacement in modern times of patriarchy by what Antoinette Fouque calls "fratriarchy," see, in addition to the works by Pateman and Fouque already cited, MacCannell, *The Regime of the Brother*. Miming the allegedly historical succession of patriarchy by fratriarchy, feminists—but not only feminists—are now turning their attention away from the regime of the father to the regime of the brother(s). As I write, fratriarchy is quickly replacing patriarchy as the order most inimical to women's liberation.

7. Sand, *Little Fadette*, p. 7/33, emphasis added. This and all subsequent double references to *Little Fadette* in the notes and the text are to the English and French editions, respectively.

8. Sand, "L'Auteur au lecteur," in *La Mare au diable*, p. 30, emphasis added.

9. Cf. N. Miller, "Arachnologies: The Woman, the Text, and the Critic" and "The Knot, the Letter, and the Book" in *Subject to Change*, pp. 77–101 and 125–61, respectively. In her essay "Let's Go to the Fountain," Berger interprets this attempt to retrieve and make audible the oral and dialectal language of the peasant as a desire to retrieve "the mother's tongue, as though it were the living source of her artistic language" (p. 57).

10. My reference to a "first-stage" feminist reading alludes to histories of feminist criticism that generally equate the infancy of feminist criticism with a focus on "images of women" (particularly in male-authored texts). See, for example, Moi, *Sexual/Textual Politics*.

11. Deutsch, *The Psychology of Women*, p. 304. Cf. Cate, *George Sand*, for yet another biographical reading of what he terms a "juvenile version of *The Taming of the Shrew*": "The village brat was quite obviously (though the author may not consciously have realized it) her own daughter Solange" (p. 606), with whom Sand had a famously stormy relationship.

12. Danahy, "Growing Up Female," p. 50. See also Danahy, "*La Petite Fadette*: The Dilemma of Being a Heroine," in *The Feminization of the Novel*, pp. 159–91.

13. Danahy, *The Feminization of the Novel*, p. 180.

14. Moers, *Literary Women*, p. 53.

15. de Lauretis, *Alice Doesn't*, p. 137.

16. It is symptomatic of the novel's peculiar split structure that over the years critics have had a hard time deciding who is the central character, choosing to focus either on Fadette (Deutsch, Danahy), to the exclusion of the twins, or on one of the twins—see, for example, Grant's focus on Landry in his article "George Sand's *La Petite Fadette* and the Problem of Masculine Individuation"—to the exclusion of the other twin and Fadette. As we shall see below, my own double reading ends up by focusing on the most neglected figure in the triangle, Sylvinet, who certainly deserves an article of his own.

17. Bogaert, introduction to Sand, *La Petite Fadette*, pp. 18–19.

18. Bettelheim, *The Uses of Enchantment*, p. 91.

19. Girard, *Violence and the Sacred*, p. 57.

20. On woman as *coupure*, see Lemoine-Luccioni, *Partage des femmes*, pp. 91 and 98.

21. Here I part ways with Pateman, who sees the fraternal pact as a perpetuation of the conjugal rights of the patriarch. Following Freud's anthropological fable in *Totem and Taboo*, the brothers bound by the fraternal compact share the women monopolized by the primal father. In *Fadette*, however, there is no sharing, because there is only one available woman. See Pateman, *The Disorder of Women*, esp. pp. 36–46.

22. Sand, *Nanon*, p. 81.

23. There are many comparisons to be made among these three figures, and especially between Nanon—who is described as having a "coeur simple" (p. 95)—and Félicité, in relation to the acquisition of knowledge.

24. MacCannell, *The Regime of the Brother*, p. 39.

25. Hecquet, *Mauprat de George Sand*, esp. chapter 3, "L'Ere des contrats ou l'apprentissage de la patience: Sand et Rousseau," pp. 69–92.

5. Transmissions: *Histoire de ma vie*

1. Sand, *Story of My Life*, p. 800/*Oeuvres autobiographiques*, 1:1107. All subsequent double references in the notes and the text are to the English translation, then the French.

2. Lubin, introduction to Sand, *Oeuvres autobiographiques*, 1:xxi. The bon mot is from Pontmartin, *Nouvelles causeries littéraires*, p. 360. Cf. the parodistic tone of the *Voyage en Auvergne*, Sand's earliest (1827) attempt at writing her memoirs, where in an explicit ellipsis she cavalierly alludes to the family history she will *not* write in order to get to her own more quickly: "Let's move on to chapter 1, to follow the rules of the art, I should say something about my parents' history and even go back two or three generations back to their parents, but since I don't have the time, and I intend to finish

my work before dinner, I'm moving on to my story" (*Oeuvres autobiographiques*, 2:508). It is interesting to note that in this early autobiographical sketch, Sand acknowledges the existence of rules of the genre only to flaunt them. Suppressed in the *Voyage en Auvergne*, the obligatory genealogy returns with a vengeance in the much later *Histoire de ma vie*.

3. Mason, "The Other Voice," p. 231.

4. Taine, "George Sand," in *Derniers essais*, pp. 126–27.

5. Goux, *Symbolic Economies*, p. 222.

6. This chapter bears the traces of two conferences where early versions of the material were presented: to the "Transmissions" conference held at Dartmouth in May 1988 I owe the emphasis on transmission, which is in fact a key notion in Sand's *Histoire de ma vie*. Thus she writes, "We carry within us from birth instincts which are only the result of the blood that has been transmitted to us" (p. 82/1:24), and further, "Thus, you artisans who are learning to write, don't forget your departed ones any longer. Hand down the life of your forefathers to your sons" (p. 86/1:28). Fainter traces of the conference entitled "The Novelist and the Life," held at Stanford in February 1989 to honor Joseph Frank and Ian Watt can also be made out in the footnotes.

7. In the growing Sand bibliography, something of a split seems to be developing between the "motherists" and the "fatherists." The first, inspired by Brée's pioneering article "George Sand: The Fictions of Autobiography," take the position that the maternal and writing are indissolubly linked in Sand's fiction. The second, exemplified by Crecelius's *Family Romance*, argue that Sand's identification with her "good" (and/but also conveniently dead) father authorized her to write. The fatherist reading of the autobiography is made by Verjat who writes apropos of Sand's treatment of her mother in *Histoire de ma vie*: "In her narrative her role is rather unpleasant. It is set against the paternal hagiography and the idealization of the grandmother. We conclude from it that the motor of Sand's autobiographical model might well be the production of the mourning for the father and the evacuation of the mother" ("Formes et fonctions," p. 37). To the extent that I accept this split, I must at least initially make common cause with the fatherists.

8. Frank, *Dostoevsky*, p. 101.

9. The case could be made that, for Sand, autobiography is in fact a detail genre. She notes, for example: "It is in the detail, in the apparently insignificant deeds that one grasps the secret of the human conscience" (p. 185/1:180).

10. Sand, *Oeuvres autobiographiques*, 2:509.

11. Assoun, "Freud aux prises avec l'idéal," p. 100. In addition to this superb article, on which I have relied heavily throughout what follows, I would single out as particularly enlightening one other article that appeared in the same extremely rich special issue of the *Nouvelle Revue de Psychanalyse*: André Green's "L'Idéal."

12. Freud, "Family Romances," 9:238.

13. By undertaking what he terms an "archeology of idealism," Goux brilliantly argues the case for the link between the paternal and the ideal in the history of Western thought, notably in Marxist and Freudian theory. According to him, this association of the paternal and the ideal is rooted in the earliest theories of reproduction, where man

is the giver of form and woman the provider of matter: "*Idealism is first of all a conception of conception*" (*Symbolic Economies*, p. 213). Although carried out in a Marxist rather than a feminist perspective, Goux's theories can be described as feminist to the extent that his recuperation of the mother matter repressed by idealism is consonant with the philosophy of Luce Irigaray, who has sought to recover the founding materialism of Western thought by undertaking an archaeology of materialism, which is also inevitably of idealism. Of all the philosophers Luce Irigaray has "romanced" none, at least among her contemporaries, is closer to her than Goux.

But where I would disagree with Goux is in his endorsement of the irreconcilability of idealism and materialism. If the male idealist tradition he so lucidly analyzes cannot think of the maternal–nature as active—"*Generative* nature is the unthought absolute of an idealism that can conceive only a material nature" (p. 227)—as we shall see below, Sand is not far from inventing a sort of feminist idealism that incorporates the maternal.

14. Freud, *The Ego and the Id*, 19:31.

15. Freud, "Some Psychological Consequences," 19:257.

16. Freud, *The Ego and the Id*, 19:32.

17. Sand's identification with her father will be transferred onto her son Maurice, about whom she writes: "Maurice has all my habits, the very character I had then. Seeing his life begin, I feel I am rereading mine" ("Sketches and hints," in *Oeuvres autobiographiques*, 2:594). Following her own resolutely motherist reading of Sand, Berger reads the initial section of *Histoire de ma vie* less as the story of the father and hence of Sand's identification with the paternal figure than as "the marvelous story of a mother and son and their reciprocal passion" (p. 58). Citing a crucial passage from the autobiography describing the love of the sexless teenage son for his mother as ideal, superior to that of the daughter for the mother, Berger argues that Sand's apparent male identification masks a double female identification: "The ideal son is indeed a daughter; the loving son represents the ideal daughter of the mother, the one George Sand did not have but the one she was herself. It is in this way that George Sand identifies with her father; not with a paternal figure but with the son of the mother, even of two mothers" ("Let's Go to the Fountain," p. 59). It is only when she becomes a grandmother, at a remove as it were, that Sand comes to identify with a female relative, her favorite granddaughter, Aurore, to whom she wishes to transmit her legacy.

18. Lacan, *Les Complexes familiaux*, p. 65.

19. Hartmann and Loewenstein, "Notes on the Superego," p. 61.

According to Green, a similar rescue operation occurs on the metapsychological plane, as the elaboration of the very notion of the Ideal gives narcissism, a concept Freud had somewhat hastily introduced and abandoned in 1914, a new lease on life: "If narcissism is hardly mentioned at all after the final theory of drives and the second topography, it lives on at least under the auspices of the Ideal" ("Un Autre, neutre," p. 44).

Cf. Robert's remarks regarding the egotistical benefits of idealization in the family romance scenario: "The offspring of divine parents can only be an infant god. Thus the apologist is the first beneficiary of his idols' presumed virtues: the love he bestows is reciprocated, he basks in the reflected light of his parents' glory and the magnifying mirror of his admiration reflects his own image suitably enlarged" (*Origins of the Novel*,

p. 23). Much in Robert's work is useful for theorizing idealism in the novel, but her division of all novels into two categories (both derived from the family romance), the regressive (and idealizing) novel of the foundling and the adult novel of the "Realist Bastard" suffers both from the crudeness inherent in such striking generalizations and the complete phallocentrism of the conceptual apparatus and fictional examples.

20. Although Chasseguet-Smirgel recognizes that the ego ideal evolves in Freud's writings, where it becomes over the years "less the projection of narcissism on to the parents than the incorporation of idealized parents" (*The Ego Ideal*, p. 244), she rejects (without ever naming its principal theorizer) the Lacanian distinction between *idealich* and *ichideal*, saying: "Only the most passionate exegetists (in France) have been able to try and find some significance in what was simply a linguistic device to try and avoid repetition" (pp. 244–45). She does, however, recognize the importance of some of those theorists who have introduced what amounts to a "separate concept to designate the more archaic modalities of re-uniting ego and ideal" (p. 245).

21. Freud, "On Narcissism," 14:94.

22. As quoted in Chasseguet-Smirgel, *The Ego Ideal*, p. 245.

23. Martin, *Woman and Modernity*, p. 199.

24. Freud, *The Ego and the Id*, 19:37.

25. Riley, *Am I That Name*, pp. 40, 41.

26. Watt, *The Rise of the Novel*, p. 137.

27. Flaubert, as we have already noted, belongs in this tradition. There is no cruder expression of the grounding of male moral superiority in female anatomical lack than these remarks drawn from Flaubert's correspondence with one of his cronies: "Women have no notion of *Right*. The best of them do not scruple to listen behind doors, to unseal letters, to advise and practice thousands of little betrayals, etc. Everything comes from their organ. Where man has an Eminence, they have a Hole!" (*Correspondance*, 3:57).

28. Pateman, *The Disorder of Women*, p. 23. Pateman then goes on to rehearse much of the material covered in the previous pages.

29. Berger proposes another means by which Sand reconciles the mother and idealization. Arguing first that in Sand's "life and work it is the mother who guarantees access to the symbolic order," Berger goes on to suggest that "the path of idealization" ("Let's Go to the Fountain," p. 62) in Sand runs parallel to the "first education" of the child by the mother in "matters of cleanliness": "Does not the law of existence of George Sand's characters consist in having them march in the direction of the dry and clean? Is not learning to speak well a way of pleasing the mother by sublimating the erotic impulses and displacing them from the anal-genital zone to the mouth?" (p. 63). Interestingly enough, one of the prime examples of this scenario of maternal acculturation of a wild child saved from drowning is to be found in *François le champi*, but Berger makes nothing of the crucial fact that the relationship between the symbolic mother and the child is, as in the paradigmatic Mosaic version of this story, not biological but adoptive.

30. Mirecourt, *George Sand*, pp. 85–86.

6. Living On: Flaubert's Idealism

1. Flaubert, *Letters*, 2:235/*Oeuvres*, p. 181. Hereafter abbreviated FL and FOe, respectively.

2. Ibid., 2:239/393.

3. FL, 2:222; Sand and Flaubert, *Correspondance Flaubert-Sand*, 505 (hereafter abbreviated CFS).

4. Quoted in Flaubert, *Three Tales*, p. 15/FOe, p. 176.

5. I am obviously alluding here to Bloom's notions in *The Anxiety of Influence*.

6. Cf. Martin's account of the conventional interpretation of the Salomé-Nietzsche relationship: "It is not surprising that so much ink has been spilled in the effort to prove that it was Salomé who desired and seduced Nietzsche; that it was she who gained more from the relationship, both intellectually and personally; that she was, in effect, his product.... Nietzsche is restored to the position of Master" (*Women and Modernity*, p. 62). In both instances, rethinking the vectors of influence is inseparable from rethinking the nature of intersexual friendship, from turning to account the complex interplay of intellectual and erotic seduction.

7. Jacobs, preface to CFS, p. 11.

8. FL 2:234/CFS 533; emphasis added.

9. Debray-Genette, *Métamorphoses du récit*, p. 152; emphasis added.

10. The allusion here is clearly to Gilbert and Gubar, *The Madwoman in the Attic*.

11. I do not mean to suggest here that Sand was not as aware as Flaubert of the opacity and above all the plasticity of language as a means of intersubjective communication. Thus in *Indiana* she writes with reference to Raymon de Ramière's linguistic talent for self- and other-deception: "Nothing is so easy and so common as to deceive one's self when one does not lack wit and is familiar with all the niceties of the language. Language is a prostitute queen who descends and rises to all roles, disguises herself, arrays herself in fine apparel, hides her head and effaces herself; an advocate who has an answer to everything, who has always foreseen everything, and who assumes a thousand forms in order to be right" (p. 94/130; the reference is to the English and French editions, respectively). As Naginski shows, *Indiana* is a novel about writing, about language; see her *George Sand*, pp. 53–76.

12. Flaubert, *Madame Bovary*, p. 169/260. The reference is to the English and French editions, respectively.

13. "Vers moi et à ma place," Derrida, *Circonfession*, pp. 24, 26–27, 28.

14. Cf. the interesting work on (European, nineteenth-century) networks of correspondences being done by Hoock-Demarle, as in "Un Lieu d'interculturalité."

15. Mlle Leroyer de Chantepie, in Flaubert, *Correspondance*, 2:684.

16. *Sand-Flaubert Letters*, pp. 5–6 (hereafter abbreviated SFL)/CFS, p. 64.

17. Ibid., pp. 118–9/CFS, p. 213.

18. In a superb recent article, Reid makes or at least touches on many of the same points as I do. Thus she sees at work in the Sand-Flaubert correspondence what she calls "the two axes" that inform all correspondences—the axis of identification (here we agree)

and that of negation (here we differ) ("Flaubert et Sand," pp. 64–65). Reid is on the whole far more pessimistic in her reading than I, emphasizing in this instance the ways in which the apparent dialogue of such a correspondence masks a solipsistic monologue, where one is constantly missing the other, corresponding only with oneself via the addressee. And yet, while rejecting the influence thesis, Reid proposes a term that beautifully describes the nature of the Flaubert-Sand relationship, the untranslatable French word "connivence," which is to say a form or more exactly a space of complicity:

> The correspondence has an anchoring point where Sand and Flaubert answer each other. This anchoring point, which is carefully constructed and regularly nourished in the two writers' relationship, could be called *connivence*—in that the exchange of letters implies some sort of intimacy, a personal space that, however small, is shared with the other, a certain way of "closing one's eyes" together, of maintaining some secret. (p. 59)

19. SFL, pp. 47–48/CFS, pp. 119–20.

20. CFS, p. 53.

21. SFL, p. 20/CFS, p. 84; translation modified.

22. Flaubert, *Correspondance*, 2:696.

23. SFL, p. 49/CFS, p. 122.

24. Here again I part ways with Reid, who, discussing many of these same issues and passages, concludes pessimistically that conventional notions of sexual difference and its concomitant misogyny prevail in the correspondence: "The difference remains essential—with the flaws one attributes to women and the qualities one attributes to men" ("Flaubert et Sand," p. 62).

25. SFL, p. 46/CFS, p. 118; translation modified.

26. FL, 2:102/CFS, p. 122.

27. SFL, p. 170/CFS, p. 295.

28. Sand, *Story of My Life*, p. 899/*Oeuvres autobiographiques*, 2:126.

29. For more of Sand on Rollinat, see her *Correspondance* 2:702–4, as well as the fourth letter in *Lettres d'un voyageur* (*Oeuvres autobiographiques*, 2:735–57).

30. FL, 2:90/CFS, pp. 91–92.

31. SFL, p. 227/CFS, p. 352.

32. Cf. in *Histoire de ma vie*, when she contrasts the egotism of love with the disinterestedness of friendship. Sand writes: "The great goal we must all pursue is to kill the great evil that gnaws at us—the cultivation of self-love" (*Story of My Life*, p. 902/*Oeuvres autobiographiques*, 2:131). The very same depersonalization, which is to say deindividualization, makes possible the highest form of friendship and of love, the one being a training ground for the other: "If you go on to seek ideal love, you will see that ideal friendship has admirably prepared your heart to receive its benefits" (p. 902/2:131).

33. SFL, p. 249/CFS, p. 382.

34. CFS, p. 405.

35. SFL, p. 290/CFS, p. 428.

36. CFS, p. 505.

37. FL, 2:230/CFS, p. 521.

38. James, *French Poets and Novelists*, p. 225.

39. FL, 2:227/CFS, p. 513; translation modified.

40. Quoted in Flaubert, *Three Tales*, p. 15/*Trois Contes*, p. 29.

41. Culler, *Flaubert*, p. 210.

42. Quoted in Flaubert, *Three Tales*, p. 15/*Trois Contes*, p. 29.

43. Brombert, *The Novels of Flaubert*, p. 238: "The compassionate account of this simple woman at times comes close to hagiography." Brombert qualifies any reading that fails to take note of this tender tonality a misreading but gives the "satirical overtones" of the tale their due.

44. Chambers, "An Invitation to Love," p. 137.

45. Schor, "Fetishism and its Ironies."

46. Chambers, "An Invitation to Love," p. 138.

47. Debray-Genette, *Métamorphoses du récit*, p. 162.

48. There are, of course, exceptions to this rule. See, for example, Bellemin-Noël's psychoanalytic reading of *Un Coeur simple* in his *Le Quatrième Conte*. According to Bellemin-Noël, Félicité is stuck—better, mired—in the anal stage. He, too, emphasizes masculine inadequacy in the tale (p. 33).

49. Girard, *Deceit, Desire, and the Novel*, p. 152.

50. Flaubert, *Trois Contes*, p. 7.

51. Flaubert, *Three Tales*, p. 42/*Trois Contes*, p. 66; emphasis added. All subsequent double references in the text and the notes are to the English and French editions, respectively.

52. Cixous and Clément, *La Jeune Née*, p. 276.

53. FL, 1:130/Flaubert, *Correspondance*, 1:708. Writing to Mlle Leroyer de Chantepie, who identifies strongly with Madame Bovary, he recalls his earlier project, suggesting that his original protagonist would have been a more appropriate candidate for identification for his unmarried, presumably virgin correspondent: "The first idea I had was to make her a virgin, living in the provinces, growing old in misery and reaching the last stages of mysticism and of dreamt-of passion. I foresaw such difficulties in the first outline that I did not dare" (*Correspondance*, 2:697).

54. Flaubert, "A Simple Heart," in *Three Tales*, p. 30.

55. This detail is also noted by Bellemin-Noël (*Le Quatrième Conte*, pp. 43–44), but he does not draw out the implications of the observation, because it is not germane to his reading of the tale. See also, Jameson, "The Realist Floor-Plan," who reads the "little temple of Vesta" first in its objectal manifestation as a "sign of bourgeois taste," a decorative "ironic allusion," second and more importantly in its function as a clock as an agent for "the rationalization of time and the organization of the modern labour process" (p. 379). For Jameson, the sort of reading I am proposing, which interprets the temple of Vesta "as staging a very immediate symbolic reference to the destinies of the two women protagonists—themselves virtual vestal virgins in the isolation of the bourgeois household" (p. 381), is not so much "*wrong*"—like Chambers, he sees no need to decide the conflict of interpretations—as dated, a "high modernist longing for symbolic

6. Living On: Flaubert's Idealism

unification which seeks to convert the work of art into an immense organic totality" (p. 382).

56. Goux, "Vesta," p. 94. Cf. on the influence of gender on the idealism/realism paradigm by the same author, "Sexual Difference and History" in *Symbolic Economies*, pp. 213–44.

57. Or, as Bellemin-Noël would have it, sexual difference is never even attained, as Félicité never makes it out of the preoedipal stage: "Félicité's drama is played out before an authentic oedipal triangulation, before a realization of sexual difference" (*Le Quatrième Conte*, p. 34).

58. Derrida, "Une Idée de Flaubert," p. 323.

59. Cf. these remarks earlier, apropos of the Spinozan aspects of the Devil's discourse at the end of *La Tentation*:

> The devil, is of course not an atheist, no one is less of an atheist than the devil; but no more than Spinoza he does not exclude the extension and thus the matter of God, which terrifies Anthony, just as he is overwhelmed by the total dehumanization of a God which, while lacking all anthropomorphic subjectivity, must be without love, without anger, without any feeling, without any form, without providence and without finality. (ibid., pp. 310–11).

60. Culler, "The Uses of *Madame Bovary*," p. 6.
61. SFL, p. 261/CFS, p. 356.

WORKS CITED

Albistur, Maïté, and Daniel Armogathe. *Histoire du féminisme français*, 2 vols. Paris: des femmes, 1977.

Armstrong, Nancy. *Desire and Domestic Fiction*. Oxford: Oxford University Press, 1987.

Assoun, Paul-Laurent. "Freud aux prises avec l'idéal." *Nouvelle Revue de Psychanalyse*, special issue, *Idéaux* 27 (1983): 85–123.

Auerbach, Erich. *Mimesis: The Representation of Reality in Western Literature*. Willard R. Trask, tr. Princeton: Princeton University Press, 1968.

Barthes, Roland. *S/Z*. Richard Miller, tr. New York: Hill and Wang, 1974.

Beauvoir, Simone de. *The Second Sex*. H. M. Parshley, tr. New York: Vintage, 1974.

Bellemin-Noël, Jean. *Le Quatrième Conte de Gustave Flaubert*. Paris: PUF, 1990.

Belsey, Catherine. *Critical Practice*. London: Methuen, 1980.

Bénichou, Paul. *Le Temps des prophètes: Doctrines de l'âge romantique*. Paris: Gallimard, 1977.

Bennington, Geoffrey, and Jacques Derrida. *Jacques Derrida*. Paris: Seuil, 1991.

Berger, Anne. "Let's Go to the Fountain: On George Sand and Writing." In *Writing Differences: Readings from the Seminar of Hélène Cixous*. Susan Sellers, ed. New York: St Martin's, 1988, pp. 54–65.

Béteille, Arlette. "Où finit Indiana? Problématique d'un dénouement." *Recherches Nouvelles: Groupe de Recherches sur George Sand*. C.R.I.N. 6–7 (1983): 62–73.

Bettelheim, Bruno. *The Uses of Enchantment: The Meaning and Importance of Fairy Tales*. New York: Vintage, 1977.

Biermann, Karlheinrich. *Literarisch-politische Avantgarde in Frankreich, 1830–1870: Hugo, Sand, Baudelaire, und andere*. Stuttgart: W. Kohlhammer, 1982.

Works Cited

Bloch, Ernst. *The Utopian Function of Art and Literature: Selected Essays.* Jack Zipes and Frank Mecklenburg, trs. Cambridge: MIT Press, 1988.

Bloom, Harold. *The Anxiety of Influence: A Theory of Poetry.* London: Oxford University Press, 1973.

Bogaert, Geneviève van den. Introduction to George Sand, *La Petite Fadette.* Paris: Garnier-Flammarion, 1967, pp. 15–24.

Bossis, Mireille. "L'Homme-dieu ou l'idole brisée dans les romans de George Sand." In *George Sand: Colloque de Cerisy.* Simone Vierne, ed. Paris: SEDES, 1983, pp. 179–87.

—"Les Relations de parenté dans les romans de George Sand." *Cahiers de l'Association Internationale des Etudes Françaises* 28 (1976): 297–314.

Brecht, Bertolt. "Against Georg Lukács." In Theodor Adorno, Walter Benjamin, Ernst Bloch, Bertolt Brecht, Georg Lukács, Fredric Jameson, *Aesthetics and Politics.* Ronald Taylor, tr. and ed. London: Verso, 1980, pp. 68–85.

Brée, Germaine. "George Sand: The Fictions of Autobiography." *Nineteenth-Century French Studies* 4 (1976): 438–49.

— "Le Mythe des origines et l'autoportait chez George Sand et Colette." In *Symposium and Modern Literature: Studies in Honor of Wallace Fowlie.* Marcel Tetel, ed. Durham: Duke University Press, 1978, pp. 103–12.

Brombert, Victor. *The Novels of Flaubert.* Princeton: Princeton University Press, 1966.

Brooks, Peter. *Reading for the Plot: Design and Intention in Narrative.* New York: Vintage, 1985.

Brunetière, Ferdinand. *Discours de Combat.* Paris: Perrin, 1903.

— "La Transformation du lyrisme par le roman." In *L'Evolution de la poésie lyrique en France au dix-neuvième siècle: Leçons professées à la Sorbonne,* vol. 1. Paris: Hachette, 1913, pp. 291–326.

— *La Renaissance de l'idéalisme.* Paris: Firmin-Didot, 1896.

Butler, Judith. "Bodies that Matter." In *Engaging with Irigaray.* Carolyn Burke, Naomi Schor, and Margaret Whitford, eds. New York: Columbia University Press, forthcoming.

Butler, Judith. *Gender Trouble: Feminism and the Subversion of Identity.* New York: Routledge, 1990.

Butler, Marilyn. "Feminist Criticism, Late-Eighties Style." *TLS* 4432 (March 11–17, 1988): 283–84.

Caors, Marielle. Preface to George Sand, *Le Meunier d'Angibault.* Grenoble: Aurore, 1990, pp. 5–24.

— Afterword to George Sand, *Le Meunier d'Angibault.* Grenoble: Aurore, 1990, pp. 295–98.

Carlut, Charles. *La Correspondance de Flaubert: Etude et répertoire critique.* Columbus: Ohio State University Press, 1968.

Cate, Curtis. *George Sand: A Biography.* New York: Avon, 1975.

Cellier, Léon. *La Porporina: Entretiens sur Consuelo. Actes du colloque de Grenoble,* 4–5 octobre 1974. Grenoble: Presses Universitaires de Grenoble, 1976.

Works Cited

Chambers, Ross. *L'Ange et l'automate: Variations sur le mythe de l'actrice de Nerval à Proust. Archives* 128 (1971).

— "An Invitation to Love: Simplicity of Heart and Textual Duplicity in 'Un Coeur simple.' " In *Story and Situation: Narrative Seduction and the Power of Fiction.* Minneapolis: University of Minnesota Press, 1984, pp. 123–50.

Champfleury [Jules François Félix Husson] and George Sand. *Du Réalisme: Correspondance.* Paris: Cendres, 1991.

Chasseguet-Smirgel, Janine. *The Ego Ideal: A Psychoanalytic Essay on the Malady of the Ideal.* Paul Barrows, tr. Christopher Lasch, intro. New York: Norton, 1985.

— *Ethique et esthétique de la perversion.* Paris: Champ Vallon, 1984.

Chonez, Claudine. "George Sand et le féminisme." *Europe* 587 (March 1978): 75–79.

Chow, Rey. "The Politics and Pedagogy of Asian Literatures in American Universities." *differences* 2.3 (1990). 29–51.

Cixous, Hélène, and Catherine Clément. *La Jeune Née.* Paris: 10/18, 1975.

Cornell, Drucilla. "The Doubly-Prized World: Myth, Allegory, and the Feminine." *Cornell Law Review* 75.3 (March 1990): 644–98.

Coward, Rosalind, and John Ellis. *Language and Materialism: Developments in Semiology and the Theory of the Subject.* London: Routledge and Kegan Paul, 1977.

Crabbé, Brigitte, Marie-Luce Delfosse, Lucia Gaiardo, Ghislaine Verlaeckt, and Evelyne Wilwerth. *Les Femmes dans les livres scolaires.* Brussels: Pierre Mardaga, 1985.

Crecelius, Kathryn. *Family Romance: George Sand's Early Novels.* Bloomington: Indiana University Press, 1987.

Culler, Jonathan. *Flaubert: The Uses of Uncertainty.* Ithaca, N.Y.: Cornell University Press, 1974.

— "The Uses of *Madame Bovary.*" In *Flaubert and Postmodernism.* Naomi Schor and Henry Majewski, eds. Nebraska: University of Nebraska Press, 1984, pp. 1–12.

Czyba, Lucette. "La Femme et le prolétaire dans *Le Compagnon du tour de France.*" In *George Sand: Colloque de Cerisy.* Simone Vierne, ed. Paris: SEDES, 1983, pp. 21–29.

Danahy, Michael. *The Feminization of the Novel.* Gainesville: University of Florida Press, 1991.

— "Growing Up Female: George Sand's View in *La Petite Fadette.*" In *The George Sand Papers: Conference Proceedings* 1978. Natalie Datlof, Edwin L. Dunbaugh, Frank S. Lambasa, Gabrielle Savet, William S. Shiver, Alex Szogyi, and Joseph G. Astman, eds. New York: AMS Press, 1982, pp. 49–58.

Debray-Genette, Raymonde. *Métamorphoses du récit: Autour de Flaubert.* Paris: Seuil, 1988.

DeJean, Joan, and Nancy K. Miller, eds. *Displacements: Women, Tradition, Literatures in French.* Baltimore: Johns Hopkins University Press, 1991.

de Man, Paul. "Allegory (*Julie*)." In *Allegories of Reading: Figural Language in Rousseau, Nietzsche, Rilke, and Proust.* New Haven: Yale University Press, 1979, pp. 188–220.

Delacroix, Eugène. *Oeuvres littéraires.* Vol. 1, *Etudes esthétiques.* Paris: Bibliothèque Dionysienne, G. Grès & Cie., 1923.

de Lauretis, Teresa. *Alice Doesn't: Feminism, Semiotics, Cinema*. Bloomington: Indiana University Press, 1984.

Derrida, Jacques. "Circonfession." In *Jacques Derrida*. Geoffrey Bennington and Jacques Derrida. Paris: Seuil, 1991, pp. 7–291.

— "Deconstruction in America: An Interview with Jacques Derrida." *Critical Exchange* 17 (1985): 1–33.

— "Une Idée de Flaubert: La Lettre de Platon." In *Psyché: Inventions de l'autre*. Paris: Galilée, 1987, pp. 305–25.

— "The Politics of Friendship." *The Journal of Philosophy* 85.11 (November 1988): 632–44.

— *Séminaire*, 1990–91. Unpublished lecture given in Paris, November 11, 1990.

Deutsch, Helene. *The Psychology of Women: A Psychoanalytic Interpretation*, vol. 1. New York: Grune and Stratton, 1944.

Deutelbaum, Wendy, and Cynthia Huff. "Class, Gender, and Family System: The Case of George Sand." In *The (M)other Tongue: Essays in Feminist Psychoanalytic Interpretation*. Shirley Nelson Garner, Claire Kahane, and Madelon Sprengnether, eds. Ithaca, N.Y.: Cornell University Press, 1985, pp. 260–79.

Dickenson, Donna. *George Sand: A Brave Man, the Most Womanly Woman*. Oxford: Berg, 1988.

Didier, Béatrice. Introduction to George Sand, *Lélia*, vol. 1. Grenoble: Aurore, 1987, pp. 5–50.

— Preface to George Sand, *Indiana*. Paris: Gallimard Folio, 1984, pp. 7–32.

— Preface to George Sand, *Le Meunier d'Angibault*. Paris: Poche, 1985, pp. 5–17.

Eagleton, Terry. *Criticism and Ideology: A Study in Marxist Literary Theory*. London: Verso, 1976.

Ehrard, Antoinette. "L'Esthétique de Zola: Etude lexicologique de ses écrits sur l'art." *Cahiers Naturalistes* 58 (1984): 133–50.

Eliot, George. *Adam Bede*. Harmondsworth: Penguin, 1980.

— *Essays of George Eliot*. Thomas Pinney, ed. New York: Columbia University Press, 1963.

Faguet, Emile. *Dix-Neuvième Siècle: Etudes littéraires*. Paris: Boivin, 1887.

Felman, Shoshana. "Modernité du lieu commun: En Marge de Flaubert—*Novembre*." *Littérature* 20 (1975): 32–48.

Ferguson, Priscilla Parkhurst, Philippe Desau, and Wendy Griswold, eds. *Critical Inquiry*, special issue, *The Sociology of Literature* 14.3 (Spring 1988).

Flaubert, Gustave. *Correspondance*, 3 vols. Jean Bruneau, ed. Paris: Pléiade, 1973–92.

— *The Letters of Gustave Flaubert*, 2 vols. Francis Steegmuller, tr. Cambridge: Harvard University Press, 1982.

— *Madame Bovary*. Paul de Man, ed. and tr. New York: Norton, 1965.

— *Madame Bovary*. Paris: Garnier-Flammarion, 1966.

— *Les Oeuvres de Gustave Flaubert*, vol. 16. Lausanne: Editions Rencontre, 1965.

— *Three Tales*. Robert Baldick, tr. Baltimore: Penguin, 1961.

Works Cited

— *Trois Contes*. Pierre-Marc de Biasi, ed. Paris: Flammarion, 1986.

Foucault, Michel. "What Is an Author?" In *Textual Strategies: Perspectives in Post-Structuralist Criticism*. Josué V. Harari, ed. Ithaca, N.Y.: Cornell University Press, 1979, pp. 141–60.

Fouque, Antoinette. "Women in Movements: Yesterday, Today, and Tomorrow. An Interview." Arthur Denner, tr. Anne Berger, ed. *differences* 3.3 (1991): 1–25.

Fowler, Bridget. *The Alienated Reader: Women and Popular Romantic Literature in the Twentieth Century*. London: Harvester, 1991.

Frank, Joseph. *Dostoevsky: The Seeds of Revolt, 1821–1849*. Princeton: Princeton University Press, 1976.

Freadman, Anne. "Of Cats, and Compagnons, and the Name of George Sand." In *Grafts: Feminist Cultural Criticism*. Susan Sheridan, ed. London: Verso, 1988, pp. 125–56.

Freud, Sigmund. " 'A Child Is Being Beaten': A Contribution to the Study of the Origin of Sexual Perversions." In *The Standard Edition of the Complete Psychological Works of Sigmund Freud*. London: Hogarth Press, 1959, 19:175–203.

— "Creative Writers and Day-Dreaming." In *The Standard Edition of the Complete Psychological Works of Sigmund Freud*. London: Hogarth Press, 1959, 9:141–53.

— *The Ego and the Id*. In *The Standard Edition of the Complete Psychological Works of Sigmund Freud*. London: Hogarth Press, 1959, 19:3–66.

— "Family Romances." In *The Standard Edition of the Complete Psychological Works of Sigmund Freud*. London: Hogarth Press, 1959, 9:235–42.

— "Female Sexuality." In *The Standard Edition of the Complete Psychological Works of Sigmund Freud*. London: Hogarth Press, 1959, 21:221–44.

— "Femininity." In *The Standard Edition of the Complete Psychological Works of Sigmund Freud*. London: Hogarth Press, 1959, 22:112–35.

— *Group Psychology and the Analysis of the Ego*. In *The Standard Edition of the Complete Psychological Works of Sigmund Freud*. London: Hogarth Press, 1959, 18:67–143.

— "On Narcissism: An Introduction." In *The Standard Edition of the Complete Psychological Works of Sigmund Freud*. London: Hogarth Press, 1959, 14:67–102.

— "On the Universal Tendency to Debasement in the Sphere of Love." In *The Standard Edition of the Complete Psychological Works of Sigmund Freud*. London: Hogarth Press, 1959, 11:178–90.

— "Some Psychological Consequences of the Anatomical Distinction between the Sexes." In *The Standard Edition of the Complete Psychological Works of Sigmund Freud*. London: Hogarth Press, 1959, 19:241–60.

— *The Standard Edition of the Complete Psychological Works of Sigmund Freud*. 24 vols. London: Hogarth Press, 1959.

Gallagher, Catherine. *The Industrial Reformation of English Fiction (1832–1867)*. Chicago: Chicago University Press, 1985.

Gallop, Jane. *Around 1981: Academic Feminist Literary Theory*. New York: Routledge, 1992.

— *Reading Lacan*. Ithaca, N.Y.: Cornell University Press, 1985.

Works Cited

Gasché, Rodolph. "The Stelliferous Fold: On Villiers de l'Isle-Adam's *L'Eve future*." *Studies in Romanticism* 22.2 (Summer 1983): 293–327.

Gilbert, Sandra, and Susan Gubar, *The Madwoman in the Attic: The Woman Writer and the Nineteenth-Century Literary Imagination*. New Haven: Yale University Press, 1979.

Gilman, Sander. "Black Bodies, White Bodies: Toward an Iconography of Female Sexuality in Late Nineteenth Century Art, Medicine, and Literature." *Critical Inquiry*, special issue, *Race, Writing, and Difference*, Henry Louis Gates, Jr., ed., 21.1 (Autumn 1985): 204–42.

Girard, René. *Deceit, Desire, and the Novel*. Yvonne Freccero, tr. Baltimore: Johns Hopkins University Press, 1965.

— *Violence and the Sacred*. Patrick Gregory, tr. Baltimore: Johns Hopkins University Press, 1972.

Goux, Jean-Joseph. "Vesta, or the Place of Being." Wm. Smock, tr. *Representations* 1.1 (1983): 91–107.

— *Symbolic Economies: After Marx and Freud*. Jennifer Curtis Gage, tr. Ithaca, N.Y.: Cornell University Press, 1990.

Grant, Richard. "George Sand's *La Petite Fadette* and the Problem of Masculine Individuation." In *L'Hénaurme siècle*. W. McLendon, ed. Heidelberg: Carl Winter, 1984.

Green, André. "L'Idéal: Mesure et démesure." *Nouvelle Revue de Psychanalyse*, special issue, *Idéaux* 27 (1983): 8–33.

— "Un Autre, neutre: Valeurs narcissiques du même." In *Narcissisme de vie, narcissisme de mort*. Paris: Minuit, 1983, pp. 31–79.

Grimm, Reinhold R. "Les Romans champêtres de George Sand: L'Echec du renouvellement d'un genre littéraire." *Romantisme* 16 (1977): 64–70.

Hartmann, Heinz, and Rudolph M. Loewenstein. "Notes on the Superego." In *The Psychoanalytic Study of the Child*, vol. 17. New York: International University Press, 1962, pp. 42–81.

Heath, Stephen. "Realism, Modernism, and 'Language-Consciousness.' " In *Realism in European Literature*. Nicholas Boyle and Martin Swales, eds. Cambridge: Cambridge University Press, 1986, pp. 103–22.

Hecquet, Michèle. *Mauprat de George Sand: Etude critique*. Lille: Presses Universitaires de Lille, 1990.

— *Contrats et symboles: Essai sur l'idéalisme de George Sand*. Doctoral dissertation, 1990.

— "Contrats et symboles: Essai sur l'idéalisme de George Sand." *CRIN*, special issue, *George Sand: Une Oeuvre multiforme. Recherches Nouvelles* 2, Françoise van Rossum-Guyon, ed., 24 (1991): 29–41.

Hegel, Georg Wilhelm Friedrich. *Philosophy of Right*. T. M. Knox, tr. Oxford: Clarendon Press, 1967.

Heilbrun, Carolyn. *Writing a Woman's Life*. New York: Norton, 1988.

Hémon, Félix. *Cours de littérature*. Vol. 30, *Romanciers*. Paris: Delagrave, n.d.

Hernnstein Smith, Barbara. *Contingencies of Value: Alternative Perspectives for Critical Theory*. Cambridge: Harvard University Press, 1988.

Works Cited

Hirsch, Michèle. "Questions à *Indiana*." *Revue des Sciences Humaines* 165 (1977): 117–29.

Hoock-Demarle, Marie-Claire. "Un Lieu d'interculturalité franco-allemande: Le Réseau épistolaire de Coppet." *Romantisme* 73 (1991-III):19–28.

Hume, Katherine. *Fantasy and Mimesis*. New York: Methuen, 1984.

Iknayan, Marguerite. *The Idea of the Novel in France: The Critical Reaction, 1815–1848*. Geneva: Droz, 1961.

Jacobs, Alphonse. Preface to George Sand and Gustave Flaubert, *Correspondance Flaubert-Sand*. Paris: Flammarion, 1981, pp. 7–24.

James, Henry. *French Poets and Novelists*. New York: Grosset and Dunlap, 1964.

Jameson, Fredric. *Marxism and Form: Twentieth-Century Dialectical Theories of Literature*. Princeton: Princeton University Press, 1971.

— "Reflections in Conclusion." In Theodor Adorno, Walter Benjamin, Ernst Bloch, Bertolt Brecht, Georg Lukács, Fredric Jameson, *Aesthetics and Politics*. Ronald Taylor, tr. and ed. London: Verso, 1980, pp. 196–213.

— "The Realist Floor-Plan." In *On Signs*. Marshall Blonsky, ed. Baltimore: Johns Hopkins University Press, 1985, pp. 373–83.

Jauss, Hans Robert. "The Idealist Embarrassment: Observations on Marxist Aesthetics." *New Literary History* 7:1 (Autumn 1975): 191–208.

— "The Perfect as the Fascinosum of the Imaginary." In *Questions and Answers: Forms of Dialogic Understanding*. Michael Hays, tr. and ed. Minneapolis: University of Minnesota Press, 1989, pp. 10–25.

— "On the Origins of the Differentiation between Fiction and Reality." In *Questions and Answers: Forms of Dialogic Understanding*. Michael Hays, tr. and ed. Minneapolis: University of Minnesota Press, 1989, pp. 4–10.

Johnson, Barbara. "Gender and Poetry: Charles Baudelaire and Marceline Desbordes-Valmore." In *Displacements: Women, Tradition, Literatures in French*. Joan DeJean and Nancy K. Miller, eds. Baltimore: Johns Hopkins University Press, 1991, pp. 163–81.

Juin, Hubert. *Lectures du dix-neuvième siècle*, vol. 2. Paris: 10/18, 1977.

Kaminsky, Alice. *Georges Henry Lewes as Literary Critic*. Syracuse: Syracuse University Press, 1968.

Kant, Immanuel. *The Critique of Judgement*. James Creed Meredith, tr. Oxford: Clarendon Press, 1952.

— *Critique of Pure Reason*. Norman Kemp Smith, tr. London: Macmillan, 1929.

Kaplan, Cora. *Sea Changes: Essays on Culture and Feminism*. London: Verso, 1986.

— " 'Like a Housemaid's Fancies': The Representation of Working-class Women in Nineteenth-Century Writing." In *Grafts: Feminist Cultural Criticism*. Susan Sheridan, ed. London: Verso, 1988, pp. 55–75.

Knoepflmacher, U. C. *George Eliot's Early Novels: The Limits of Realism*. Berkeley: University of California Press, 1968.

Kristeva, Julia. *Tales of Love*. Leon S. Roudiez, tr. New York: Columbia University Press, 1987.

Works Cited

Lacan, Jacques. *Les Complexes familiaux*. Paris: Navarin, 1984.

Laclos, Pierre Choderlos de. *Oeuvres complètes*. Maurice Allem, ed. Paris: Pléiade, 1951.

Lalou, René. *Histoire de la littérature française contemporaine*. Vol. 1, 1879 à nos jours. Paris: PUF, 1941.

Langbauer, Laurie. *Women and Romance*. Ithaca, N.Y.: Cornell University Press, 1990.

Larnac, Jean. *George Sand révolutionnaire*. Paris: Editions Hier et Aujourd'hui, 1947.

Lazarus, Neil. "Doubting the New World Order: Marxism, Realism, and the Claims of Postmodernist Social Theory." *differences* 3.3 (1991): 94–134.

Lemoine-Luccioni, Eugénie. *Partage des femmes*. Paris: Seuil, Points, 1976.

Lerminier. "Poètes et romanciers comtemporains: Seconde phase. I. Mme Sand." *Revue des Deux Mondes* 6 (1844): 84–117.

— "Des Femmes philosophes." *Revue des Deux Mondes* 2 (1843): 673–91.

Leroux, Pierre. *De l'egalité*. Boussac: Pierre Leroux, 1848.

— *Oeuvres de Pierre Leroux* (1825–1850). Paris: Louis Netré, 1859–61.

Levin, Harry. *The Gates of Horn: A Study of Five French Realists*. New York: Oxford University Press, 1963.

Lewes, G. H. "Balzac and George Sand." *Foreign Language Quarterly* 33 (1844): 265–98.

— "George Sand's Recent Novels." *Foreign Language Quarterly* 37 (1846): 21–36.

— *The Principles of Success in Literature*. Boston: Allyn and Bacon, 1891.

Lubin, Georges. Introduction to George Sand, *Oeuvres autobiographiques*, vol. 1. Paris: Pléiade, 1970, pp. xiii–xxviii.

MacCannell, Juliet Flower. *The Regime of the Brother: After the Patriarchy*. New York: Routledge, 1991.

Macherey, Pierre. "Un Roman panthéiste: *Spiridion* de George Sand." In *A quoi pense la littérature? Exercices de philosophie littéraire*. Paris: PUF, 1990, pp. 37–51.

Martin, Biddy. *Women and Modernity: The (Life)styles of Lou Andréas-Salomé*. Ithaca, N.Y.: Cornell University Press, 1991.

Mason, Mary G. "The Other Voice: Autobiographies of Women Writers." In *Autobiography: Essays Theoretical and Critical*. James Olney, ed. Princeton: Princeton University Press, 1980, pp. 207–35.

Mathewson, Rufus W. *The Positive Hero in Russian Literature*. Stanford: Stanford University Press, 1975.

Maurois, André. *Lélia: The Life of George Sand*. Gerard Hopkins, tr. New York: Harper and Brothers, 1953.

Mayr, Joseph. *Studien zur Rezeption des Art social: Die Sozialromane George Sands in der zeitgenossischen Kritik*. Frankfurt am Main: Peter Lang, 1984.

Meese, Elizabeth. "Sexual Politics and Critical Judgment." In *After Strange Texts: The Role of Theory in the Study of Literature*. Gregory S. Jay and David L. Miller, eds. University: University of Alabama Press, 1985, pp. 85–100.

Michaud, Stéphane. "En miroir: Flora Tristan et George Sand." In *Un Fabuleux Destin: Flora Tristan*. Stéphane Michaud, ed. Dijon: Editions Universitaires de Dijon, 1984.

Michel, Arlette. "Structures romanesques et problèmes du mariage chez George Sand, d'*Indiana* à la *Comtesse de Rudolstadt*." *Romantisme* 16 (1977): 34–45.

Works Cited

Michel, Régis. *Le Beau Idéal ou l'art du concept.* Paris: Réunion des Musées Nationaux, 1989.

Michelson, Annette. "On the Eve of the Future: The Reasonable Facsimile and the Philosophical Toy." *October* 29 (Summer 1984): 3–21.

Miller, J. Hillis. *The Ethics of Reading.* New York: Columbia University Press, 1987.

— "The Geneva School." *Critical Quarterly* 8.4 (1966): 305–21.

Miller, Nancy K. *Subject to Change: Reading Feminist Writing.* New York: Columbia University Press, 1988.

Mirecourt, Eugène de. *George Sand.* Paris: J.-P. Roret, 1854.

Moers, Ellen. *Literary Women: The Great Writers.* Garden City, N.J.: Doubleday, Anchor Books, 1977.

— "Fraternal George Sand." *The American Scholar* 48 (Spring 1979): 221–26.

Moi, Toril. *Sexual/Textual Politics: Feminist Literary Theory.* London: Methuen, 1985.

Naginski, Isabelle Hoog. *George Sand: Writing for Her Life.* New Brunswick, N.J.: Rutgers University Press, 1991.

Nesbit, Molly. "What Was an Author?" *Yale French Studies,* special issue, *Everyday Life,* Alice Kaplan and Kristin Ross, eds., 73 (1987): 229–57.

Nochlin, Linda. *Realism.* Harmondsworth: Penguin, 1971.

Nouvelle Revue de Psychanalyse, special issue, *Idéaux* 27 (Spring 1983).

O'Brien, Dennis. "George Sand and Feminism." In *George Sand Papers: Conference Proceedings* 1976. Natalie Datlof, Edwin L. Dunbaugh, Frank S. Lambasa, Gabrielle Savet, William S. Shiver, Alex Szogyi, and Joseph G. Astman, eds. New York: AMS Press, 1980, pp. 76–91.

Orcel, Michel, and François Boddaert. *Ces imbéciles croyants de liberté, 1815–1852.* Paris: Hatier, 1990.

Orr, Linda. *Headless History: Nineteenth-Century French Historiography of the Revolution.* Ithaca, N.Y.: Cornell University Press, 1990.

Panofsky, Erwin. *Idea: A Concept in Art Theory.* Joseph J. S. Peake, tr. Columbia: University of South Carolina Press, 1968.

Pateman, Carol. *The Disorder of Women: Democracy, Feminism, and Political Theory.* Stanford: Stanford University Press, 1989.

Pellissier, Georges. *Le Mouvement littéraire au dix-neuvième siècle.* Paris: Hachette, 1889.

Perdiguier, Agricol. "Lettres choisies d'Agricol Perdiguier, de sa femme Lise et de George Sand." In Jean Briquet, *Agricol Perdiguier: Compagnon du tour de France et représentant du peuple, 1805–1875.* Paris: Butte aux Cailles et Jean Briquet, 1981, pp. 383–535.

Perrot, Michelle, ed. *Histoire de la vie privée.* Vol. 4, *De la Révolution à la Grande Guerre.* Paris: Seuil, 1987.

— "Un Entretien avec Michelle Perrot: La Guerre sans dentelles." *Nouvel Observateur* 1361 (December 6–12, 1990): 170–71.

Petrey, Sandy. "George and Georgina Sand: Realist Gender in *Indiana.*" In *Sexuality and Textuality.* Michael Worton and Judith Still, eds. Manchester, England: Manchester University Press, forthcoming.

Works Cited

Pointon, Marcia. *Naked Authority: The Body in Western Painting,* 1830–1908. Cambridge: Cambridge University Press, 1990.

Pontmartin, Arnold de. *Nouvelles Causeries littéraires.* Paris: Michel Lévy, 1855.

Poovey, Mary. "Mary Wollstonecraft: The Gender of Genres in Late Eighteenth-Century England." *Novel* 15.2 (1982): 111–26.

Prawer, S. S. *Karl Marx and World Literature.* Oxford: Clarendon, 1976.

Prendergast, Christopher. *The Order of Mimesis.* Cambridge: Cambridge University Press, 1986.

Proudhon, P. J. *Du principe de l'art et de sa destination sociale.* Paris: Garnier, 1865.

— *Les Femmelins: Les Grandes Figures romantiques.* Paris: A l'écart, 1989.

Rabine, Leslie. "George Sand and the Myth of Femininity." *Women and Literature* 4 (1976): 2–17.

Rachilde [Mme de la Vallette]. *Monsieur Vénus.* Paris: Flammarion, 1977.

Radway, Janice A. *Reading the Romance: Women, Patriarchy, and Popular Literature.* Chapel Hill: University of North Carolina Press, 1984.

Rancière, Jacques. *Aux bords du politique.* Paris: Osiris, 1990.

Reid, Martine. "Flaubert et Sand en correspondance." *Poétique* 85 (February 1991): 53–68.

Rescher, Nicolas. *Ethical Idealism: An Inquiry into the Nature and the Function of Ideals.* Berkeley: University of California Press, 1987.

Riley, Denise. *Am I That Name: Feminism and the Category of "Women" in History.* Minneapolis: University of Minnesota Press, 1988.

Robert, Marthe. *Origins of the Novel.* Sacha Rabinovitch, tr. Bloomington: Indiana University Press, 1980.

Robin, Régine. *Le Réalisme socialiste: Une Esthétique impossible.* Paris: Payot, 1986.

Robinson, Christopher. *French Literature in the Nineteenth Century.* Newton Abbot, England: David & Charles, 1978.

Robinson, Lillian S. "Treason Our Text: Feminist Challenges to the Literary Canon." In *The New Feminist Criticism: Essays on Women, Literature, Theory.* Elaine Showalter, ed. New York: Pantheon Books, 1985, pp. 105–21.

Rocheblave, Samuel. Introduction to George Sand, *George Sand: Pages choisies des grands écrivains.* Paris: Armand Colin, 1924.

Roustan, M. *La Littérature française par la dissertation.* Vol 3, *Le Dix-Neuvième Siècle.* Paris: Librairie Classique Mellottée, n.d.

Said, Edward. "Opponents, Audiences, Constituencies, and Community." *Critical Inquiry* 9.1 (September 1982): 1–26.

Sainte-Beuve, Charles Augustin. *Les Grands Ecrivains français: Dix-Neuvième Siècle, les romanciers.* Paris: Garniers Frères, 1927.

Salomon, Pierre. *George Sand.* Paris: Hatier-Borcier, 1953.

Sand, George. *Le Compagnon du tour de France.* Grenoble: Presses Universitaires de Grenoble, 1988.

— *Le Compagnon du tour de France,* vol. 1. Paris: Michel Lévy, 1869.

— *Correspondance,* 25 vols. Georges Lubin, ed. Paris: Garnier, 1964–90.

— "*L'Education sentimentale* par Gustave Flaubert." In *Questions d'art et de littérature.*

Works Cited

Henriette Bessis and Janis Glasgow, eds. Paris: des femmes, 1991, pp. 353–63.

— *Indiana*. George Burnham Ives, tr. Chicago: Academy Chicago, Publishers, Cassandra Editions, 1978.

— *Indiana*. Béatrice Didier, ed. Paris: Gallimard Folio, 1984.

— *Isidora*. Paris: des femmes, 1990.

— *Jean Ziska: Episode de la guerre des Hussites*. Brussels: Société belge de librairie, 1843.

— *The Journeyman Joiner; or, The Companion of the Tour of France*. Francis Geo. Shaw, tr. New York: Howard Fertig, 1976.

— *Lélia*. Paris: Garnier, 1960.

— *Lélia*. Maria Espinosa, tr. Bloomington: Indiana University Press, 1978.

— *Lélia*, 2 vols. Béatrice Didier, ed. Grenoble: Aurore, 1985.

— *Lettres à Marcie*. Paris: Perrotin, 1835.

— *Little Fadette*. Eva Figes, tr. London: Blackie, 1967.

— *La Mare au diable*. Paris: Garnier-Flammarion, 1964.

— *Mauprat*. Stanley Young, tr. Chicago: Academy Chicago, Publishers, Cassandra Editions, 1977.

— *Le Meunier d'Angibault*. Grenoble: Aurore, 1990.

— *Nanon*. Grenoble: Aurore, 1987.

— *Nouvelles*. Eve Sourian, ed. Paris: des femmes, 1986.

— *Oeuvres autobiographiques*, 2 vols. Georges Lubin, ed. Paris: Pléiade, 1970–71.

— *Le Péché de Monsieur Antoine*. Grenoble: Aurore, 1982.

— *La Petite Fadette*. Paris: Garnier-Flammarion, 1967.

— *Questions politiques et sociales*. Paris: des femmes, 1991.

— *Souvenirs et impressions littéraires*. Paris: Hetzel, 1862.

— *Story of My Life: The Autobiography of George Sand*. A Group Translation. Thelma Jurgau, ed. State University of New York Press, 1991.

Sand, George, and Gustave Flaubert. *Correspondance Flaubert-Sand*. Paris: Flammarion, 1981.

— *The George Sand–Gustave Flaubert Letters*. Aimee L. McKenzie, tr. New York: Liveright, 1921.

Satiat, Nadine. Introduction to Villiers de l'Isle-Adam, *L'Eve future*. Paris: GF-Flammarion, 1992.

Schor, Naomi. *Breaking the Chain: Women, Theory, and French Realist Fiction*. New York: Columbia University Press, 1985.

— "Female Fetishism: The Case of George Sand." In *The Female Body in Western Culture*. Susan Rubin Suleiman, ed. Cambridge: Harvard University Press, 1986, pp. 363–72.

— "Fetishism and Its Ironies." In *Fetishism as a Cultural Discourse*. Emily Apter and William Pietz, eds. Ithaca, N.Y.: Cornell University Press, forthcoming.

— "The Portrait of a Gentleman: Representing Men in (French) Women's Writing." *Representations* 20 (1987): 113–33. In *Misogyny, Misandry, and Misanthropy*. R. Howard Bloch and Frances Ferguson, eds. Berkeley: University of California Press, 1989.

— *Reading in Detail: Aesthetics and the Feminine*. New York: Methuen, 1987.

Works Cited

— "Re-reading in Detail: or, Aesthetics, the Feminine, and Idealism." *Criticism* 32.3 (Summer 1990): 309–24.

Scott, Joan Wallach. "The Sears Case." In *Gender and the Politics of History*. New York: Columbia University Press, 1988, pp. 167–77.

Scriven, Michael, and Dennis Tate, eds. *European Socialist Realism*. Oxford: Berg, 1988.

Showalter, Elaine. *The New Feminist Criticism: Essays on Women, Literature, and Theory*. New York: Pantheon, 1985.

Sivert, Eileen. "*Lélia* and Feminism: French Texts/American Contexts." *Yale French Studies* 62 (1981): 45–66.

Slama, Béatrice. "De la littérature féminine à l'écriture-femme': Différence et institution." *Littérature* 44 (1981): 51–71.

Sourian, Eve. Preface to George Sand, *Isidora*. Paris: des femmes, 1990, pp. 7–32.

Suleiman, Susan R. *Subversive Intent*. Cambridge: Harvard University Press, 1990.

Suvin, Darko. *Metamorphoses of Science Fiction: On the Poetics and History of a Literary Genre*. New Haven: Yale University Press, 1979.

Swales, Martin. "The Problem of Nineteenth-Century German Realism." In *Realism in European Literature*. Martin Swales and Nicholas Boyle, eds. Cambridge: Cambridge University Press, 1986, pp. 415–23.

Sychrava, Juliet. *Schiller to Derrida: Idealism in Aesthetics*. Cambridge: Cambridge University Press, 1990.

Taine, Hippolyte. *Derniers essais de critique et d'histoire*. Paris: Hachette, 1894.

— *Philosophie de l'art*, 2 vols. Paris: Ressources, 1980.

Tallis, Raymond. *In Defence of Realism*. London: Edward Arnold, 1988.

Tanner, Tony. *Adultery in the Novel*. Baltimore: Johns Hopkins University Press, 1978.

Thomas, Edith. *George Sand*. Paris: Editions Universitaires, 1959.

Thomson, Patricia. *George Sand and the Victorians: Her Influence and Reputation in Nineteenth-Century England*. New York: Columbia University Press, 1975.

Todorov, Tzvetan. *Theories of the Symbol*. Catherine Porter, tr. Ithaca, N.Y.: Cornell University Press, 1982.

Tompkins, Jane. *Sensational Designs: The Cultural Work of American Fiction, 1790–1860*. New York: Oxford University Press, 1985.

Van Tieghem, Philippe. *Histoire de la littérature française*. Paris: Fayard, 1949.

Vareille, Kristina Wingard. *Socialité, sexualité, et les impasses de l'histoire: L'Evolution de la thématique sandienne d'Indiana (1832) à Mauprat (1837)*. Uppsala: Almqvist and Wiskell, 1987.

Verjat, Alain. "Formes et fonctions du discours autobiographique." In *George Sand: Colloque de Cerisy*. Simone Vierne, ed. Paris: SEDES, 1983, pp. 31–40.

Vickers, Nancy. "Diana Described: Scattered Woman and Scattered Rhyme." *Critical Inquiry*, special issue, *Writing and Sexual Difference*, Elizabeth Abel, ed., 8.2 (Winter 1981): 265–80.

Vierne, Simone, ed. *George Sand: Colloque de Cerisy*. Paris: SEDES, 1983.

Villiers de l'Isle-Adam. *L'Eve future*. Nadine Satiat, intro. Paris: GF-Flammarion, 1992.

Waller, Margaret. *The Male Malady: Fictions of Impotence in the French Romantic Novel*. New Brunswick, N.J.: Rutgers University Press, forthcoming.

Works Cited

Warner, Marina. *Monuments and Maidens: The Allegory of the Female Form*. New York: Atheneum, 1985.

Watt, Ian. *The Rise of the Novel: Studies in Defoe, Richardson, and Fielding*. Berkeley: University of California Press, 1957.

Weil, Kari. "Feminocentric Utopias and the Paris of the Saint-Simoniennes." Unpublished paper.

Weinberg, Bernard. *French Realism: The Critical Reaction, 1830–1870*. London: Oxford University Press, 1937.

Williams, Raymond. *The Country and the City*. New York: Oxford University Press, 1973.

Woolf, Virginia. *Three Guineas*. New York: Harvest/HBJ Book, 1966.

Zola, Emile. *Mes haines*. In *Ecrits sur l'art*. Paris: Gallimard, "Tel," 1991.

— *Oeuvres complètes*, 11 vols. Paris: Cercle du Livre Précieux, 1968.

INDEX

Index

Beauvoir, Simone de, 13, 24, 32, 38, 131, 196, 231*n*18

Béguin, Albert, 218*n*8

Bellemin-Noël, Jean, 249*nn*48, 55, 250*n*57

Bellori, 27

Belsey, Catherine, 226*n*48, 235*n*7

Bénichou, Paul, 14

Berger, Anne, 242*n*9, 245*n*17, 246*n*29

Berkeley, George, 10

Bettelheim, Bruno, 143

Biermann, Karlheinrich, 112, 116, 238*nn*26, 27

Biography/biographers, 160, 165; of Sand, 161, 180, 220*n*12

Blanc, Louis, 109

Bloch, Ernst, 123, 125–28, 129

Bloom, Harold, 247*n*5

Boddaert, François, 225*n*40

Bogaert, Geneviève van den, 243*n*17

Bossis, Mireille, 63, 64–66, 231*n*15, 231*n*16

Bouchardeau, Huguette, 180

Brecht, Bertolt, 45, 84

Brée, Germaine, 244*n*7

Brombert, Victor, 9, 249*n*43

Brontë, Charlotte, 118, 221n15

Brontë sisters, 27

Brooks, Peter, 227*n*51

Brotherhood, 131, 134–36, 152; and fraternity, 242*n*2

Brothers, 134–35, 153, 242*n*6, 241*n*70; idealized society of, 151; in religion, 152; society of, 136, 143, 199; tale of two, 145, 147, 148, 149, 151; *see also* Fraternity

Brunetière, Ferdinand, 30–32, 83, 223*n*22, 224*n*34, 236*n*12

Butler, Judith, 86, 219*n*17, 232*n*29

Butler, Marilyn, 219*n*15

Byron, George Gordon, Lord, 13, 218*n*11

Cabet, Etienne, 114

Calmann-Lévy, 21

Canon, 2, 3, 4, 18, 24–26, 186, 213, 214, 228*n*60; French, 187; of French

literature, 236*n*12; Flaubertian, 204; male, 231*n*21; and token woman, 219*n*2

Canonization, 8, 25; literal, 180

Caors, Marielle, 109, 114, 119, 239*n*36

Capitalism: agrarian, 110, 125; industrial, 125, 127; rising, 118, 128; versus socialism, 124

Carlut, Charles, 228*n*58

Castration, 104, 199, 205

Cate, Curtis, 242*n*11

Cellier, Léon, 26, 215

Chakiris, George, 182

Chalon, Jean, 180

Chambers, Ross, 50, 204–5, 206, 249*n*55

Champfleury, Jules François Félix Husson, 23, 229*n*64, 231*n*21

Chasseguet-Smirgel, Janine, 65–66, 231*n*16, 238*n*22, 246*nn*20, 22

Chateaubriand, François-René, 48, 215, 229*n*72

Chodorow, Nancy, 147

Chonez, Claudine, 232*n*32

Chopin, Frédéric, 180, 181, 182

Chow, Rey, 114

Christofle, 181

Cixous, Hélène, 74, 81, 207, 234*n*47

Clare, John, 218*n*11

Class, 92–94; asymmetry, 97; axis of, difference, 102; cleavages, 112; differences, 97, 101, 124, 142, 165, 206; fusion of, 116, 122, 154; and gender, 237*n*13; privilege, 106, 154–55, 176; relations, 113; struggle, 107; in Taine, 161; in *Un Coeur simple*, 205–8; upper, 115

Colet, Louise, 201, 217*n*1, 220*n*2, 237*n*18

Commune, 200, 211

Constructionism, 85, 120

Contract, 154; era of, 155; Faustian, 148; fraternal, 136, 154; sexual, 136; social, 121, 130, 134, 151; social and sexual, 242*n*6; social theories, 154–55; theories, 240*n*54

Conventionalism, 235*n*8

Corneille, 40, 41, 50

266

Index

Index

Index

Index

274

Index

Sozialroman, 100, 111–14, 116, 119

Spinoza, Baruch, 13, 210, 250*n*59

Staël, Germaine de, 2, 220*n*4

Starobinski, Jean, 9, 218*n*8

Stendhal, 99, 229*n*74

Stern, Daniel, 220*n*2

Stowe, Harriet Beecher, 226–27*n*50

Sue, Eugène, 121

Suleiman, Susan R., 228*n*59

Suvin, Darko, 127, 129, 240*n*65

Swales, Martin, 47, 229*n*65

Swift, Jonathan, 38

Sychrava, Juliet, 218*n*11

Symbol, 58, 59, 127–28

Symbolic (n.), 101–2, 104, 106, 141, 146, 149, 176, 178, 194; revolution of the, 241*n*70

Taine, Hippolyte, 35, 39, 42, 46, 108, 161, 176, 223*n*20, 224*n*34

Tallis, Raymond, 226*nn*48, 49, 227*n*52

Tanner, Tony, 88, 228*n*60

Tate, Dennis, 237*n*20

Thomson, Patricia, 33

Tompkins, Jane, 226–27*n*50

Transference, 150

Transmission, 157–183

Trilogy, 137, 138

Triptych, 100, 117, 124, 137, 151

Tristan, Flora, 219*n*2

Turin, Adela, 159

Universalism, false, 134

Utopia, 54, 100, 101, 106, 227*n*50, 234*n*46, 240*n*65, 241*n*67; absurd utopian theories, 222*n*18; in Bloch, 127; dreams, 136; feminist, 132; fictions (pre-1848), 130, 131, 151; Sand's, 121;

socialist, 81, 136; utopian closure, 239*n*33; utopian fraternal elan, 136; utopian ideal, 152; utopianism, 15, 81, 117, 127, 129; utopian novels, 153; utopian politics, 180, 239*n*44; utopian thought, 194; utopian trilogy, 138

Value, 213

Van Tieghem, Philippe, 27

Vareille, Kristina Wingard, 81, 106, 232–33*n*33, 239*n*33

Verjat, Alain, 244*n*7

Verne, Jules, 50

Véron, Louis-Désiré, 108

Vesta, temple of, 209, 249*n*55

Vickers, Nancy, 237*n*17

Vico, Giambattista, 30

Vierne, Simone, 232*n*29

Villiers de L'Isle-Adam, 18–19, 20, 219*n*21

Virginity, 208–10

Waller, Margaret, 215, 230*n*4

Warner, Marina, 67

Watt, Ian, 177, 244*n*6

Weil, Kari, 234*n*46

Weinberg, Bernard, 219*n*18, 221–22*n*17, 223*n*19

Williams, Raymond, 236*n*11

Wollstonecraft, Mary, 120, 226–27*n*50

Women: novelists, 34; writers, 12, 24

Woolf, Virginia, 24, 27, 43, 220*n*12

Wordsworth, William, 218*n*11

Zola, Emile, 4, 44, 99, 121, 224*n*34, 227*n*54

Zulawski, Andrzej, 180

Designer: Teresa Bonner
Text: Garamond #2
Compositor: Impressions
Printer: Edwards Brothers
Binder: Edwards Brothers